Plato and Freud

To My Parents And To My Children

Plato and Freud
Two Theories of Love

Gerasimos Santas

Basil Blackwell

First published 1988
Basil Blackwell Limited
108 Cowley Road, Oxford OX4 1JF, England

Basil Blackwell Inc.
432 Park Avenue South, Suite 1503
New York, NY 10016, USA

British Library Cataloguing in Publication Data

Santas, Gerasimos
Plato and Freud: two theories of love.
1. Plato—Contributions in concept of love
2. Freud, Sigmund—Contributions in concept of love
3. Love
I. Title
152.4 B398.L9

ISBN 0-631-15914-2

Printed and bound in the USA

Contents

As I rode forth one day not long ago,
Pensive about my journey and distressed,
I met Love, like a traveller, humbly dressed,
Coming along my path, forlorn and slow.
He might have been a monarch dispossessed.

Dante

Vain is the glory of the sky,
The beauty vain of field and grove,
Unless, while with an admiring eye
We gaze, we also learn to love.

Wordsworth

Preface

My modest aim in this book has been to elucidate two grand, coherent and influential theories of love. It has not been an easy task. Like life itself, love seems to be a large mystery. Desire, reason, pleasure, the continuation of the human species, creation in the arts and sciences, immortality, the theory of Ideas, beauty and the good, the human soul and the divine – all these and more Plato brings into his study of love. To these Freud adds the crude facts of anatomy and physiology, the evolution of the species, the inchoate helplessness of the infant, the vicissitudes of human development in family and culture, the anatomies, dynamics and economics of the psyche, and the secret irrationalities of the unconscious. Does the study of love have any natural boundaries?

In addition our authors discussed love in several of their writings, sometimes implicitly, not always confidently, and sometimes in frank speculation. They also seem to have changed their minds several times, and they both approached the mysteries of love with an intimidating reverence and modesty. The humility of Socrates in the *Symposium* and the *Phaedrus* goes beyond the usual Socratic disclaimers. Freud never did write the book on 'the love life of man,' which Ernest Jones tells us that he had announced, but near the end of his life he said that we know very little about love. And of course the secondary literature on both authors amply testifies to reasonable differences in interpretation of many of the crucial texts that we discuss. I have even heard it disputed that Freud had a theory of love, as distinct from his general theory of sexuality, as I maintain; though of course I agree that his theory of love is essentially based on his theory of sexuality.

For all these reasons, putting together the views of each author on love and 'reconstructing' them as 'theories of love' is a more difficult and risky undertaking than might appear at first sight. Nevertheless, making due allowances for differing views in different works, development of ideas, and difficulties of interpretation, I maintain that both Plato and Freud had grand, coherent – and fairly consistent over time – theories of love. I hope that the effort to bring them together in a clear light, as theories of love, will help us understand their views better, understand something about love, and perhaps stimulate further study and discussion.

The general plan of the work is to sketch briefly the nature and aims of this study, to reconstruct each theory of love in its own context and in some detail, to compare them, and finally to raise some critical questions. In the introductory chapter I make some distinctions in the study of love and I give some reasons for the selection of Plato and Freud. I also try by a series of questions to indicate roughly the aims and scope of a theory of love, and I sketch some of the linguistic background in which Plato's theory of love is set. In chapters 2, 3 and 4 I give a detailed critical exposition of Plato's theories of eros, friendship and familial love. In chapter 5 I expound briefly Freud's new conception of sexuality, highlighting the elements most relevant to his theory of love; and in chapter 6 I expound that theory in some detail. Finally, I compare the two theories in chapter 7, and I end the book by raising some critical questions.

It is impossible to acknowledge in detail all the help I have received in the last eight years while I was studying the theories of love of Plato and Freud and trying to write this book. My students here at the University of California at Irvine and Stanford, where I taught courses on Plato's and Freud's theories of love, raised many sharp questions which mixed cool skepticism with my admiration for these two great authors. Bury's great edition of the *Symposium* I could not have done without. And Dover's sharp disagreements with Plato's view of eros were an earthly antidote to the magic of Plato, who for many of us is still what Parmenides was to him, 'an awesome and reverent figure' – even Freud calls him 'the Divine Plato'. For the literary, dramatic, and religious rituals in which Plato sometimes embeds his views I received valuable help from Guthrie. Vlastos' and Moravcsik's challenging work on Plato's theory of love has been a considerable influence. And I must also thank Professor David Halperin, Chris Slupik, and several anonymous readers for many helpful comments. I am especially indebted to Professor Charles Kahn, who read an earlier version of the manuscript and saved me from many errors of omission and commission in the case of Plato; I am most grateful for the generous giving of his time. In trying to understand Freud's views and their development, I have relied considerably on James Strachey's editorial work and the great intellectual biography of Ernest Jones; and to a lesser extent on the work of Ellenberger, D. Rappaport, Wollheim and Sullaway. I am especially indebted to Professor Irvin Yalom, who read an earlier version of the Freud chapters and raised many helpful questions, and in whose seminar on Freud at the Stanford Medical School I learned a great deal about the early

Freud. I am also grateful to Professor Louis Gottschalk of the University of California at Irvine Medical School, who read a later version of the Freud chapters and gave me encouragement. None of these good people are of course responsible for my interpretations or for the errors that no doubt remain. Finally, I thank my wife Ann for her friendly encouragement and constant love.

Abbreviations

PS	Kenneth Dover, *Plato, Symposium*
GH	Kenneth Dover, *Greek Homosexuality*
HGP	W. K. C. Guthrie, *A History of Greek Philosophy*
SE	ed. J. Strachey, *The Standard Edition of the Complete Psychological Works of Sigmund Freud*

1

The Study of Love

Ask not of me, love, what is love?
Ask what is good of God above ...

P.J. Bailey

Introduction

The literature on love is immense. Over the centuries love in its many forms has been described, explained, defined, depicted and eulogized by poets, men of letters, philosophers, theologians, psychologists, anthropologists and even biologists. By now several historical and comparative studies have distinguished different concepts and historical stages in the west.[1] In Plato we have the distinction between *eros* and *philia*, erotic love, friendship and familial love; in Christian literature the concept of *agape*, God's love, love of God and brotherly love; and later the developments of courtly and romantic love.

A rough but perhaps useful distinction we can make in the literature on love is between the poets, novelists, and men of letters, on the one hand, and philosophers, theologians, and scientists on the other.[2] The distinction is not meant to be invidious. Sappho, Dante, or Shakespeare can depict and portray the experience of love with a beauty, delicacy, and dramatic power that philosophers, theologians, and scientists don't even pretend to rival, even though some of them are great writers themselves. What characterizes the latter group of writers, Plato, Aquinas or Freud, is that they approach the study of love in a more systematic fashion. They seek to distinguish, classify, and define different forms of the phenomenon, they try to discover the origins and causes of love in human nature and the human condition, and also to interpret the meaning and importance of love in the context of their vision of human life and destiny. Thus in their case we may perhaps speak of *theories* of love. In this book we shall reconstruct and compare two such theories.

Why should philosophers be interested in the study of love? Part of the reason lies in history and tradition. Plato, who started so much of philosophy, devoted three important dialogues to it, the *Lysis* to friendship and the *Symposium* and the *Phaedrus* to eros. And several subsequent philosophers, for example, Aristotle, Augustine and Aquinas studied love seriously. But the fundamental reason goes beyond history. Plato and Aristotle saw friendship as a great good and an important element in happiness. Plato saw eros as a powerful motivating force capable of inspiring humans to the greatest achievements in art, science, and philosophy. In his theory of sublimation Freud takes a similar view; and he regards sexual love as providing our most intense experience of pleasure and a pattern in our search for happiness. Christian philosophers such as Augustine and Aquinas downgraded erotic love but elevated love of God into the leading principle in the life of virtue and the way to salvation. Thus the study of love connects inevitably with the study of ethics, the study of the right and the good. Whether some form of love can function as the fundamental principle of rightness is controversial – John Rawls, for example, disputes it in the case of benevolence.[3] But that we cannot develop best as human beings, achieve and be happy, without the presence of some kinds of love would, I believe, be generally acknowledged. Plato and Freud would certainly agree.

But why compare Plato and Freud? A far more comprehensive historical and theoretical study would be of great interest, I believe, for philosophy, psychology, and perhaps even for education and aesthetics: a study that reconstructed and compared the great theories of eros and friendship in Plato and Aristotle, the Christian theories of agape, the theories of courtly and romantic love, Freud's theory, and the many post-Freudian theories in this century, chiefly by psychologists. Such a giant study is beyond my knowledge and would probably be a joint project cutting across several disciplines. For my part I offer a reconstruction and comparison of two grand and coherent theories which I regard as landmarks in the history of the concept.

The choice of Plato and Freud rests on several reasons. For one thing, Freud himself invites the comparison. On several occasions he tries to elicit support for his theories of sexuality and love by reference to the 'divine Plato'; and in *Group Psychology and the Analysis of the Ego* he makes a very exact claim of comparison: 'In its origin, function, and relation to sexual love, the "Eros" of the philosopher Plato coincides exactly with the love force, the libido of psychoanalysis ...' (1921, SE, vol. XVIII, p. 91). When one considers the many fundamental differences between Plato and Freud, in language, culture, and conditions of philosophic and scientific knowledge, this is a remarkable claim worthy of investigation.

Apart from this, Plato and Freud may well be regarded as two great innovators, revolutionaries in the study of love, philosophers and scientists who had at their disposal great new theories and methods to aid them in the analysis of the concept and the understanding of the experience. Plato was the first great philosopher to study love seriously. He used his moral psychology and his theories of person and the soul to locate the origin of love in human imperfection and mortality; he used the new philosophical methods, developed by himself and Socrates, to define different kinds of love; and his metaphysical theory of Forms to show how love can elevate us and put us in touch with the divine. By his own estimate, Freud was the first man of science to approach the study of love scientifically, to try to probe its mysteries and explain its irrationalities.[4] Using his new theories of the mind and the psychosexual development of the individual, and relying on data from his patients revealed by the methods of psychoanalysis, he tried to locate the origins of all love in the early experiences of the individual, and to define and explain genetically its many forms in adult life. The results of all this are, in my opinion, impressive: two grand, coherent, and ambitious theories that throw considerable light on a range of related concepts and experiences.

To my knowledge, the two theories have not been reconstructed and compared systematically enough and in significant detail.[5] Both theories are complex and comparisons must be made carefully and with an open mind. We must not assume at the outset, for example, that Plato and Freud had the same concerns about love or that they asked exactly the same questions. Nor that they had similar theories of the human mind or similar methods of investigation. Each theory must first be reconstructed in its own terms and within each author's wider theoretical context, and the main comparisons made later. I hope this will bring out the essential features of each theory, will suggest their main virtues and defects, and also stimulate further study. This is the strategy I follow in this book.

Questions about Love

We spoke of Plato's and Freud's *theories* of love and we made a distinction between the poets' studies of love and those of the philosophers and scientists. This distinction itself may of course be challenged, as well as the implication that poets have no theories of love. Without entering this last dispute, it would clearly be useful to have some idea of what a theory of love is. We might indicate this very roughly by considering briefly the main *questions* about love that philosophers and scientists have raised and thought important enough to try to answer. This will give us some understanding of what a theory of love is supposed to accomplish, it will be a guide to the exposition and evaluation of Plato's and Freud's theories of love, and it will also offer a glimpse of the main controversies in the literature about love.

The set of questions we discuss below is reasonable or non-arbitrary in the sense that it contains questions theorists of love have thought important and have actually tried to answer. The set is not meant to be exhaustive, but I think it contains the most important questions that have been raised, and a theory that does not answer several of them may well be thought to be incomplete. Plato and Freud do not explicitly raise all these questions – hardly any single writer does – but their theories are comprehensive enough to contain or suggest answers to almost all of them.

Love is universally thought to be a relation with at least two terms, something that loves, the lover, and something that is loved, the beloved or 'the object' of love. It is also clear that love is not always mutual:[6] one's love may or may not be returned, and perhaps for this reason studies of love are usually studies of the lover. The first question that arises is about the possible ranges of 'lovers' and 'objects of love':

What sorts of things can love and what sorts can be loved?

There is minimal agreement, I think, that lovers are sentient beings, capable of some perception or thought and feeling. Animals, humans, and divine beings can fall under this characterization, but there is disagreement whether divine beings can love, and whether all non-human animals can be lovers.[7] Objects of love, on the other hand, are not universally confined to sentient beings: apparently just about everthing else can be loved, including food, country, works of art, ideas, 'causes', etc. There are perhaps differences of emphasis here, but we can say, I think, that love among humans is usually regarded as central and important, and a theory that does not satisfactorily account for this case may well be thought defective.[8]

The question of the range of lovers and objects of love is important not only for understanding the general concept, but also for distinguishing or classifying different kinds of love. It may be that the most neutral or least question-begging way to distinguish different kinds of love is purely extensionally, that is by reference only to lovers and objects of love. Familial love is just such a classification: it is love among members of families, parents and children and siblings. By way of contrast, classifying love into egoistic and altruistic love is less useful; it is question-begging at the start of an investigation since some theorists claim that all love is egoistic.[9]

With the possible exception of Christian love, it is universally thought that love involves choice. Lovers and friends do not love and befriend everyone; they choose or select, though such selections are not necessarily deliberative, rational, or even conscious. Some writers, Freud for example, thought that we cannot understand love unless we understand how lovers select. The problem of choice is highlighted in the case of 'love at first sight', where the selection seems instant and mysterious. So an important question about love is:

How does a lover choose or select a beloved?

Plato raised this quesion occasionally and his theory contains a general answer to it, as does the view he puts in the mouth of Aristophanes. Freud paid a lot of attention to this question and provided several models of selection; partly due to his influence, we now have several theories of selection, though none that has gained general acceptance.[10]

A very central question, important in itself and also to the issue of selection, is raised by every theorist of love: it concerns the origins, sources, or causal conditions of love. Why do we love at all? Or, as we might phrase it more familiarly:

What are 'the causes' of love?

Physiological, psychological and biological needs are often cited by writers in answer to this question, but there is of course much disagreement.[11] Plato makes central use of the notion of need or deficiency and gives some teleological explanations of erotic behavior, while Freud concentrates on physiology and the developmental experiences of the individual.

The literature shows as much concern for 'the effects' as for the causes of love.

What are the characteristic effects of love?

This is one of Plato's main questions about love. There is much disagreement here, the biggest controversy perhaps being whether love is always beneficial and benevolent.[12]

But the biggest contemporary controversy perhaps has been raised by the question:

What is the relation of love to sexual desire?

Plato seems to have done his best to desexualize even love between the sexes, assigning it a non-sexual final cause, namely immortality. Freud proposed an equally radical hypothesis, almost the exact opposite of Plato, and since then the disagreements have intensified.[13]

Another controversy, ancient, medieval and modern, has raged in various forms around the question:

Is love always egoistic or selfish?

Plato's theory seems to contain a positive answer to this question, and has been much criticized on that account. The question has exercised subsequent writers, and is often complicated by distinctions between different kinds of love: familial, romantic, Christian, and so on.[14]

Idealization or overestimation of the beloved was a hallmark of courtly and romantic love. It was recognized by Plato, and Freud thought of it as a sure sign of love and tried to explain it. So we have the question:

Why do lovers idealize or overestimate the beloved?

According to some theorists defining love is indispensible to understanding it. Hence the central question:

What is love?

Plato thinks it is essential to raise this question, and he takes it as a request for a non-stipulative 'real' definition. Subsequent writers have also tried to define love, but not all of them have Plato's notion of definition. Apart from stipulations, we may perhaps understand the question as calling for some sort of general characterization of love, which is true of all clear cases of love and explanatory of each. The better definitions will presumably also illuminate borderline and puzzling cases.[15]

It is difficult to find a writer on love who has resisted the temptation to talk about the value of love and to evaluate different kinds of love. We can perhaps raise this normative issue in this way:

Are some kinds of love better than others?

Plato explicitly ranks different kinds of love in his famous 'Ladder of Love', Freud speaks of 'normal love', Maslow of 'healthy love', and others of 'genuine love', or 'true love'.[16]

Our last question is clearly normative, in the sense that answers to it presuppose some criteria or standards of rightness or goodness. We shall try to reconstruct these criteria in the case of Plato and Freud.

Other questions, for example, the ones about causes and effects, seem to be empirical or experimental: answers to them should be based on and tested by investigation of actual cases. With various writers these investigations range all the way from introspection and ordinary observation of others to more systematic clinical observation and more systematic yet controlled experiments. Lacking the benefit of the empirical sciences, Plato's investigations fall somewhere in the beginning of this range; Freud relied largely on clinical observations, while some recent empirical studies are experimentally oriented and make systematic use of control groups.[17]

Some questions are neither normative nor empirical but primarily conceptual or linguistic; thus the question, whether non-sentient beings such as stones can love is presumably to be answered by reflection on the concept of love or the use of the term 'love'.

It is therefore clear that a theory which answers all our questions will be partly conceptual, partly descriptive and explanatory, and partly normative. Writers do not always make these distinctions, but it will be useful for us to bear them in mind, both in reconstructing and assessing theories of love.

Terms of Love: *Eros, Philia, Agape*

Since several languages are involved in this study, we might avoid early confusion by looking briefly at some of the main terms of love, especially in Ancient Greek which distinguishes different kinds of love more sharply than English or German.

In English the word 'love' seems to cover a rather wide variety of feelings, attitudes and behavior. We select some part of this variety by joining the word 'love' with some modifying word or phrase; thus we speak of 'parental love', 'romantic love', 'divine love', and so on. The single word common in all these phrases creates a presumption that all these varieties have something in common, a common core or source. The story is similar in German with the word 'Liebe', something Freud was impressed by and tried to take advantage of, as we shall see (SE vol. XVIII, p. 91, and chapter 6 below). But these linguistic situations did not exist in Plato's language. Instead, he uses two different words, *eros* and *philia*, and their corresponding verbs, to pick out different, perhaps overlapping portions of this variety. A third word for love, the noun *agape*, does not occur in Plato at all, and indeed does not occur in Greek till considerably later.[18] It is the word used in the New Testament to signify God's love, love of God, and love of neighbor. Plato does use the cognate verb *agapan* (to be content with) and sometimes couples it with the verb *philein* (to love), but there is no evidence to suppose he thinks it represents a significantly different concept from eros and philia.[19] We can say, trivially, that Plato had no theory of agape. Let us look briefly at some distinctions among the three terms and their relations to 'love'.

In Ancient Greek, and certainly in Plato and Aristotle, *philia* was standardly used to signify two kinds of love: familial love, whether parental, filial, or sibling, and the love of friendship.[20] *Philia*, whether among family members or friends, need not have a sexual component, and it was not standardly understood to involve sexual desire. *Eros*, on the other hand, standardly signified sexual love, that is, love between persons, whether of the same or different sex, in which sexual desire is a component.[21] Eros was also usually conceived as being more intense, more passionate and as having greater motivating power than philia, at least friendship-philia; while philia was thought to be more constant and lasting.[22] Both *eros* and *philia* normally signify relations among humans; the objects of familial philia are determined by family relations, while friendship-philia and eros involve selection or choice over all humans. In the New Testament, *agape* is used to signify God's love for his children, the love men are urged to have for God, and the love they are exhorted to have for each other. Christian agape is not supposed to have a sexual component, it is essentially benevolent, and it is supposed to be constant and abiding.[23]

This is a rough sketch of some of the distinctions between eros, philia, and agape. Since all three are covered by the English 'love', the following chart gives some of the relations among all four:

LOVE

Philia		*Eros*	*Agape*
Familial Love	Friendship[24]	Sexual Love	Christian Love
Parental		Male–Female	God–Man
Filial		Male–Male	Man–God
Sibling		Female–Female	Man–Man

It should be noted that our chart is very simplistic and does not attempt to capture complexities of usage. It indicates roughly only the denotations or semantic fields of the four terms, not their connotations or meanings. Nor does it take account of the complex uses of the cognate verbs, adjectives and concrete nouns. For these the only thing that seems clear is that *erastai* is properly rendered by 'lovers', *philoi* by 'friends', and the verbs *philein* and *eran* are best rendered by 'to love'.

Despite the simplifications, our distinctions and chart are useful in enabling us to indicate the scope of Plato's 'theory of love'. What we mean by this expression in this book is his theories of eros and philia. But though he had no theory of agape, we shall see that his theories of eros and philia have some interesting implications for 'divine love'. In any case, our remarks hopefully will serve to avoid gross semantic confusions that can arise from the fact that we are studying theories which were written in different languages.

Limits of This Study

Besides linguistic variations, the study of Plato's and Freud's theories of love also involves different cultures, different historical periods and different disciplines. We acknowledge this complexity, and because of it we need to make explicit the limits of this study.

Plato and Freud of course lived in different cultures and historical periods, and one was primarily a philosopher, the other a psychologist. Though love seems to be a universal human phenomenon, how love is conceived, practised and valued may sometimes vary with culture and historical setting. Social controls and practices of courting and mating behavior, incidence and attitudes toward homosexuality, perceptions of beauty, the state of psychobiological knowledge – all these may differ with culture and time and might influence significantly the theory constructed by a given writer. What he takes as data for his theory or as characteristic of love could be only a small and unrepresentative sample of considerable cultural and temporal variations. Even when a writer is aware of this problem, the theory he constructs may still be culture-bound simply because a wider range of data is not available to him. As we shall see, Plato was aware of cultural variations, and he was a genius at constructing and presenting honestly theories rival to his own. But he obviously lacked extensive, empirically based, medical, biological and psychological knowledge, and the cultural variations he seemed aware of were confined to the Greek culture.[25] Freud was more fortunate in all these respects. He had more extensive medical knowledge, he knew the theory of evolution, and he had available to him several anthropological and historical studies of primitive and other cultures. But his clinical practice and observations obviously had a rather narrow cultural and temporal base, and his theory can be expected to have corresponding limits.[26] Both writers were aware of cultural variations and rival theories, and both probably tried to construct theories of love that would have universal validity, but it is hardly reasonable to expect that either of them was able to escape completely the limits of culture and time.

The differences in cultures and historical times between our two authors are beyond the scope of this book. This is not a sociological or cultural study. It is mainly a critical exposition and comparison of Plato's and Freud's theories, which relies primarily on explication of texts and philosophical analysis. Fortunately, there are many able cultural and historical studies of the two periods, some of which we consult in the sequel, and some of which our readers can consult to form a more complete picture of conceptions of love in Plato's and Freud's times.

Notes

1 In this category fall the studies of, e.g., Nygren, A., *Agape and Eros*; Singer, I., *The Nature of Love*; Hunt, M.M., *The Natural History of Love*; Morgan, D.N., *Love: Plato, the Bible and Freud*; and de Rougemont, D., *Love in the Western World.*

2 A similar distinction is drawn by Freud in the opening paragraph of his first essay on love, 'A Special Type of Choice of Object Made by Men,' Standard Edition (SE), vol. XI. He actually draws the distinction between 'creative writers' or 'artists' and 'science', and

says that he is going to extend 'a strictly scientific treatment to the field of human love' (p. 165). It is unclear in what category Freud would place the philosophers and theologians who studied love before him; his first sentence suggests that he would put them under 'creative writers,' and so does SE, vol. XXIII, 1938, p. 149, n. 1.

3 *A Theory of Justice*, 1971, p. 190. For a different interpretation of agape as a fundamental principle, see Donagan, A., *The Theory of Morality*, pp. 57–66, and of course Nygren, *Agape and Eros*.

4 SE, vol. XI, p. 165.

5 The only comparisons of the two theories that I know of, brief and somewhat fragmentary, are by Morgan, *Love*; Nachmanson, M., 'Freuds Libidotheorie verglichen mit Eroslekre Platos', *Internationale Zeitschrift für Auztliche Psychoanalyse*; Pfister, O., 'Plato als Vorlanger der Psychoanalyse', *Internationale Zeitschrift für Psychoanalyse*; Gould, T., *Platonic Love*; and Simon, B., *Mind and Madness in Ancient Greece*, Cornell, 1978.

6 In technical language, love is a non-symmetric relation. It is also non-transitive and non-reflexive. See, e.g., I.M. Copi, *Symbolic Logic*, pp. 141–3; Copi actually gives love as an example of a relation with all these three properties.

7 As we shall see, Plato has a conception of love and of divine beings from which it follows that gods cannot love. This is in obvious disagreement with conceptions of Christian love. Lower non-human animals which reproduce asexually are dubious candidates for lovers. See Daly, M. and Wilson, M., *Sex, Evolution and Behaviour*.

8 Plato may be a case in point: love of the Form Beauty, an abstract entity, is the highest kind of love in his system, and his theory of love of persons is sometimes thought to be inadequate partly for this reason. Freud concentrates on love among humans and regards this as the central or 'nuclear' case; love of inanimate objects is analysed by means of the mechanisms of displacement, inhibition and sublimation.

9 Hazo's *The Idea of Love* seems to me sometimes defective because he uses the egoistic-altruistic distinction as a basic classification.

10 Grant, V.W., 'Sexual Love' in *The Encyclopedia of Sexual Behavior*, gives a useful review of recent theories of selection, as well as Freud's.

11 Variants of this question are extensively discussed in contemporary literature. See Daly and Wilson, *Sex*; Ellis, ed. *The Encyclopedia*; and Montague, A., ed., *The Meaning of Love*.

12 Plato raises this question explicitly in terms of the *erga* (works) of eros. A whole range of effects – physiological, psychological and cultural – is covered by this question.

13 This question is complicated by distinctions between different kinds of love: familial, Christian, romantic and courtly, and so on.

While Christian love is normally regarded as not having a sexual component and romantic love as having one, familial love has become a controversial case. And of course, even in the case of nonfamilial love between different sexes writers have tried to distinguish between sexual desire and love. See e.g., Grant, 'Sexual Love' (in Ellis).

14 This question has been discussed by Vlastos, G., 'The Individual as Object of Love in Plato' in *Platonic Studies*; Nygren, *Agape and Eros*; McDougal, W., *Social Psychology*; and others.

15 Other than stipulations and dictionary reports of usage, theoretical definitions of love are rarely attempted, difficult to construct, and hard to justify. Plato thought that the construction of a definition is essential to successful investigation, but subsequent writers do not seem to share this view. Still, some try, for example, Montague.

16 Systematic evaluations, revealing the criteria for the rankings, are rare. Plato, Freud, and Maslow, for example, all rank love, but it is difficult to discover their criteria.

17 H.F. Harlow's study (some of it in Montague) is a good example of the last, though it is confined to animals.

18 But Dover cites an apparently fourth or fifth century vase of a half-naked woman bearing the name 'agape', *Greek Homosexuality* (GH), p. 50. In any case, here we are speaking of *agape* as it occurs in the New Testament, and as expounded by Nygren in his great study *Agape and Eros*, especially the chapters on the Gospels and St. Paul.

19 The most recent illuminating discussion of the three terms, especially *eros* and *philia* is in Dover, GH, pp. 42–54.

20 Philia in the sense of friendship, is Socratically investigated in Plato's *Lysis*, and some account of it is given in the *Republic*. See Ch. 5, and Vlastos, *Platonic Studies*, pp. 6–19. Aristotle's masterful analysis of it occurs in *Nicomachean Ethics*, Bks VIII, IX. Philia, in the sense of familial love, is briefly discussed and compared to eros by Phaedrus in *Symposium* 179bc. For these two uses of *philia* see also *A Greek–English Lexicon*.

21 Dover thinks that in the classical and Hellenistic periods 'the connotation of this group of words [*eros, eran, erasthai*] is so regularly sexual that other uses of it can fairly be regarded as sexual metaphor', GH, p. 43. In note 11 of the same page he claims that 'Plato's concept of eros differed from everyone else's', and on p. 156 he says that Socrates 'uses "erastes" figuratively (e.g. *Rep*. 501d)'. Whether Plato divorces eros from sexuality so much that his use of the term becomes metaphorical I shall consider in ch. 2.

22 For some of these contrasts between philia and eros see Vlastos, ibid., p. 4, n. 4, Dover, GH, pp. 49–50. For the intensity of eros Dover cites Prodicus' definition of eros as 'desire doubled' and his comment that 'eros doubled is insanity'. Dover, GH, p. 43.

23 This is supposed to be pre-eminently true of God's agape for us, which Nygren takes as the model for interpreting the commandments to love God and neighbor.

24 'Friendship' seems to present an exception to the statement that in English there is a single word for all kinds of love (a point sharpened by the differences between 'friends' and 'lovers'), though it is difficult to supposed that friendship is not a kind of love.

25 Some of the cultural variations Plato was aware of are given in the preliminary speeches in the *Symposium*; see ch. 2. For two recent studies of the Greek culture of eros see Dover, GH, and Carson, A., *Eros: The Bittersweet*.

26 For a recent study of the culture in which Freud was brought up and in which he practised, see Zanuso, B., *The Young Freud*, especially chs 1 and 2, in which the authoritarian and repressive structure of the Viennese society and family are clearly brought out.

2

Plato's Theory of Eros in the *Symposium*

Love and desire are the spirit's
wings to great deeds.

Goethe

Introduction

Plato's *Symposium* has been justly described as 'one of the masterpieces of classical literature,' by 'the subtlest and most brilliant of artists in prose.' With 'the throbbing pulse of life as his theme' Plato 'matches that theme by the dramatic verve and vigor of his style'.[1]

Plato's theme is eros, and the dramatic setting a dinner party at the house of Agathon, the young poet who had won a victory in a drama contest a day earlier. Besides the host, the guests included Socrates and his pupil Aristodemus (from whom the narrator Apolodorus heard of the proceedings); Phaedrus with whom Socrates discusses eros also in the *Phaedrus*; Pausanias who is in love with the beautiful Agathon; the sober physician Eryximachus; the great comic poet Aristophanes; and eventually the wild and brilliant Alcebiades who delivers a drunk but glorious closing speech in praise of Socrates.

Early in the proceedings Eryximachus suggests that instead of heavy drinking they take turns praising Eros, a theme proposed to him by Phaedrus, who had complained that one finds treatises in praise of everything – even salt – but no encomia of the great god Eros. Socrates accepts, remarking that neither he nor Aristophanes can very well refuse, since he himself knows nothing but 'erotics', while Aristophanes divides his time between Dionysus and Aphrodite. Accordingly they take turns at praising Eros, proceeding from left to right around the couches, Phaedrus first and Socrates last. In content, style, and tone the speeches display an amazing variety: from the conventional to the profound, from pedantry to poetry, from soberness to burlesque, from the sublime to the ridiculous.

Plato does not tell us explicitly why he chose such a setting in which to present his own theory of eros, presumably in the speech of Socrates and the wise woman Diotima. But it is characteristic of his middle dialogues (such as the *Phaedo*, the *Republic*, and the *Phaedrus*, with which the *Symposium* is usually grouped) to present his own views against a background of traditional and contemporary alternative or opposing ideas. Thus it seems reasonable to take the first five speeches as representing at least Plato's perception of the various traditions about Eros in the Greek culture: in poetry and art, in pre-Socratic speculations, in medicine and law, and in courting and mating practices.[2] And indeed we shall find some evidence of this.

Moreover, Plato often portrays his speakers as star-examples, in character and background, of the views they express. Thus, for example, the beautiful young poet Agathon gives us a pretty eulogy of Eros as he appears in poetry and the arts; the solemn Eryximachus propounds medical theories and cosmic pre-Socratic speculations; Aristophanes buffoons around in a typical display of fantasy and sexual frankness, combined with some serious thoughts. And Socrates? In questioning Agathon he starts with a typical display of Socratic logic. But under the guidance of the prophetess Diotima he elevates eros from sexuality and bodily beauty to philosophic love of wisdom and Beauty itself. The dramatic entrance of Alcebiades, noisy, unseemly and drunk, seems to take us from the sublime to the ridiculous, and even from the noble to the corrupt. But in Alcebiades' speech Socrates emerges as the star example of the philosophic lover, one who turns down seemingly irresistible bodily charms in favor of wisdom and beauty of soul. In the final speech, through the admiration of the corrupt Alcebiades for the uncorrupted Socrates, we are perhaps meant to see a personal example of the union of passion and reason in which Plato's abstract theory of eros culminates.[3]

Some Preliminary Speeches: Eros all Good, Eros Good and Bad, Eros a Cosmic Force

Phaedrus begins with an unqualified eulogy of the god Eros. Eros, he says, is a great god, a marvel among men and gods. He cites Hesiod and Parmenides that Eros is the oldest of the gods, and being oldest 'the cause of the greatest goods' (*Symposium* 178a–c).[4] Phaedrus cannot see a greater good than a young man having an honorable lover or a lover having a boy-favorite. Kinship, office and wealth do not ensure a good life as much as eros. Ambition for noble deeds and shame of base acts is most powerful among lovers, and eros is thus the greatest motivation for good, whether in private, civic, or military life. Out of eros for her husband Alcestis was willing to die for him, while his father and mother were not, which shows that eros is stronger than familial love (philia). The gods honored her, while they punished Orpheus who was not similarly willing to die for Euridice. They honored Achilles, who chose to die for his lover Patroclus, even more; for a lover is filled with divinity, whereas the noble deeds of the beloved, done without that benefit, are more admirable. In sum:

> Eros is the most venerable and honorable of the gods, the most powerful in giving virtue and happiness to men whether living or departed. (180b)

Though not rich in substance, Phaedrus' speech has some noteworthy features. It reveals the mythical tradition that there is a *god* of love, Eros, who is responsible for eros among humans. It distinguishes between eros and parental love, and it interprets three famous cases of lovers, two heterosexual and one male homosexual . The most unusual feature is Phaedrus' view that Eros is all good and its effects on man completely beneficial. This is contrary to the whole tradition about Eros before Plato, in which eros is a mixed blessing and a 'bittersweet' experience.[5] Phaedrus's speech is pure encomium.

Pausanias at once takes issue with the view that eros is all good. He also assigns definite superiority to male-homosexual eros, and is much concerned with the circumstances in which it is proper for the beloved to gratify his lover sexually.[6] Pausanias follows the tradition that makes a god or goddess responsible for eros among humans. But he distinguishes two goddesses of eros, Popular Aphrodite and Heavenly Aphrodite, he assigns different characteristics to each, and explains two kinds of eros among humans accordingly. Popular Aphrodite is younger, wanton, and partakes of both male and female. Lovers inspired by this goddess love women as well as boys, love the body rather than the soul, and care for nothing but sexual gratification. Set upon the body, this love ceases as soon as bodily beauty fades, and the beloved is abandoned for another beauty, deceived and bereft of benefit. Heavenly Aphrodite, on the other hand, is older and wiser, partakes only of the male, and is untinged with wantonness. Accordingly, lovers inspired by this Aphrodite love only boys, for males have a robuster nature and a larger share of mind; they love the soul rather than the body, and seek to impart wisdom to their beloveds. Set on the virtue of the soul, rather than the transitory beauty of the body, this love is constant and abiding, superior to popular love in the benefits it bestows on lover and beloved alike. Unlike the laws and customs of courtship in other cities, the laws in Athens reflect the superiority of this love. Only when the older man loves the boy's soul and cares for its education and wisdom is it deemed honorable for the beloved to sexually gratify his lover, for the sake of virtue (184c–185b).

Pausanias' speech fully reflects the Greek bias of male superiority. It also reflects the ambiguous standing of male homosexual love. Pausanias is apologetic of and downgrades the 'mere passion for boys'. He tries to elevate some male homosexual relationships above the level of sexuality, making soul rather than body the principle of selection and attraction, and emphasizing the intellectual benefits an older and wiser man can bestow upon a young boy. His distinctions foreshadow some of Plato's, but unlike Plato he does not weaken the connection between eros and sexual desire. Apart from Plato's own view, his speech probably represents 'the best face' that conventional Greek morality could put on male homosexual relationships.

Aristophanes is supposed to give the next speech, but he has the hiccoughs and asks Eryximachus either to give him medical help or to take his turn in speaking. The physician prescribes several remedies and takes Aristophanes' turn.

Eryximachus claims to agree with Pausanias that there are two kinds of eros, but immediately proceeds to extend the range of lovers and the objects of love far beyond what any speaker before or after him does. He says that medicine has taught him that eros 'is not merely an impulse of human souls towards beautiful men, but the attraction of all creatures to a great variety of things, which works in the bodies of all animals and all growths upon the earth, and practically in everything that is' (186a). Apparently he thinks of eros as a cosmic force, an attraction and desire among dissimilars, which brings opposites into agreement and harmony. He tries to define several arts and sciences in terms of eros; medicine, he says, is 'knowledge of the love-matters of the body in regard to repletion and evacuation' (186cd); music is a 'knowledge of love-matters relating to harmony and rhythm' (187c). He makes similar remarks about agriculture and athletics. He sees eros at work even in the yearly seasons. When the opposites heat and cold, drought and moisture, are brought together by the orderly Eros they become 'bearers of ripe fertility and health to men and animals and plants'; but 'when the wanton-spirited Eros gains the ascendant in the seasons of the year, great destruction and wrong does he wreck'

(188ab). He finally alludes to Pausanias' two kinds of eros, Heavenly and Popular, and makes similar remarks about their effects on human affairs.

Commentators have seen Eryximachus' speech as representing the tradition, in poetry and pre-Socratic philosophy, of Eros as a cosmic power, a principle of generation and reconciliation of opposites.[7] In Hesiod's *Cosmogony* Eros is 'an all-powerful cosmic force ... fairest among the immortal gods, the power of sexual generations ... necessary to set on foot the matings and births which are thought of as the sole means of generation of all parts of the universe'.[8] In Empedocles (Fragments 21 and 22, for example), Love is a cosmic force that reconciles opposites, though we must note that Empedocles does not use the word *Eros* but rather *Philia* or *Philotes*. Commentators have also related Eryximachus' speech to themes in Aeschylus, Euripides and Orphic Poetry as well as to the Hippocratic writings.[9]

Plato does not make his attitude explicit towards the main themes in Eryximachus' speech. We may note that in Socrates' view (presumably Plato's own), specific eros is essentially connected with begetting or creativity, and that it extends beyond sexuality.[10] But in Plato's theory the lover is always a human being, and Eros mediates not between opposites (such as the beautiful and the ugly or the good and the bad), but rather between 'intermediates' (what is neither beautiful or ugly) and the good or the beautiful.

The Speech of Aristophanes: Eros as Desire to Unite with One's Other Half

It is now the turn of Aristophanes who has finally mastered the hiccoughs with a fit of sneezing. Erychimachus soberly warns him to stop buffooning lest his speech appear absurd, but Aristophanes replies that he is not afraid of the absurd – that after all is native to his Muse – but only of the ridiculous. He is not afraid of being laughed with but only of being laughed at.

He begins by saying that humanity has not appreciated the power of eros, and that to do so one must learn about human nature and its sufferings. Originally our nature was not what it is now: there were not two kinds of humans, male and female, but three. This third kind, a combination of the two, has perished and only the name remains, 'man–woman'. Each of the three kinds had four arms, four legs, two faces and two genitals facing in opposite directions. These beings, a male–male, a male–female, and a female–female, did their begetting not with each other, but on the earth, 'like the crickets'. Grotesquely globular but fast and powerful, they eventually started to conspire against the gods. The gods soberly pondered the problem. Zeus found a clever way of reducing their strength without destroying them; he cut each pair in half, and asked Apollo to heal the wound and to turn the face of each to the side of the wound 'in order that everyone might be made more orderly by the sight of the knife's work upon him' (190e). In this intermediate condition, 'when our first form had been cut in two, each half in longing for its fellow would come to it again; and then they would fling their arms about each other and in mutual embrace yearning to be grafted together, till they began to perish in hunger and general indolence, through refusing to do anything apart' (191ab). On the death of a half, the other half would seek and embrace any half that would match the original pair: a male half of a male–male would seek a male, a male half of a male–female would seek a female, and a female half of a female–female would seek a female. These unions were not sexual, since they sought to rejoin each other wound to wound while the genitals were still on the opposite sides. In this condition they were perishing, and Zeus, taking pity on them resorted to a fresh device. He moved the genital parts to the wound side, an operation resulting in our present condition:

> These parts he now shifted to the front, to be used for propagating on each other – in the female member by means of the male; so that if in their embracements a man should happen on a woman there might be conception and continuation of their kind; and also if male met with male they might have some satiety of their union and a relief, and so might turn their hands to their labours and their interest to ordinary life. Thus anciently is mutual love ingrained in mankind, reassembling our earlier estate and endeavoring to combine two in one and heal the human sore. (191cd)

Aristophanes now proceeds to explain homosexual and heterosexual attractions on the basis of his story. Some men seek and love other men because they are halves of an original male–male pair, and they seek to be whole again by reuniting with their other half. Some men seek women and some women seek men because they were of the male–female pair and seek reunion with their other half. And some women are women lovers because they are of the woman–woman pair and seek similar re-union. In addition, the reason why lovers universally want to be together, to live together, and even to die together, is not merely sexual intercourse – this is too weak a reason to explain the phenomena:

> No one could imagine this to be the mere amorous connection, or that such alone could be the reason why each rejoices in the other's company with so eager a zest: obviously the soul of each is wishing for something else that it cannot express, only divining and darkly hinting what it wishes. (192c)

And that is to be made whole again by rejoining and reuniting with one's other half in the original condition.

In conclusion, Aristophanes offers a definition of eros based on his story, a definition that seems designed to give us the 'real' or 'ultimate' cause of eros:

> The cause of it all is this, that our original form was as I have described, and we were whole; and the desire and pursuit of this wholeness is called eros. (192e–193a)

Over the centuries Aristophanes' speech has exercised a strange fascination, its influence being second only to the speech of Socrates, and it has even been mistaken for Plato's own 'theory'.[11]

There is agreement that the speech, in marked contrast to the ponderousness and even pedantry of Eryximachus, provides comic relief, and that Plato does justice to the great comic genius of Aristophanes; but there is much controversy whether anything in the speech is meant seriously and if so what. Guthrie says that it is a 'wild extravaganza' and a 'comic burlesque'; as such it can hardly have a 'moral,' though he conceeds that it has a 'conclusion', the definition of eros.[12] According to Bury, the speech 'shows a very pretty wit', and is 'a masterpiece of grotesque fantasy worthy of Rabelais himself'. But its conclusion 'is not without depth and beauty'.[13] Dover maintains that the speech is 'amusing and fanciful', but it does have a 'moral'. He goes on to interpret it in a paragraph worth quoting:

> Aristophanes, unlike all the other speakers in *Symposium*, recognizes that when you fall in love you see in another individual a special and peculiar 'complement' to yourself; for your union with that individual is an end, most certainly not a means, nor a step toward some 'higher' and more abstract plane, and very often you continue to love and desire that person even when much more powerful sensory or intellectual stimuli impinge upon you from alternative sources. Having composed for Aristophanes the only speech in *Symposium* which strikes a modern reader as founded on observable realities, Plato later makes Diotima reject and condemn its central theme.[14]

It may not be possible to reconcile all these views and many more besides. But though there are big differences in emphasis, there is much agreement that the speech is both amusing and serious; indeed, we might say, a masterful combination of the absurd, the clever and the profound. So let us have our laugh and then remove the comic mask and look at what remains.

The comedy, the burlesque, the grotesqueness, the sexual frankness, the pretty wit, are all evident and abundant. But what is serious? To this question we may never find a generally agreed answer, but for a related question we have clear evidence. Did Plato take anything in Aristophanes' speech seriously? In a clear reference to this speech Plato has Diotima make a fundamental criticism of Aristophanes' definition of eros: Eros is not for our other half, nor for wholeness, nor for what is our own or what belongs to us, but only for the good.[15] Conceivably, Plato is objecting to the narcissism implicit in Aristophanes' view (what we love is a part of us or someone like ourselves), but he is certainly objecting to the concept of eros as attachment without valuation. Neither goodness or beauty or any other value term characterizes the objects of Aristophanic eros, whereas such valuation is essential in Plato's view.

Moreover, we have plenty of evidence that Freud took Aristophanes' view seriously.[16] Contrary to Plato, he may have found Aristophanic narcissism congenial, but in any case he certainly adopted the guiding idea in Aristophanes' speech: that to understand eros, and indeed all love, we need to look into human nature and its development. As we shall see, all of Freud's explanations of love were genetic or developmental (at first ontogenetic, referring to the development of the individual from infancy, and later philogenetic as well, referring to the development of the species).

Apart from whether they were meant seriously, there are other noteworthy features in Aristophanes' view. One is the attempt to explain the facts of homosexual and heterosexual selection in love – facts that any theory of love would need to explain. Though this part of the story is not entirely clear and has been criticized as 'a little confused',[17] the main idea is clear enough: what selection we make depends on what our other half was, male or female, in the original human condition.

Another noteworthy feature is that Aristophanes elevates eros above sexual reproduction and even above sexual union. Reproduction cannot be the aim or even a main aim of eros since it is not present in all cases of eros. This is reflected in Aristophanes' speech, where reproduction is made a by-product of one kind of eros, male–female, in our present human condition. In the intermediate stage reproduction is non-sexual and totally independent of eros; while in the original condition there is non-sexual reproduction and eros is totally absent! Sexual union or sexual intercourse is present in all three cases of eros in our present human condition, but it is nevertheless not the aim of eros, though it is useful in leading to reproduction in one case and in providing relief in the others. This is shown both by the definition of eros, in which the aim is given as wholeness rather than sexual union, and also by the fact that in the intermediate stage there is desire and eros for wholeness, but not for sexual union.

Aristophanes locates the origin of eros in an essential incompleteness in the human being – separation from other humans, and assigns to eros the aim of bringing us together – completion and wholeness by union with another person. This thought is indeed not without depth and beauty. Plato agrees that eros arises from some incompleteness, but disagrees on what the incompleteness is, and on how eros remedies it.

We see, then, that when we remove the comic mask the speech shows considerable insight and sophistication: it does some of the main things we expect a theory of love to do. It attempts to get at the origin or causal conditions of eros, it sees the need to explain the main facts of selection of beloveds, and does so genetically; it also assigns roles to reproduction and sexuality, and it attempts to define the concept. For this alone Freud's respect for it is deserved. And when we bring back the masterful blend of myth and fantasy, the sexual frankness, the pretty wit, its charm and fascination become understandable. Who but Plato could have written it? Perhaps only Aristophanes!

The Speech of Agathon: Good and Beautiful Eros is Eros of Beauty and Goodness

> Were beauty under twenty locks kept fast,
> Yet love breaks through and picks them all at last.
>
> Shakespeare

The pretty speech of Agathon follows as a flowery climax. Drawing freely from art and poetry in a euphonious eulogy of Eros, Agathon floods us with a stream of fine phrases. He begins by saying that he will first speak of the nature of the god Eros, which no one else has adequately described, and then he will tell of the blessings he bestows on mankind. Of all the gods he is best among them. Young, delicate, soft, of beautiful hue and shapely grace, he loves soft and delicate bodies and souls, shuns their opposites, and inspires love of these qualities in others. He is just in not injuring or causing others to injure, temperate in controlling pleasures and desires since no pleasure is stronger than Eros. He is brave, for he can capture even Ares; wise and skillful, a 'composer so accomplished that he is a cause of composing to others'. Eros is the source of life, for 'the composing of all forms of life is Eros' own craft, whereby all creatures are begotten and produced'. Anyone in the arts and crafts who has Eros as his teacher turns out 'a brilliant success'; even Apollo invented archery and medicine and divination 'under the guidance of desire and Eros'. The great god has no concern with ugly things, but is Eros of beauty only. Since he arose, all benefits among men and gods have come from the love of beautiful things. Finishing with a flourish Agathon piles up the fine phrases in a paragraph that would try any translator:

> He casts out alienation, draws intimacy in; he brings us together in all such friendly gatherings as the present; at feasts and dances and ovations he makes himself our leader; politeness contriving, moroseness outdriving; kind giver of amity, giving no enmity; gracious benign; a marvel to the wise, a delight to the gods; coveted of such as share him not, treasured of such as good share have got; father of luxury, tenderness, elegance, graces and longing and yearning; careful of the good, careless of the bad; in toil and fear, in drink and discourse, our trustiest helmsman, boatswain, champion, deliverer; ornament of all gods and men; leader fairest and best, whom every one should follow, joining tunefully in the burthen of his song, wherewith he enchants the thought of every god and man. (197de)

The speech was followed by 'tumultuous applause from all present, at hearing the youngster speak in terms so appropriate to himself and the god'. But as Bury remarks, 'Agathon does little more than formulate the conventional traits of the god as depicted in poetry and art ...'[18] The substance of Agathon's talk is that Eros personifies, more than any other god, happiness, beauty, and goodness, but also that Eros is love *of* beauty; that Eros inspires love of beautiful things in others and is a tremendous force for creativity in the arts. As we shall soon see, Plato takes over the idea that Eros is love of beauty, and that he is a creative force, but criticizes the notion that Eros is beautiful and good, or indeed a god.

Agathon's speech completes Plato's own account in the *Symposium* of the Greek culture of eros, the cultural context in which his own theory is set. Several prominent features stand out.

With the exception of Eryximachus, all the speakers think of eros as a relation among humans, which unlike familial love includes a sexual component. Agathon also alludes to eros among the gods, in accordance with stories about eros between, for example, Ares and Aphrodite. Eryximachus' view, that eros is a cosmic force that extends beyond and relates even non-living things, seems to represent a different tradition that Plato is aware of but does not utilize: in Plato a lover is always a sentient being.

All the speakers also agree that eros is a powerful human motive, perhaps the most powerful. But they do not agree about its source and origin. Most are content to think that the god Eros is the source and cause of eros among humans, while Aristophanes tries to show that some need or deficiency is the cause of eros, a deficiency which can be traced back to human nature and its development.

Phaedrus and Agathon think that eros is all good and its effects completely beneficial, but Pausanias introduces the important notion that there are better and worse kinds of eros, and some kinds can be inconstant, harmful and deceitful. Even in the worst case of eros, though, the association between eros and some sort of beauty is preserved, a relation that Plato takes over and refines.

All speakers see eros as the source of life, the motive that leads to reproduction and the preservation of the species, as well as a motive for creation in the arts and crafts; and this too is a thought that Plato takes over.

A significant feature implicit or explicit in all the speeches is the attitude towards homosexuality, especially male. What is important here is not so much the existence and prevalence of homosexuality, but the attitude of the speakers towards it, especially of Phaedrus, Pausanias, and Aristophanes: male homosexuality was not regarded as a 'deviation' or 'abnormality', but on the contrary as the highest and best kind of eros, at any rate under certain circumstances, and in any case higher and better than male–female eros. Plato does not share this view, that homosexual love is the best kind of eros. But the prevalence of and favorable attitude to homosexuality influences all the theories in the *Symposium*. It dictates that biological reproduction be assigned a secondary role: since reproduction is not possible in all cases of eros, especially the 'better' ones, it cannot be a universal aim or function of eros. Moreover, when this attitude is joined with the notion that eros is a *creative* force, the notion that we find in Eryximachus and Agathon, a substitute creation for biological offspring has to be found in the case of homosexual love, works in the arts and sciences. These are essentially the directions that Plato's own theory takes. But as we shall see, Plato does not stop here. The speeches we have reviewed, with the possible exception of Eryximachus, retain a close connection between eros and sexuality: eros is not identical with sex, but it always has sexual desire as an essential element (this is what we earlier called sexual love: not love which is identical with sex, but love which includes sexual desire). Plato sometimes seems to sever this connection. As he proceeds from heterosexual to homosexual eros, not only does he substitute artistic and scientific creation for biological offspring, but he also downgrades radically bodily beauty and attraction; and, what is more radical yet, as he goes further up the ladder of love he seems to sever the connection between eros and human sexuality. To explain and understand this final leap, we need to look not to the Greek traditions of Eros before Plato, but to Plato's ethics and metaphysics, his theories of goodness, beauty, and immortality.

The Speech of Socrates: Introductory

It is now Socrates' turn and he makes a long and complex speech, usually taken to present Plato's own theory of eros in the *Symposium*. Characteristically, Socrates begins his speech by changing the aims of the discourse, from eulogies and encomia of Eros to a search for the truth about what eros is and what are his works.[20] Also characteristically, he undertakes an elenchus, a cross-examination and refutation of an important part of Agathon's view, that Eros is the most beautiful and the best and happiest of the gods. But the refutation is not purely negative: it reveals Plato's view that eros arises out of some imperfections or deficiencies in the lover, lack of goodness or beauty, and that the lover desires these very things. Somewhat uncharacteristically, Socrates next introduces the wise woman Diotima as having taught him all he knows about eros: he explains how she practiced the very same cross-examination on him; how she distinguished between generic eros and specific forms of it; how she defined eros generally as well as the specific form usually called eros; and finally how she introduced him into the higher mysteries of love, Plato's famous Ladder of Love, which elevates eros from desire of a beautiful body to love of Beauty itself.

Carefully crafted, subtle and complex, variously understood, immensely influential, the speech requires and deserves close study. Paying most attention to its philosophical divisions and tenets, we shall try to understand it by following it systematically and in some detail.[21] We shall proceed by listing the main propositions that constitute the theory, marking them by the letter 'E'. Propositions on which Plato relies but are not part of the theory and belong rather to his metaphysics or ethics or moral psychology we shall mark with the letter 'P'. Some propositions Plato lays down without argument or takes over from previous speakers; here we shall indicate the source. Other propositions Plato derives or deduces from previously laid down propositions, and these will be preceded by the word 'hence'. In accompanying comments we shall indicate context and raise problematic questions.

As I interpret it, Plato's theory has four main parts:

1 Eros is linked with desire, and Plato's deficiency and egoistic models of desire are applied to eros.
2 A distinction is made between generic eros and specific forms of it, and a definition of generic eros is constructed.
3 A definition of the specific form usually called eros is reconstructed from the text.
4 The famous ladder of love is described, that is, the normative part of Plato's theory.

In the next four sections of this chapter we shall take up these parts of the theory in turn.

The Deficiency and Egoistic Models of Desire Applied to Eros

> Every theory of love, from Plato down, teaches that each individual loves in the other sex what he lacks in himself.
>
> G. Stanley Hall

Socrates begins his speech by remarking that he thought they were supposed to say what is true about eros, rather than pile up fine praises whether true or not, as Agathon had done. But he approves of Agathon's introduction in which he said that he would show, first, what Eros is, and second, what his works are. These are two of our questions from Chapter I, and Socrates takes these to be the main questions he will try to answer. Throughout Socrates' speech 'Eros' signifies a god or a demon and is symbolic of the lover,[22] while 'eros' signifies love or the lover. Plato has a myth or story about the origin and nature of eros, and a theory about eros, and he makes the story cohere with the theory.

Without argument, Socrates elicits from Agathon agreement to three propositions, and on the basis of them refutes Agathon's claim that Eros is beautiful:

Eros is eros of something. (199e) E1
Eros desires that of which it is eros. (200a) E2
Of necessity, a desiring subject desires something it lacks, and when it does not lack something it does not desire it. (200ab) P1

The first proposition simply says that Eros must have an object, something that is loved; the second that desire for the object is a component of eros, or possibly that eros is a species of desire.[23] The third proposition is what we shall call 'the deficiency model of desire'.[24] Socrates illustrates it with several examples, and makes an important qualification. A tall or strong man, a healthy or wealthy man, cannot desire to be tall, strong, healthy, or wealthy – these things he already is or he already has. However, a man who is or has these things may desire to be or have them also in the future. This qualification is apparently necessary to avoid the seeming paradox that would otherwise obtain from the conjunction of E2 and P1, namely that a man could not love the things he already had or would cease to love them as soon as he made them his own. In making desire a component of eros Plato is implying that erotic love cannot be merely an appreciating or liking of what we are or what we have.

Socrates now puts together Agathon's last admissions with Agathon's claim, which he accepts, that Eros is of beauty, and refutes Agathon's other claim, that Eros is beautiful:

Hence, Eros lacks that which it desires. (From E2 & P1) E3
Eros loves and desires beauty. (From Agathon) E4
Hence, Eros lacks beauty, or Eros is not beautiful.[25] (From E3 and E4) E5

Socrates next lays down a new proposition without argument, a standard Platonic doctrine:

Good things are beautiful. (201c) P2

And from E5 and P2 he infers:

Hence, Eros also lacks good things. E6

And finally, from E5 and E6 he infers that, contrary to Agathon:

Hence, Eros is neither beautiful nor good.[26] E7

This completes the application of the deficiency model of desire to erotic love. Its consequences are far reaching. Let us look at some of them.

If Agathon's view represented the Greek traditional conception of the god Eros in art and poetry, Plato's conclusion seems to contradict that whole tradition. There are two possible explanations of this. One is that in art and poetry Eros was a confused or at least confusing symbol: Plato takes Eros to be symbolic of the lover, but others may have taken it as symbolic of love of beautiful things or of the beloved. At 204c Socrates is himself represented as having made the mistake of thinking of Eros as the beloved, and thus thinking, as Agathon did, that Eros was beautiful and good. On this explanation, Plato is reinterpreting, not contradicting, the poetic and artistic tradition. But there is a deeper, though more speculative explanation, in which the contradiction remains at a deeper level. This is that Eros represented the lover, but love was conceived not on a deficiency model but on a narcissistic one, on a model of self-love. On this model, Eros, being beautiful and good, loves these qualitities in himself, or loves himself insofar as he has these qualities; and loves others insofar as they have the same qualities. Love of others arises out of love of oneself. This goes with the ancient Greek notion that the like loves its own like, a notion that Plato takes up and rejects in the *Lysis*. This model seems incompatible with the deficiency model, in which love of another arises out of the perception of some deficiency or need in oneself, and the perception that some quality in the object will satisfy the deficiency. Of course, one can love both oneself and others. The dispute arises about the origin of the emotion in human beings, and about the causal primacy of the one over the other (self-love and love of objects). Reflections on this dispute re-emerge in Freud. And in some modern theories Plato's model of deficiency is given some support, though not in Plato's terms. In these theories, the infant's love for the mother is seen as the first experience of the emotion, and it is seen as developing out of the satisfaction of the infant's needs by the mother.[27] The deficiency model of love makes it difficult for Plato to have a coherent notion of self-love. If we can love only what we lack, how can we love ourselves? If loving ourselves implies loving what we *are*, the concept is excluded by Plato's deficiency model. But Plato's theory allows that if we somehow attained the objects of our desire and love we could still desire and love them in the sense of wanting to have them also in the future; it also allows love of an idealized self (Freud's 'ego ideal', for example) since this is perfectly compatible with the deficiency model.

In any case, the central point of the deficiency model is that eros arises out of some deficiency or incompleteness in the lover. In this

Socrates is in agreement with all the previous speakers including Aristophanes: in all of them the lover desires to have something he lacked or to become something he was not or to accomplish something he had not. But when Plato joins the deficiency model to Agathon's view that Eros is of beauty and, further, connects beauty with goodness, he gives his theory a new direction contrary to Aristophanes, as Diotima explicitly points out:[28]

> And certainly there runs a story, she continued, that all who go seeking their other half are in love; though by my account love is neither for half nor for whole, unless this happens to be something good. For men are prepared to have ... their own feet and hands cut off if they feel these belongings to be harmful. The fact is, I suppose, that each person does not cherish his belongings except where a man calls the good his own property and the bad another, since what men love is simply and solely the good. (205E)

Eros does not arise out of the separateness of one human being from another, but out of lack, deficiency of beauty or goodness. Its object is not oneself or what belongs to one, but the good. As we shall see in chapter 4, this criticism of Aristophanes' speech is also crucial for understanding Plato's view of philia in the *Lysis* and the *Republic*.

Socrates now introduces the wise woman Diotima,[29] as his teacher of all he knows about eros, and relates how he asked her a natural question about the deficiency model: If Eros is not beautiful or good, is he ugly and bad? She explains that just as there is an intermediate condition between knowledge and ignorance, namely true belief, so there is a third condition between beauty and ugliness, and between good and bad. Eros is in these three intermediate conditions. The deficiency model dictates that Eros, the lover of beauty, cannot be permanently beautiful, and good, and still love. But it is also Plato's view that someone who is thoroughly ignorant, evil, and ugly, also cannot love, a view that Plato also affirms in the *Lysis* about philia. The main reason he gives for this view is that an ignorant man would not be aware of his own defects and thus would have no desire for the good and beautiful things that would remedy them. At one extreme, the gods have no desire and love for wisdom – and other good and beautiful things – because they are permanently wise and good and beautiful. At the other extreme a completely ignorant man would not be aware of his ignorance – and his lack of other good and beautiful things – and so would have no desire and love either. Love and desire for good and beautiful things arises when we both lack them and are also aware of this lack (204a). Thus the deficiency model and the familiar Socratic notion of wisdom and ignorance provide the foundation of the view that the lover must be in these intermediate conditions.

In an interesting sidelight Diotima gives Socrates a proof that Eros cannot be a god, as Agathon and other speakers had supposed. The proof is built on the deficiency model and Plato's conception of divinity: All the gods are happy and beautiful; those are happy who possess good and beautiful things; Eros lacks good and beautiful things; therefore, Eros is not a god (202b–d). The proof is interesting because it follows from the conclusion that a god cannot love (erotically). This shows clearly enough that eros, as symbolized here by Eros, is essentially different from Christian agape. A Christian would presumably deny that his God is deficient in beauty and goodness, and yet he would also say that God loves his children. The explanation of this difference between agape and eros is probably either that the deficiency model does not apply to agape, or that the objects of agape need not always be beautiful or good, or both. The explanation may be different for the three types of Christian agape, parental, filial, and sibling: our love of God perhaps arises out of our deficiencies or needs and we may love God as the supreme good; but God's love does not arise out of any deficiencies nor does he love us only if we are beautiful or good. And brotherly love may possibly arise out of our needs but it is not commanded on account of the beauty or goodness of our neighbor.[30]

In a mythical interlude Diotima relates a myth about the origin and nature of Eros. Eros is a daemon, a spirit between the divine and the human, 'the son of Resource and Poverty', poor in lacking good and beautiful things, but aware of his lack and resourceful in pursuing these. He communicates divine things to humans and human things to gods. The myth climaxes with a proof that since wisdom is among the most beautiful things and Eros is of beautiful things, Eros is also a lover of wisdom, a philosopher! (202e–204c). The myth accords with the theory laid down so far, and it perhaps foreshadows the ladder of love in which eros enables us to get in touch with divine things, such as the Form Beauty, and become philosophers.

Socrates now asks: If this is what Eros is, what is its use to mankind? (204c). In response Diotima engages Socrates in two interchanges which show that eros is conceived as having an egoistic aim.

> 'The lover of beautiful things, what does he love?'
>
> 'That they may be his,' I replied.
>
> 'But your answer craves a further query', she said, 'such as this: What will he have who gets beautiful things?' This question, I declared, I was quite unable to answer offhand. (204d)

Since Socrates is unable to answer her second question, Diotima drops the inquiry about eros of beautiful things – it will be taken up later – and raises two exactly parallel questions about eros of good things, questions which Socrates finds easy to answer.

> 'Well', she proceeded, 'imagine that the object is changed and the inquiry is made about the good instead of the beautiful. Come, Socrates, I say, the lover of good things, what does he love?'
>
> 'That they may be his,' I replied.
>
> 'And what will he have who gets good things?'
>
> 'I find this easier to answer,' I said. 'He will be happy.'
>
> 'Yes', she said, 'the happy are happy by the possession of good things, and we have no more need to ask for what end a man wants to be happy; the answer is final.' (204e–205a)

We can understand Diotima's questions by drawing a distinction between the object and the aim of eros, parallel to the distinction Freud draws between the object and the aim of the sexual instinct: the object is that from which the attraction emanates or which the lover finds attractive; the aim is that towards which the instinct of eros strives.[31] Diotima gives the object in her questions, the beautiful in the first case, the good in the second, and she asks for the aim. Socrates' two answers in the second interchange reveal a standard Platonic doctrine, that

> Happiness is the final aim of all desire, and it consists in the possession of good things. P3

His answers also give us a new proposition about eros of good things:

> The lover of good things loves the good things to be his for the sake of his own happiness. E8

It is this proposition that expresses what I have called the egoistic model of eros. Eros is egoistic relative to its aim: in loving good things the aim of the lover is to make them *his own* for the sake of *his own* happiness. And insofar as the lover is successful in attaining his aim eros would bring happiness to the lover. In the case of love of things, as distinct from love of persons, this conception of love is perhaps natural; it is natural to think that when a man loves, say, wisdom and health, he loves to be healthy and wise; though when we add 'for the sake of his own happiness' we add an important qualification, since others' having wisdom and health is thereby not included as part of Platonic eros. When we come to love of persons, the egoistic model begins to cut deeper. We have to suppose that when one loves another person, conceiving him or her to be good, the lover's aim is to possess or make him or her his own for the sake of his own happiness. Care for the beloved, concern for his or her good or happiness is not excluded as incompatible with this love, but neither is it included in the aims of the lover. Benevolence toward the beloved is not necessarily part of Platonic eros. If the lover's own happiness is the final aim of eros, concern for the good of the beloved will presumably be present if it is seen by the lover as a means to his own happiness. We shall find these implications of the egoistic nature of eros confirmed in subsequent passages. For the present, we note that the deficiency and egoistic models of eros go well together. If one supposes that the source of eros is a perceived deficiency in the lover, it is natural to think that the lover's aim will be to make up that deficiency in himself: he will love others insofar as he perceives them to be useful or valuable to himself in making up his deficiencies. This seems to be the conception that Plato has also of philia in the *Lysis*.

Generic Eros: Desire for the Good to be One's Own Forever

With Diotima's switch from eros of beautiful things to eros of good things we have entered the passage where the latter is defined. Let us first look at the distinction between the two kinds of eros, and then at the definition itself.

Having agreed that the lover desires to possess good things for his own happiness, Diotima and Socrates also agree that the desire and love of good things and of happiness is common to all men. Yet, she remarks, not all men are said to love (*eran*); some are said to love and others not, a situation that Socrates finds puzzling. The explanation for this, she says, is that 'we have singled out a certain form of eros, and applying thereto the name of the whole, we call it eros' (205b). She adds that 'there are other names that we commonly abuse,'[32] and gives an illustration: poetry (poiesis) is the art that causes the composition or making of anything (shoes, buildings, statues, tragedies) and all its practitioners are poets (poietai); but not all these are *commonly* called poetry and poets (poiesis and poietai), but only the business of music and meters is called poiesis and only its practitioners poietai. Generically, poetry is the composing of all these things, but common linguistic practice gives the name of the whole to only a part of it. Presumably, this common linguistic use is an abuse because it hides the whole–part or genus–species relation that exists between poetry in general and that part of it concerned with music and meters. Similarly, Diotima continues, generically (*to men kephalaion*) eros is all desire for good things and happiness, but those who pursue him in a variety of ways – in money making, sports, philosophy – are not said to love (*eran*) and are not called lovers (*erastai*), whereas those who pursue him in one particular form are given the name of the whole, are said to love, and are called lovers (205d). This too is a linguistic abuse, presumably for the same reasons: it hides the relation of whole–part or genus–species, which according to Plato's theory holds between eros of good things and eros of beautiful things. Plato, then, is consciously and explicitly extending the scope of the Greek concept of eros beyond what he conceeds to be the contemporary Greek linguistic use of the term.[33] The linguistic use he refers to is that of all the previous speakers, except Eryximachus. All of them used the term eros to refer to a relation among persons, male–male, male–female, female–female, a relation in which the object of eros was a beautiful person, a relation that included a sexual component. Plato is now saying that this is only one part of eros, a part of eros of good things generally.[34]

Diotima now proceeds rapidly to construct the definition of generic eros, out of three elements previously agreed on: men love the good; they love the good to be theirs, and to be theirs forever (always).[35] So, generically,

Eros is for the good to be one's own forever. (206a) E9

We may note briefly that eros, as defined here, satisfies both the deficiency and egoistic models, and that (given E8) it contains an implicit reference to happiness. Taken in context, the definition says that the object of generic eros is the good or good things, and that the aim of the lover is to make these things his own forever for the sake of his own happiness. There is perhaps a serious question whether eros so defined has any connection with eros as conceived by the previous speakers, but in his distinction between generic and specific eros Plato seems to acknowledge this. In his own grand theory Plato wants to make eros of beauty a species of the desire for the good.

Specific Eros: Desire to Create Offspring in Beauty for the Sake of Immortality

Immediately after the definition of generic eros has been constructed and has received Socrates' emphatic approval, Diotima asks:

> Now if eros is always for this, she proceeded, what is the method of those who pursue it, and what is the behavior whose eagerness and straining would be called eros? What is actually its characteristic work (*ergon*)? (206b)

The phrase 'would be called eros' signals that Diotima is now asking about that part of generic eros to which contemporary Greek linguistic practice gave the name 'eros'; in short she is asking about specific eros.[36]

Socrates does not know the answer, and she gives it at 206b:

> The characteristic work of specific eros is the begetting of offspring on a beautiful object by means of body or soul.[37] E10

Socrates does not understand, and she elaborates. All men, she says, are 'pregnant in body or soul' and at a certain age 'our nature desires to beget'; we cannot beget on the ugly but only on the beautiful. The conjunction of man and woman is such begetting, and this pregnancy and begetting is something divine and immortal in the mortal animal. In almost lyric language she describes the role of the beautiful in begetting:

> When the pregnant approaches the beautiful it becomes not only gracious but so exhilarate, that it flows over with begetting and bringing forth .... When a person is big and teeming ripe he feels himself in sore flutter for the beautiful, because its possessor can relieve him of his heavy pangs. (206d–e)

Right after this, Diotima makes a correction in the reply Socrates had given back at 204d, when they were talking about eros of the beautiful and Diotima had asked: 'The lover of beautiful things, what does he love?' Socrates had replied, 'That they may be his.' She now says:

> For you were wrong, Socrates, in supposing that eros is of the beautiful.
>
> What then is it?
>
> It is of engendering and begetting upon the beautiful. (206e)[38]

Hence, unlike the case of generic eros, it is the beautiful rather than the good that is the attracting object; and unlike the former case where possession of the good was the aim, here the aim is not to possess the beautiful but to generate offspring on it – a point already implicit in E10.

> Diotima now asks further: Why (is eros) of (for) this begetting?
>
> Because this is something ever-existing, and immortal in our mortal life. From what has been admitted it is necessary that we desire immortality no less than the good, if eros is for the good to be one's own forever. Of necessity it follows from this definition that eros is also of immortality. (207a)

Here Diotima has made two moves: she infers the proposition that eros is (among other things) desire for immortality from the definition of generic eros; and she claims that this desire for immortality explains the (desire for) begetting offspring on a beautiful object, which is characteristic of eros proper. Let us consider briefly these two moves.

The inference seems appropriate, in the sense that if eros proper is a part or species of generic eros, it will have all the features that are definitionally true of generic eros; while presumably the desire to beget on a beautiful object by means of body or soul will be the distinguishing mark of eros proper. The inference, though, seems puzzling. One problem has to do with the scope of *aei* (forever, always) in the definition of generic eros. If someone told us that he wanted to have good things forever, say, health, wealth, knowledge, or happiness, by 'forever' we would naturally understand him to mean 'during his whole lifetime'. But this clearly does not amount to immortality in any of the senses which Plato subsequently defines.[39] Aside and independently of this problem, the inference apparently detaches *aei* from the definition and treats it as if this expression can signify a separate aim – and this too seems puzzling. Expressions such as 'to have good things forever' or 'to be happy always' can be used to signify aims, but 'always' and 'forever' do not seem to be expressions that can by themselves signify aims. How then can we infer from someone's wanting to be happy always that he has two aims, to be happy and to be immortal? Laying aside these puzzles, we can state the proposition derived as follows:

Eros is also desire for the lover's own immortality. Ell

Let us now consider Diotima's second move. At 207a she makes more explicit her previous question ('Why is eros of begetting?'): What is the cause of this eros and desire (to beget offspring on a beautiful object)? What is to be explained is the desire for begetting offspring, which she takes to be a fact and we take as characteristic of eros proper. She constructs the explanation by appealing to the desire for immortality, to a definition of immortality (208b) and to certain facts about mortal nature, animal and human (207d–208c). Insofar as this explanation is satisfactory, we may regard it as confirming the desire for immortality as part of eros, which now plays the role of an explanatory hypothesis.

Diotima begins with the case of animals: she describes the behavior of mating and rearing offspring and asks for the cause of it (207b). Socrates does not know the answer, and she gives it at 207ed, intending to cover both the case of animals and humans, though humans so act on the promptings of reason while presumably animals act from instinct:

> Well then, she said, if you believe that eros is bent on what we have repeatedly admitted, you may cease to wonder. For here too [the case of humans as well as animals], on the same principle as before, the mortal nature ever seeks, as best it can, to be immortal. In one way only can it succeed, and that is by generation; since so it can leave behind it a new creature in the place of the old.

She proceeds to argue that all mortals change with respect to all their properties, whether of body (hair, flesh, bones, blood), or soul (manners, habits, opinions, desires, pains, pleasures, fears). This is so, she claims, even with respect to knowledge:

> with regard to the possession of sciences, not merely do some of them grow and others perish, so that neither in what we know are we ever the same persons; but a like fate attends each single sort of knowledge. What we call learning implies that our knowledge is departing; since

> forgetfulness is an egress of knowledge, while learning substitutes a fresh one in place of that which departs, and so preserves our knowledge enough to make it seem the same. ... every mortal thing is preserved in this way; not by being always the same in all respects like the divine, but by replacing what goes off or is antiquated with something fresh in the semblance of the original. Through this device, Socrates, a mortal thing partakes of immortality, both in its body and all other aspects; by no other means can it be done. So do not wonder if everything naturally values its own offshoot; since all are beset by this behavior and love for the sake of immortality. (208ab)

In these passages we have the following elements: a definition of divine immortality; the claim that no mortal, animal or human, can become immortal in this sense; the claim that a mortal can partake of this immortality as far as possible only by begetting offspring and thus replacing itself in the semblance of itself; and the claim that given these facts Ell explains the mating and begetting and offspring-rearing behavior characteristic of eros proper.[40] We can perhaps cast Diotima's explanation in the form of an argument:

Eros is desire for immortality and all animals have this desire. E11

A thing is divinely immortal if and only if for any property it has at any one time it has the very same property at all times. P3

All animals change eventually with respect to all their properties. P4

Hence, no animal can ever be divinely immortal. P5

During its lifetime and through change an animal continues to exist as 'the same animal' in the sense of giving up properties or parts and replacing them by similar properties or parts. P6

Animals approach or to some degree partake of divine immortality by begetting offspring similar to themselves and thus replacing themselves after death. (A process conceived somewhat analogously to the way they remain 'the same' during life.) P7

Hence, animals become erotically disposed, beget and rear offspring for the sake of partaking in immortality insofar as it is possible for them to do so. E12

It is on the basis of this explanation and of the role of the beautiful described above, that I reconstruct a definition of specific eros:

Specifically, eros is desire for begetting offspring on a beautiful object by means of body or soul for the sake of the lover's own immortality. E13

I wish to note at once that this definition does not occur in the text. But I claim that all the elements in it and their relations are clearly in the text, and I have expounded Diotima's views in detail to secure this claim.[41]

Several things are noteworthy about eros proper as defined here. It is constituted by two desires, the desire to beget offspring, and the desire for the lover's own immortality. Both desires satisfy the deficiency model, and the desire for immortality satisfies the egoistic model. Eros is presumably beneficial to the lover insofar as immortality is something good. This eros may also be beneficial to the offspring, at least in cases where the offspring is a sentient being, animal or human; but concern and care of the offspring is conceived as a means to the lover's own immortality. Since the lover's own immortality is the final aim of this eros, eros proper can appropriately be said to be egoistic. We shall see shortly that this is fully confirmed by Diotima's subsequent explanations. Second, the definition contains an implicit reference to the relation between the two desires, that is, between begetting offspring and immortality: a means–end relation. In humans this relation is recognized by reason, as Diotima remarks; in animals presumably by instinct. Third, possession of the beautiful object referred to in the definition is not the aim of either desire; rather, its role seems to be as the attracting object which sparks or releases the desire to beget. Later, in the ladder of eros, beautiful objects also seem to assume the role as well of model for the creation of offspring. Thus, the structure of eros proper seems different from that of generic eros: in the latter it is the good rather than the beautiful that is the attracting object – or perhaps happiness – and it is possession of it, not generation or creation, that is the aim. Finally, in the explanation we have reconstructed, the desire for immortality assumes a new role, independent of its problematic derivation from generic eros: even if this derivation is mistaken, as it may be, the hypothesis of the desire for immortality may have genuine validity insofar as it explains the behavior of courting, mating, and offspring-rearing behavior in animals and humans. In modern biological theories representation of an individual , animal or human, in succeeding generations is taken as explanatory of mating and breeding behavior.[42] To be sure, such explanations are now cast in an evolutionary rather than a teleological model. Plato's explanation can perhaps be viewed as the teleological analogue of such explanations, and in the case of humans, at any rate, it is not obviously without value.

So far (208c), Diotima has been speaking mainly of begetting biological offspring. But Plato could hardly have confined eros proper to such cases; for male–male eros (and even female–female) was a widely recognized cultural phenomenon and previous speakers took up such cases as prominent, and even the best cases of eros. Of course in such cases there is no biological offspring. And Diotima from the beginning (206b,c) characterized specific eros as the desire to generate offspring on a beautiful object by means of body *or soul*. So she now takes up generation by means of soul, where offspring is not biological but actions and *logoi*, such as discourses, poems, constitutions, the arts, crafts and sciences (208c–209e). As the range of 'offspring' expands, so does the range of 'beautiful objects' that attract the lover, from bodies to souls and abstract objects. In all these new cases her explanations contain the same elements as before and confirm the view that eros proper (as well as generic eros) is essentially egoistic.

At 208c Socrates professes some skepticism about such explanations and Diotima tries to convince him by piling case upon case of lovers who acted and created for the sake of their own immortality: they all had eros for 'winning a name and laying up fame immortal for all time to come' (208c). Alcestis would not have died for Admetus (female–male eros) nor Achilles for Patroclus (male–male eros) 'had they not expected to win an immortal memory for virtue'(208d).

> I hold it is for immortal virtue and such illustrious fame as this that they do all they do, and so much more in proportion to their excellence. They love (erosin) the immortal. (208c)

These cases are noteworthy, for they might normally be cited to show not only the great motivating power of eros, but also its non-egoistic nature, since they seem to be cases in which the lovers sacrificed their very lives for their beloveds. But Diotima clearly implies that the lovers so acted as to secure 'immortal fame' for themselves and that they would not have so acted had they not expected to secure this fame. She goes on to cite a number of other cases of creations of *logoi* – the poems of Homer and Hesiod, the constitutions of Solon and Lycurgus – explaining all of them on the same principles. She apparently takes all of them to confirm the structure of specific eros, and the desire for immortality to be explanatory of them. This explanation of the range of cases of specific eros is preparatory to the ladder of eros, probably the most influential part of Plato's theory.

The Ladder of Love: From Eros of a Beautiful Body to Eros of Beauty Itself

> If things were seen as they truly are, the beauty of bodies would be much abridged.
>
> Sir Thomas Browne

Diotima now warns Socrates that she is about to enter into the higher mysteries of eros and asks him to do his best to follow her. In a justly famous passage, in grand, elegant, and elevating language, she describes how one who would proceed rightly in erotics would ascend from loving a particular beautiful body to loving Beauty itself. The passage is worth quoting almost in full:

> He who proceeds rightly in this ... must ... in the first place be in love with one particular body, and engender beautiful discourse therein; but next he must remark how the beauty attached to this or that body is cognate to that which is attached to any other, and that if he means to ensure beauty in form, it is a gross folly not to regard as one and the same the beauty belonging to all ... But his next advance will be to set a higher value on the beauty of souls than on that of the body ... bringing forth and soliciting such discourse as will tend to the betterment of the young; and ... he may be constrained to contemplate the beautiful as appearing in our observances and our laws, and to behold it all bound together in kinship and so estimate the body's beauty as a slight affair. From observances he should be led on to the branches of knowledge, and there also he may behold a province of beauty, and by looking thus on beauty in the mass may escape from the mean, meticulous slavery of a single instance ...; and turning rather towards the main ocean of the beautiful may by contemplation of this bring forth in all their splendor many beautiful truths of discourse and meditation in a plenteous crop of philosophy ....
>
> When a man has been thus far tutored in the lore of love ..., in the right and regular ascent, suddenly he will have revealed to him ... a wonderful vision, beautiful in its nature; and this, Socrates, is the final object of all these previous toils. First of all it is ever-existent and neither comes to be nor perishes, neither waxes nor wanes; next, it is not beautiful in part and in part ugly, nor is it such at such a time and other at another, nor in one respect beautiful and in another ugly, nor so affected by position as to seem beautiful to some and ugly to others ... existing ever in singularity of form independent by itself, while all the multitude of beautiful things partake of it in such a way

that, though all of them are coming to be and perishing, it grows neither greater or less, and is affected by nothing ....

But tell me, what would happen if one of you had the fortune to look upon essential beauty entire, pure and unalloyed; not infected with the flesh and color of humanity, and ever so much more of mortal trash? What if he could behold the divine beauty itself, in its unique form? ... Do but consider, she said, that there only will it befall him, as he sees the beautiful through that which makes it visible, to breed not illusions but true examples of virtue, since his contact is not with illusion but with truth. So when he has begotten a true virtue and has reared it up he is destined to win the friendship of heaven; he, above all men, is immortal. (212–13; tr. Lamb)

This first and most famous *scala amoris* is the normative part of Plato's theory: it places different cases of eros in a developmental series, ranks them from the less to the more valuable, and it describes an ascent to the most valuable. The structure of the ladder and the ascent have been well reconstructed by Moravcsik;[43] though he does not explain the rest of the theory and place the ladder in it, his account is in agreement with our results and I follow it for the most part. After discussing briefly the structure of the ladder and the ascent, I concentrate on a question not discussed adequately in the literature: What are Plato's criteria for his evaluative ranking of different kinds of eros?

I take the ladder of love to be about eros proper rather than generic eros. This is clear from the fact that at every step of the ladder we have creation of offspring, which is characteristic of eros proper, and the fact that at the top we have the Form Beauty rather than the form of the Good. But since eros proper, the love of beauty, is a part or species of generic eros, the love of the good, we should expect to find some relation between beauty and the good, and some relation between the ladder of love and another famous ladder, the Divided Line in the *Republic* in which the Form of the Good *is* at the top. This relation has an important bearing on our main question about criteria for ranking.

To understand the structure of the ladder and the ascent, we must distinguish between steps in the ladder and ascents from step to step. If our reconstruction has been correct so far, we should expect to find all the elements of eros proper at each step: a lover, the 'perception' of an attracting beautiful object, the desire to beget offspring 'on' the beautiful object, and the desire for immortality for the sake of which the begetting takes place.[44] Plato does not always provide all these elements at each step. For example, he does not always tell us what the lover creates. Similarly, he does not bring in immortality until the top. This seems to have misled recent commentators, who do not make the distinction between aim and object, into underestimating or not recognizing at all the element of immortality in the theory. But as we have seen, Plato is clear that immortality is the final aim of eros proper, and the question of the egoism of Platonic love is to be understood in terms of it.

The lover's ascent from step to step involves a change of attracting object and a change of offspring, and it is initiated and directed by reason. It is by 'understanding' that the beauty of one body is akin to the beauty of another that the lover ascends to the love of the beauty of body; and it is by 'perceiving' a new kind of beauty (the beauty of soul), that the lover ascends to the love of beauty of souls and laws. Thus, as reason 'perceives' a new beautiful object or a new kind of beauty, the lover becomes attracted to it, and is inspired to create new offspring. In this sense reason initiates the ascent, and emotion and creation follow reason. As Moravcsik has noticed we find three kinds of terms in the ladder passage: cognitive, emotional, and creative. Cognition always leads the way and passion and creativity follow. And this is very Platonic indeed.

Though this much seems clear about the ladder, several unclarities remain. One, a subject of controversy in the literature,[45] is whether Plato means that the lover is supposed to give up all previous objects as he ascends or only that he sees them in a truer perspective and proportions his attachments accordingly. The former seems very radical: the lover who reached Beauty itself would neither love nor value any of the lower objects, including not only beautiful bodies but the whole world of the fine arts, the world of shape and color and sound. Can it really be correct to suggest that a lover who reached the form Beauty should no longer love Mozart's fortieth symphony? Would it not still have some beauty and value for him? If, ideally, our loves are to be proportioned to the value or beauty of their objects, a principle that seems very Platonic, the ladder cannot plausibly be said to be 'exclusionary'.

A second unclarity is how Plato conceives the change of attachment or emotion: is the original emotional attachment to a single beautiful body transferred to the beauty of bodies, and later to the beauty of souls, and so on, or is the original desire extinguished and a new one takes its place? An answer to this question would make a difference on whether we can interpret the ascent as a series of successive 'sublimations', another controversy in the literature.[46] In the *Symposium* there seems to be no clear evidence for answering these questions, but in the *Phaedrus* and the *Republic* we shall find some evidence that bears on them.

Beauty, Immortality and the Good

> She, like a guide who has his goal in sight
> began to speak again: We have ascended
> from the greatest sphere to the heaven of pure light.
> Light of the intellect, which is love unending;
> love of the true good, which is wholly bliss;
> bliss beyond bliss, all other joys transcending.
>
> Dante

The ladder of love is 'normative', not 'descriptive'. It ranks evaluatively different kinds of eros, apparently according to the value of their objects; and it tells us not how lovers in fact 'progress' from step to step, but how they would progress if they had the right guidance, that is, if they were guided by some one who had these rankings. Hence the question we postponed earlier: What are Plato's criteria for ranking evaluatively different kinds of eros? In a passage before the ladder, soul eros is ranked above body-eros. Speaking of soul lovers, Diotima says:

> Equally with him he shares the nurturing of what is begotten, so that men in this condition enjoy a far fuller community with each other than that which comes with children, and enjoy a far surer friendship (philia), since the children of their union are more beautiful and more immortal. (209c)

Here soul-eros is ranked above body-eros on the ground that soul-lovers have a fuller community and a far surer friendship than body-lovers; and this in turn on the ground that the offspring of soul-lovers is more beautiful and immortal. It would seem then that greater degrees of beauty and immortality in the offspring make for better eros as we go up the ladder. Insofar as the offspring is modeled on the attracting beautiful object, presumably degrees of beauty and immortality in the offspring will reflect degrees of beauty and immortality in that object. And insofar as degrees of beauty and immortality in the offspring reflect the lover, its creator, he too as he goes up the ladder will presumably become more beautiful and immortal.

Two questions arise here: first, how are we to construe degrees of immortality and beauty? Second, why should greater degrees of immortality and beauty make eros better?

It is fairly easy to construe degrees of immortality. In the ladder only beauty itself, being a Form, is divinely immortal; all the other attracting objects below it, being non-Forms, wax and wane, increase and decrease, come into being and perish (211ab). These attracting objects are more or less like the divinely immortal Beauty in lasting more or less; the poems of Homer, for example, had already lasted longer than any biological offspring, so they are more immortal than biological offspring and more like, in that respect, the divinely immortal Beauty. Degrees of beauty are perhaps more difficult to interpret. The only clue that Plato gives us here is in the description of Beauty itself as being beautiful without qualification: 'It is not beautiful in part and ugly in part, nor is it beautiful at one time and not at another, nor beautiful in comparison with one thing and ugly with another, nor is it so affected by position so as to seem beautiful to some and ugly to others' (211a). So presumably, the attracting beautiful objects below the top are beautiful with one or more of these qualifications and are less beautiful in this sense. This is probably Plato's view. The double characterization of beauty itself, as at once divinely immortal and beautiful without qualification, provides the ideal standard by which degrees of lesser immortality and beauty are to be judged.

But why should Plato suppose that greater degrees of beauty and immortality, in the attracting object and the offspring, make eros better? Two answers already hinted at or suggested by the theory seem insufficient. The first is hinted by the passage just quoted (209c). Soul eros, where a lover is attracted by the beauty of another's soul and creates a poem or a constitution about justice, is ranked above body eros, on the ground that since the offspring of their love is more beautiful and more immortal, the lovers enjoy 'a far fuller community' and a 'far surer friendship' than biological lovers. Granting the benefits of such community and friendship, this answer does not seem general enough to cover all of the ladder, and especially the top. For at the top of the ladder the attracting object is not a human being but an abstract entity, a Form, and no other human being besides the lover need be involved in such a case of eros; community and friendship need not come into it at all , and yet this is to the best kind of eros. The second answer, internal to the theory, is general enough but does not by itself go far enough. According to the theory we have reconstructed, in every case of eros proper the lover's final aim is his own immortality. And according to the ladder, as the lover ascends from step to step he realizes his aim more and more, since he is attracted to more immortal objects and creates more immortal offspring; and at the top of the ladder he realizes this aim as much as it is possible for humans to realize it. So, relative to realizing the final aim of eros proper, the lover is better off as he goes up the ladder, and best off at the top. I think that this answer does not go far enough because it does not reveal sufficiently Plato's criteria for the ranking. I think that generally for Plato we are not necessarily better off achieving what we want or aim for unless what we want or aim for is good to begin with. I wish therefore to supplement this answer by bringing in Plato's theory of the Form of the Good in the *Republic* at least as interpreted by me in a recent paper.[47] The theory shows the connection, for Plato, between the two characterizations of Beauty itself in the *Symposium* – being divinely immortal and beautiful without qualification – and his concept of goodness.

Briefly, the theory of the Form of the Good assumes that in some middle dialogues, especially in the *Symposium* and the *Republic*, Plato conceived of the Forms not as properties or attributes, but as ideal exemplars or paradigms, self-exemplifying or self-predicating. On this assumption, the Form Beauty is not the attribute of being beautiful but rather something itself beautiful; the Form Circle is not the property of being circular but the ideal circle, and so on. Within this assumption, the theory distinguishes between proper and ideal (or formal) attributes of Forms. In the case of Beauty, being beautiful is a *proper* attribute of that form, that is, an attribute that Form has by virtue of being the particular Form it is. But being (divinely) immortal is an ideal attribute of that Form, i.e. an attribute that Form has by virtue of being a Form. In addition, being always beautiful, being beautiful in all parts (or aspects) of itself, being beautiful no matter compared to what, all these are also ideal attributes of the Form Beauty, in the sense that the Form Beauty has them by virtue of both being a Form and the particular Form it is.

Given these distinctions, the theory of the Form of the Good asserts that the Form of the Good is the formal cause of all the other Forms having their ideal attributes, or that all the other Forms have their ideal attributes by virtue of participating in the Form of the Good. The ideal attributes of all the other Forms are proper attributes of the Form of the Good; or, the Form of the Good consists in the ideality of the Forms. So conceived, each Form other than the Form of the Good is the best object of its kind, and it is such by virtue of participating (fully) in the Form of the Good. The attributive goodness (goodness of kind) of a sensible object is accounted for by participation (or resemblance to some degree) in the ideal attributes of the Form of its kind, and through this also participation (or resemblance to some degree) in the Form of the Good. According to the Theory of Forms, a sensible circle is, say, a circle by virtue of participating in the proper attributes of the Form Circle. According to the theory of the Form of the Good, a sensible circle is a good circle (to some degree) by virtue of participating in (or resembling to some degree) the ideal attributes of the Form Circle: for insofar as it participates in the ideal attributes of the Form Circle it also participates in the Form of the Good, since the Circle has its ideal attributes by virtue of participating in the Form of the Good.

Applying the theory of the Form of the Good to the ladder of eros we obtain the desired correlation between degrees of immortality and beauty and degrees of goodness. As we go up the ladder, the attracting object participates more and more in the ideal attributes of Beauty itself, being divinely immortal and being beautiful without qualification; and since Beauty itself has these attributes by virtue of participating in the Form of the Good, the attracting object thereby participates more and more in the Form of the Good. Insofar as the offspring is modeled on the attracting object the same characterizations apply to the offspring. And insofar as the offspring reflects the lover, its creator, the lover too, as he ascends the ladder, becomes more and more immortal, beautiful and good.

We may end this chapter by noting that the application of the theory of the Form of the Good to the case of eros proper and the ladder of love does not imply a conflation of the two theories. The theory of the Form of the Good is general and applies to all Forms. The two theories are related but distinct. The distinction between them enables us to throw some light perhaps on the distinction between generic eros and eros proper. Eros proper is concerned with the concept of beauty, has as its ultimate object (not aim) the Form Beauty, and its distinctive mark is creation of offspring in the image of Beauty. Generic eros, on the other hand, is concerned with the notion of goodness and has as its ultimate object the Form of the Good. The ladder for generic eros is presumably given by the Divided Line and the Allegory of the Cave in the *Republic*, both of which do have the Form of the Good at the top. And when philosophers of the *Republic* are called lovers (*erastai*) it is probably meant that they are generic lovers.

The distinction made in the *Symposium* between generic and specific eros demands that Plato have some appropriate distinction and relation between beauty and goodness. Unfortunately, this is unclear in the *Symposium* and in other works.[48] It is only when we combine the *Symposium* with the *Republic*, in which the Form of the Good is the most general, abstract, or fundamental Form, that we approach what is needed; though even here, lacking a definition of beauty, we cannot be sure how Plato thought of the relation between the two Forms.

What is clear in the *Symposium* is that the concepts constitutive of specific eros are desire, beauty, creativity and immortality. It is probable, I think, that the primitive models for these concepts were the attraction for the physical beauty of bodies, the creation of biological offspring to which such attraction leads, and the notion that the function of such biological procreation is the representation of the individual in future generations. It was Plato's distinctive contribution to widen these models to the attraction of the beauty of soul and even of abstract entities, to creation in the arts, the sciences and philosophy, and to the immortality such creations bring. Despite this widening, his concept of specific eros maintains connection and continuity with the sensual attachment his contemporaries would have called eros, through the special role of beauty as the attracting object – a point we shall find reaffirmed and elucidated in the *Phaedrus*.

The subsuming of specific eros under desire for the good in the *Symposium* I interpret as a *further* move, reaching towards a grand theory of *all* attachments: not only erotic attachments to beauty, concrete or abstract, but also the love of knowledge, the attachments of friendship and familial love, the love of honor and the love of gain. I interpret these other attachments to fall under desire for the good, real or apparent, but not to be erotic, in the sense of specific eros, since beauty plays no special role in them. But this grand theory has to await the new psychology of the tripartite division of the soul, implicit in the *Phaedrus* and explicit in the *Republic*, and the theory of the Form of the Good. In our analysis of philosophic eros in the *Phaedo* and the *Republic* and of friendship and familial love in the *Lysis* and the *Republic*, we shall find some confirmation of this interpretation.

Notes

1 Bury, R.G., *The Symposium of Plato*, p. iii. This is still the most detailed and useful edition of the dialogue. Bury's introduction, his dramatic

and philological analysis of the speeches, and his notes are all invaluable. Dover's much later and shorter edition is also worth consulting, though Dover explicitly warns us of a fundamental lack of sympathy with Plato's theories.

2 There is not much controversy about this, though there is about Plato's own attitude towards the views expressed in the first five speeches. How much did he oppose these views, and how much did he use them for his own purposes? For the latest review of the literature see Guthrie, W.K.C., *A History of Greek Philosophy*, (HGP) vol. 4, pp. 365ff and 380–1. See also Gould, T., *Platonic Love*, ch. 2, and Rosen, S., *Plato's Symposium*. We shall see that Plato takes over some of the views of the first five speakers and explicitly rejects others.

3 For a detailed analysis of Alcebiades' speech see Nussbaum, M., 'The Speech of Alcebiades: A Reading of Plato's Symposium', *Philosophy and Literature*.

4 References to Plato's works are given in Stephanus pages in the *Symposium*, common to all modern editions.

5 This tradition is well documented, indeed celebrated, in Carson's stunningly written recent book, *Eros: The Bittersweet*. See especially pp. 3–9.

6 For this dispute see Dover's extended discussion, GH, pp. 45–49 and 81–91. But the distinction between legitimate and illegitimate (or good and bad) eros drawn by Dover and several classical authors remains ambiguous. In Pausanias' speech it is clear that good eros does not exclude sexual intercourse, but only restricts it to certain circumstances and for certain reasons as given in the speech. But in Democritus' definition of 'legitimate eros' as 'aiming, without hybris, at the beautiful', this is not clear. We shall see that in the *Phaedrus* the best kind of eros – among males anyway – does exclude sexual intercourse, and so apparently does a passage in the *Republic* 403ab.

7 Guthrie, HGP, vol. I, p. 28, and vol. IV pp. 282–3; Bury, ibid., pp. xxviii–ix, Dover, *Plato, Symposium* (PS), pp. 105–11.

8 Guthrie, HGP, vol. I, p. 28.

9 Ibid., vol. IV, p. 382.

10 Dover suggests that Eryximachus' speech prepares the ground for this. PS, p. 105.

11 For the influence of the theory see, e.g., Lillyman, W., 'Analogies for Love: Goethe's *Die Wahwerwandtschaften* and Plato's *Symposium*', *Goethe's Normative Fiction*, ed. Lillyman. For the error, see Walster, E. and G. W., *A New Look at Love*, p. 5. Under the heading 'Plato's Theory' the authors give a brief summary of Aristophanes' speech and end the section with 'This then is the nature of love according to Plato.'

12 HGP, vol. IV, p. 383–4.

13 Bury, ibid., p. xxx. Bury has a long discussion of the controversies in the literature about Aristophanes' speech.

14 PS, p. 113.

15 Symposium 205DE: here Diotima in her criticism uses the very terms Aristophanes used in his definition; and at 212C Aristophanes tries to reply but he is interrupted by the noisy entrance of Alcebiades.

16 See, e.g., SE, vol. XVIII, p. 57, and pp. 250–3 below.

17 Guthrie gets into the spirit of the speech when he comments: 'How the present generation can obtain matching halves, when the dichotomy took place in the pre-historic past, it would be unfair to ask.' HGP, vol. IV, p. 384, n. 4.

18 Bury, ibid., p. xxxv. For a lively account of Eros in poetry and art see Harrison, J., *Prolegomena to the Study of Greek Religion*, ch. xii. But Carson's recent study shows that in the poetic tradition before Plato Eros was very much thought of as a mixed blessing. By comparison Agathon's speech is far too eulogistic.

19 See Dover's extended discussion of these issues in GH.

20 The first of these questions, what eros is, is an instance of the famous Socratic question, 'What is x?', which the Platonic Socrates thinks is the first and most fundamental question to be raised about any subject under investigation. The same point about eros is made in the *Phaedrus* 237cd. See also, e.g., *Meno* 77ab, and for a more extensive discussion the author's *Socrates*, ch. III.

21 In analyzing this speech we are concentrating on the philosophical theory contained in it. But as Guthrie says, we should not forget that Plato's aims are complex and that he did not write 'sober treatises' but dialogues 'with a consuming interest not only in ideas but in people'. HGP, vol. IV, p. xiii.

22 At 201e Socrates tells us that like Agathon he had supposed that Eros was a great god and that Diotima corrected him. And at 204e Diotima tells Socrates that he had mistakenly supposed, like Agathon, that Eros was the beloved, not the lover; whereas in her view Eros is the lover. The passage is clear: in Diotima's view, and in Socrates' corrected view, Eros symbolizes the lover, not the beloved. The remaining alternative, that Eros symbolizes neither but rather love itself, the relation, is not even considered. Consequently, the deficiency model discussed below is to be applied to the lover.

23 For the connection between eros and desire in the Greek language and culture, see Dover, GH, pp. 42–49, and Carson, A., *Eros: The Bittersweet*, pp. 10–11. Recall also that Prodicus had defined eros as 'desire doubled'.

24 The deficiency model is also applied to the analysis of friendship in the *Lysis* 215b: 'And if a man has no need (lack) of anything he will not cherish anything ... and he who does not cherish will not love ... and one who loves not is no friend.' See also *Lysis* 221d, *Gorg*. 496d, *Phileb*. 35a, for direct applications to desire. Carson claims that Eros

and lack of the object of love always went together in the poetic tradition before Plato, p. 11

25 Controversy has arisen about the meaning of the conclusion and the soundness of the argument, due to alleged unclarity about what 'Eros' symbolizes: is it the lover, the beloved, or the relation itself – love? See Allen, R.E., 'A Note on the Elerchus of Agathon: Symposium 199c–201c', *The Monist*, no. 50, p. 460, Dover, PS, pp. 135–36, and Guthrie, HGP, vol. IV, pp. 375, 385. We saw (n. 22) that Socrates clears up the alleged ambiguity later: 'Eros' is to be taken as a symbol for the lover. But the deficiency model being applied to Eros is also clear: it is the desiring subject (to epithumoun, 200bl) who lacks what he desires, not the desire itself. What sense would the latter make? The parallel passages cited in note 24 above confirm the point, and so do Socrates' examples: it is the man who is not tall or healthy or wealthy that desires to have these things. As Allen says, eros is a relation and as such it lacks nothing and desires nothing. Plato has no interest in proving that love itself is not beautiful (or good), nor does he ever say such a thing. He wants to show rather that eros arises out of imperfection or deficiency in the lover.

26 Some of these inferences such as E5 and E7, have been understandably criticized; see, e.g. Nussbaum, 'The Speech of Alcebiades', *Philosophy and Literature*, nos 3,2 (1979). pp. 146–7 and *The Fragility of Goodness*, p. 178. Granting Plato's premises, if Alcebiades loves the beauty of Agathon, it follows only that Alcediades lacks *that* beauty, not that he lacks *all* beauty; he might have beauty of soul or another token of the same type. True, but it should be noted that Plato is not speaking here of human lovers or beloveds, but of Agathon's god Eros. This god's very nature is to love, and hence it is plausible to suppose that, on Agathon's view, he loves all beauty. From this and the deficiency model it follows that he lacks all beauty, as indeed Socrates concludes at 201b 6–7; and similarly with goodness, given that (all) good things are beautiful. Plato does not suppose, however, that all human lovers always love all beauty: in the lower stages of the ladder of love one may love a beautiful body or just the beauty of bodies. And similarly with goodness. Given this, the deficiency model does not require that human lovers lack all beauty or goodness, but only the beauty or goodness they happen to love. This is sufficient for Plato's theory as he develops it, and it does justice to his central insight here: that erotic love arises out of some incompleteness in the lover, some imperfection in beauty, goodness or immortality, and that it is essentially a movement toward these perfections. For Dover's attack on this part of Plato's argument and some recent defences, see Carson, *Eros*, pp. 10–11, and Stokes, *Plato's Socratic Conversations*, pp. 129ff.

27 See, e.g. A. Montague, ed., *The Meaning of Love*, Montague's introduction.

28 The content of her criticism leaves no doubt that she is criticizing the view of Aristophanes (her key terms, translated 'whole', 'half', 'what belongs to one', are the very terms Aristophanes used to characterize the objects of eros), and it has been universally so taken. But dramatically her criticism is somewhat anomalous, since not having been present at the party she had not heard the speech of Aristophanes.

29 The question has been raised, why Plato's doctrine of eros is put in the mouth of Diotima, 'the only woman whose "voice" is heard at the party', as Kahn remarks. Cornford and Guthrie raise only the question why another person is introduced as having taught Socrates about eros. See *Principium Sapientiae*, p. 84, *The Unwritten Philosophy*, p. 71, and HGP, vol. IV, p. 385. Dover (PS, 137–8) approaches the question, why a woman, and though he is unsympathetic to Plato's views, hints at some elements from which we might try to construct a speculative answer (Plato does not tell us). The introduction of a woman to an all male party, where male–male eros had already been ranked above others on the ground that males are superior in intelligence and courage, is certainly striking. Moreover, Diotima introduces Socrates into the higher 'mysteries' of eros where the Form Beauty is brought in and sharply distinguished from its earthly manifestations. And according to the theory of the *Republic* Bk V, philosophers are those who have a passion for truth and who can distinguish between Forms and their sensible participants. By that theory it would appear that Diotima is a woman philosopher. And in that same book Plato proposes that women be treated on the basis of their ability to perform social functions, rather than on the basis of sex. It would seem then that the introduction of a woman into the investigation about the nature of eros can be taken seriously. Women too are capable of the highest kind of eros and can even be men's teachers of it!

30 Interpretations of Christian agape differ on many of these points. In Nygren's justly famous interpretation, God's agape for us, the agape in the Gospels and in St Paul , is taken as a model for the agape we are commanded to have for God and neighbor. God's agape is for all of us, whether Jew or Greek, godly or ungodly, good or evil (*Agape* and *Eros*, pp. 63–7). Moreover, it does not arise from any need or imperfection, but it is 'spontaneous' and 'unmotivated.' (Ibid., pp. 75–7); and further yet, 'agape is indifferent to value', i.e. to merit or value in the object, and indeed 'it does not recognize value but creates it' (p. 78). As I interpret Platonic eros, nothing can be further from it than God's agape of us *à la Nygren*. Moreover, since Nygren interprets the love we are commanded to have for God and neighbor on the model of God's agape, the former is nearly as different from Platonic eros. To be sure, God's agape for us flows from his very nature whereas our agape for God and neighbor does not; we can

love thus only when God infuses agape in us (p. 129). But this nevertheless is the agape we are commanded to have: we are not to love God and neighbor out of need, nor are we to love God as 'the highest good'. (p. 92). It should be noted, though, that Nygren has a rather special interpretation of Christian agape, in the Gospels and St Paul, which he himself opposes to other interpretations. Moreover, later views of Christian love are different. According to Nygren's detailed interpretation of Augustine, for example, our love of God is the model, rather than God's love, and we can love God as the supreme good.(Ibid, part II, ch. II). Thus, given the long history of the concept of Christian love comparisons to Plato are a complex matter, something that sometimes writers forget when they object to Nygren's thesis that Christian agape and Platonic eros have nothing in common. If we restrict this thesis to Nygren's interpretation of agape in the Gospels and St Paul and to Plato's theory of eros in the *Symposium*, the thesis seems to me essentially correct. For a somewhat different conception of eros and agape, and hence different relations between them, see, e.g., Adams, R.M., 'Pure Love', *Journal of Religion and Ethics.*

31 Freud, *Three Essays on Sexuality*, SE vol. VII, pp. 135–6. It may seem anachronistic to apply the distinction to Plato, but I think it is implicit in his grammar, where the object is given by a genitive and the aim by an infinitive construction. See my 'Hintikka on Knowledge and its Objects in Plato', *Patterns in Plato's Thought*, ed. J.M.A. Moravcsik, 1973, pp. 36–43. The distinction is also necessary in order to understand Diotima's questions, 'The lover of good things, what does he love?' and 'The lover of beautiful things, what does he love?' Here the object is already given in the question and what is requested has to be something else – I suggest the aim. The distinction also enables us to resolve the controversy between Nygren and Vlastos as to whether Platonic eros is 'idiocentric' rather than 'egocentric' or 'acquisitive'. Vlastos, G., 'The Individual as Object of Love in Plato', *Platonic Studies*, pp. 20, 30. Our reconstruction supports the answer that both generic and eros proper are egoistic relative to their aims and idiocentric relative to their objects. At the top of the ladder the Form Beauty is the object, not the aim of eros; though to get to the top and 'see' the Form Beauty is the aim *of the ascent*. The issue of egoism belongs with the aim, not the object. The distinction between aim and object is also implicit in the speech of Aristophanes: the object or eros is one's other half in the original human condition, and the aim is union with it. As we shall see, Freud makes powerful use of this distinction.

32 The translation is Lamb's. The word Plato uses is *katachrometha*. Dover says 'here its connotation is "use thoughtlessly"'. (PS, p. 145). Cornford says of this passage: 'The name Eros has been wrongly restricted in common speech ....' 'The Doctrine of Eros in Plato's

Symposium' (*The Unwritten Philosophy*, ed. W.K.C. Guthrie, p. 72). In both the case of 'eros' and 'poiesis', the generic use was the older, so Plato is probably speaking of current use. See Bury, *The Symposium*, pp. 106–7.

33 This is by no means without linguistic warrant. Dover notes that in Homer 'eros' means 'desire for a woman, for food and drink ... and for other things ...', (GH, p. 43). So Plato is going back to older uses of the term for his generic eros. Dover also claims that in Plato's time and later 'the connotation of this group of words is so regularly sexual that other uses of it can be fairly regarded as sexual metaphor.' (p. 43). Here Dover does not explicitly note Plato's linguistic move, nor the definition of generic eros as desire for the good, nor the distinction between generic and specific eros. Partly perhaps as a consequence of this he calls Plato's use of 'erastes' in *Rep.* 501d and elsewhere 'figurative'. (GH,pp. 156ff.) But the older linguistic use together with Plato's distinctions render Dover's point dubious. In calling philosophers 'erastes' in the *Republic* Plato means that they are lovers of the good, and this can be literal within the older use. Lacking a term such as 'love' which we use to cover all kinds of love, Plato reaches back to an older use and makes the appropriate distinctions. The case of specific eros may be a different story: whether Plato's use of 'eros' at the top of the ladder of eros is 'sexual metaphor' or 'figurative' is a more difficult question.

34 Some form of the distinction between generic and specific eros has been noted by the commentators. See Bury, *The Symposium*, pp. 12, 37, and 109; Guthrie, HGP, vol. IV, p. 375, Dover, PS, p. 145, and most recently Stokes, p. 157ff, who speaks of a 'wider' sense of eros and a specific form of it, on the analogy of Diotima's analysis of 'poetry'. But there is much obscurity and disagreement about the relations between the two. According to Bury, generic eros is defined as 'desire for the abiding possession of the good', and specific eros as 'desire for procreation in the beautiful'. I am in basic agreement with the former, but find the latter incomplete.

35 Where has the third element. 'to be theirs *forever* (always)', been agreed to and on what basis? I owe to Prof. Charles Kahn the suggestion that perhaps this third element comes from the analysis of desire discussed at 200bd, when the deficiency model was applied to desire and love: the man who desires what he does not have desires to have it at some future time; and the man who already has something and still desires it is explicitly said to want to have it also in the future. The aim of desire love, at 204d also implies this: *genesthai auto* literally means 'that [they] come into being to him.' And at 205b, in the case of desire for good things, Diotima explicitly added this element: 'when we say that all men love the same things [good things] always'. We may note, though, that the aim of desire always referring to something in the future is not sufficient for

claiming that we want that state of affairs always. If I now want to eat an ice cream cone, either I am not now eating one or I want to continue eating one (or want another one). and in both cases the reference is to the future; but in neither case does it follow that I want to eat an ice cream cone forever! Since Diotima does not introduce 'forever' or 'always' explicitly till the case of love and desire for good things, we might plausibly speculate that she holds this element to be true only in the case of good things, and things that are always or invariably good. Eating an ice cream cone is sometimes good for me and sometimes not, and it certainly would be destructive for me to be eating ice cream cones forever. But the opposite would seem to be true of such things as health and wisdom: I would not want to be ever without them. Since Socrates does elsewhere make the distinction between things that are invariably good and beneficial and things that sometimes are and sometimes are not, we may plausibly attribute this position to Plato. See, e.g. Kahn, C., 'Drama and Dialetic in Plato's *Gorgias*, *Oxford Studies in Ancient Philosophy*, ed. Julia Annas, pp. 467–8. It is not a point just about desire, but about desiring invariably good things. For the most recent discussion of Dover's criticisms see Stokes, M.C., *Plato's Socratic Conversations*, pp. 157–9.

36 For the shift to specific eros see Bury, *The Symposium*, p. 109.

37 It is important to notice that from the very beginning of her discussion of specific eros Diotima includes begetting by means of soul (206b,206c). Begetting by means of body is sexual, as in the cases of animals and men and women, the cases she starts with. When later (208c) she moves on to spiritual begetting, this is begetting by means of soul, creations of poems, constitutions, and so on. Thus we need not suppose that here she is switching back to generic eros. All her examples of spiritual begetting at 208, 209, exemplify the structure of specific eros.

38 It is this move that Marcus has emphasized claiming that it represents a 'radical change of perspective' and 'a new picture' of love. 'The Dialectic of Eros in Plato's Symposium', *Plato vol. II*, ed. G. Vlastos, pp. 255ff. Vlastos corrects this (*Platonic Studies*, p. 20, n. 56), pointing out the connection to the definition of generic eros. It is true, as I discuss below, that the desire for immortality is inferred directly from the definition of generic eros. I don't think, though, that 'birth in beauty' follows from that definition or that Diotima claims that it does, as Vlastos writes. We have rather a less direct inference through the new, independent proposition that only through begetting in beauty can mortals share in immortality. This I think coheres well with the idea that eros proper is a part of or species of generic eros.

39 Professor Charles Kahn has suggested an interesting defence of Plato's inference, from wanting the good to be one's own forever to

wanting immortality. 'To want to have good things always (*aei*) means to want them in the future as well as for the present. Plato's point is that desire is essentially future-oriented: no one's desires are restricted to the time before death, though of course their satisfaction may be (I want to go to the theater on Saturday, even if I *may* die on Friday). But if my desires go on indefinitely into the future, then in so far as I want to satisfy them (and that is presumably trivially true: having a desire *means* wanting to satisfy it), to that extent I want to continue existing indefinitely into the future. So my desire for future happiness (i.e. for obtaining future goods) includes or entails a desire to go on living indefinitely into the future.' Perhaps this more adequately represents Plato's thinking. Of course I may have desires whose satisfaction in the future does not require my existence then: for example, I may want this book to be read long after I am dead, or I may want my son to become president or my children to prosper after I am gone or my descendants to be always healthy and happy. But even in cases where the aim of my desire is a future state of myself, it is not clear to me that wanting something always entails wanting to exist indefinitely into the future or to be immortal. Thus I may want to speak the truth always, but that may mean no more than 'Whenever I speak I want to speak the truth'. There seems to be no contradiction in my wanting to always speak the truth and yet not wanting to live forever.

40 It is worth emphasizing that Diotima explicitly tries to *explain* the erotic desire and behavior of generating offspring on beautiful objects. The desire for immortality, derived from the definition of generic eros, is introduced explicitly in explanatory terms (*aition, aitian*) at 207a, 207c, and again at 208b. This part of the theory is descriptive or explanatory, not normative; and the desire for immortality gains status as an explanatory hypothesis, independent of its problematic derivation.

41 Bury is the only author I know who recognizes a definition of specific eros, though less complex than the one I give. Bury also points out that the idea that mortals, humans or animals, can partake of immortality by creation of offspring – immortality by replacement – is also found in Plato, *Laws*, 773 and in Aristotle, *De Anima* 415a 26ff. Immortality by replacement has its analogue in modern evolutionary theory in which procreation is seen as representative of the individual in future generations. It should be noted that the two kinds of immortality Plato talks about in the *Symposium*, divine immortality and immortality by replacement, are different from the immortality of the soul he talks about in the *Phaedo, Phaedrus* and *Republic*. In these works the soul is claimed to be immortal in the sense of being everlasting and having always two properties, that of being self-moving and alive. This is clearly not divine immortality, since it is compatible with the soul changing in other respects; and it

is clearly not immortality by replacement through offspring, since this does not entail everlastingness of one and the same entity. Immortality by replacement can be achieved only through creation of offspring, biological or spiritual, whereas the immortality of the *Phaedo* every soul has no matter whether it creates anything. It may seem puzzling that in the *Symposium* Plato has Diotima say that mortals can share in immortality *only* through creation of offspring, whereas in the other works he claims that every soul is immortal in the sense of being everlasting, always selfmoving and alive. Professor Vicki Harper is probably right in the suggestion she made to me: that in the *Symposium* Plato is speaking of personal immortality, the immortality of a person as constituted by a body, a soul, and a particular lifetime; whereas in the other works he is speaking of souls that inhabit several bodies and have no distinctive association. This makes the dialogues consistent, though it may raise troublesome questions about the identity of souls.

42 See, e.g. Daly, M. and Wilson, M., *Sex, Evolution and Behaviour*, chs 2 and 4.

43 'Reason and Eros in the "Ascent" Passage in the *Symposium*', 1971.

44 Moravscik concentrates on reconstructing what I call ascents from step to step (he calls the ascents steps, and my steps levels). When one considers the fact that he does not reconstruct or even bring in at all the theory of eros within which the ladder belongs, his reconstruction of the ascent is remarkably accurate. He finds three kinds of 'steps', steps of reason, steps of emotion, and steps of creation. Now these three kinds of things are found in every case of eros proper according to our reconstruction: the apprehension of beauty and the apprehension of the relation of creation to immortality would be reason-elements; the desire to create, the desire for immortality, and emotional attitudes to the attracting object would be emotion-elements, and the creation of offspring a creation-element. Moravscik brings out nicely the interplay between reason and emotion in the ascent, and the fact that reason guides and directs the ascent. On our reconstruction, every case of eros at all four levels (our steps) involves reason, emotion and creation. It is not clear to me that Moravscik recognizes this. Comparisons with his paper are difficult because he has not reconstructed the rest of the theory.

45 See, e.g. Irwin, T., *Plato's Moral Theory*, p. 323, n. 58, for some reasons against the so-called 'exclusive' interpretation of the ladder, according to which the lover gives up lower objects as he ascends. This issue is not to be confused with the dispute whether Platonic eros, generic or specific, is egoistic; the latter has to do with the aim of desire and eros and rises about every step whether or not one is ascending.

46 This raises difficult questions about the individuation of desires and we shall discuss it in chs 6 and 7.

47 'The Form of the Good in Plato's *Republic*', in *Essays In Ancient Philosophy*, vol. II, ed. John Anton and A. Preuss, 1983. For a shorter version of the theory see 'Two Theories of Good in Plato's *Republic*', in *Archiv für Geschichte der Philosophie*, 1985, pp. 234–9. I wish to emphasize here that the matter is quite complex; the shorter version is no substitute for the original paper; much less so is the sketch I give here.

48 The distinction and relation between beauty and goodness in Plato is notoriously obscure. As Prof. Charles Kahn notes in the *Symposium* 201c we are told that '[all] good things are beautiful', which would seem to indicate that goodness is not more general than beauty. ('Drama and Dialectic in Plato's *Gorgias*', p. 93 & n. 33). In other places, such as *Meno* 77b, Socrates also seems to hold the converse, that all beautiful things are good, since he suggests that those who desire beautiful things desire good things. And in his recent study of *Plato: Hippias Major*, p. 185. Woodruff attributes to Socrates the extensional equivalence 'the fine [beautiful] is good and the good fine'. It seems probable then that Plato held that beauty and goodness are extensionally equivalent, which does not seem to fit in well with the distinction between generic and specific eros. But we also have attempts in the dialogues, notably in the *Gorgias*, p. 474–5 and the *Hippias Major*, pp. 295–7, to define the beautiful in terms of the good; and this suggests that Plato may have also thought that though the two Forms have the same participants, Goodness is the more abstract and more fundamental notion. In any case, in the *Republic* he seems to hold the view that the Form of the Good is the most general, abstract or fundamental Form. And this does fit in well with the distinction between generic and specific eros. In the *Symposium* we have the indisputable fact that it is the Form Beauty that is at the top of the ladder of eros, not goodness or any other Form. And in view of the fact that in the same work generic eros was explicitly defined in terms of goodness, this is strong evidence that the ladder of eros is a ladder of specific eros. I think that the eros discussed in the *Phaedrus* is also specific eros, since it is uniquely related to Beauty.

Plato's distinction between specific and generic eros serves, I believe, two purposes. In his discussion of specific eros he wants to extend the concept of beauty beyond sensuous and visible beauty, and eros of beauty accordingly beyond sexual desire; but he also wants to maintain connection and continuity with the sensuous attachment his contemporaries called eros. However, in subsuming specific eros under desire for the good he is reaching beyond this, towards a unified theory of all attachments: not only erotic attachments to Beauty, but also the love of knowledge, friendship and familial love, the love of honor, and the love of gain, in which Beauty plays no special role.

3

Passionate Platonic Eros in the *Phaedrus*

Eros is desire doubled; eros doubled is madness.
Prodicus

Introduction

Plato's theory of Eros in the *Symposium* is inspiring and elevating. It subsumes all erotic love under desire for the good. Even in its 'lowest' forms, among animals and men and women, it is sparked by the attraction of bodily beauty and it is motivated by the desire for immortality, a good that all living creatures seek. In its higher forms it is transformed into a powerful force for creativity in the arts, sciences and philosophy, the highest achievements of human civilization.

For all this Plato's theory in the *Symposium* is justly famous. But it is also rather monolithic and one-sided. From Socrates and Diotima we hear nothing about the passionate irrationalities of eros, about the pleasures it brings, the conflicts it creates – all well attested phenomena in the Greek culture.[1] Nor do we hear anything about the personality and history of the lover. Even though the *Symposium* is a middle period dialogue, the tripartite division of the soul is nowhere in sight. The theory receives no help from Plato's new psychology in the *Republic* about the structure and functioning of the human personality.

The *Phaedrus* makes an important contribution on all these points: The physical passion and pleasures of eros are acknowledged and given a place in the theory; the issue of irrational eros is squarely faced; and the selection of beloved and the response to beauty are better analyzed by means of the tripartite division of the soul, the hypothesis of its previous existence, the theory of recollection and the theory of Forms.

Though there has been much controversy about the date of composition, the *Phaedrus* is usually closely associated with other middle period dialogues, such as the *Phaedo*, the *Symposium*, and the *Republic*.[2] Dramatically and philosophically, we have considerable continuity with the *Symposium*. Phaedrus, who was the father of the discourse in the *Symposium*, brings up the same subject again, eros, and the first two thirds of the work consist of three speeches about eros. The first, composed by Lysias and recited by Phaedrus, maintains that the lover's passion is a kind of madness or sickness, transient and unreliable, and that one would be better off having as a lover someone free of such a malady. This kind of eros reminds us of the 'bad' eros of Pausanias in the *Symposium*. In his own first speech Socrates takes up this theme again, but he gives Phaedrus a lesson on how to investigate such a topic, namely by classifying and defining eros first and then going into its effects – and with this too we are familiar from the *Symposium*. But in his second and much longer speech Socrates 'recants' and repudiates the substance of his previous talk: employing typical Platonic doctrines of the middle period, he builds up a theory of eros, which is continuous with the *Symposium* but also adds the new elements we noted above. In the rest of the work Socrates compares rhetoric – presumably the 'art' exhibited in Lysias' speech – unfavorably with dialectic, the art of classification and definition employed by Socrates himself.

The setting, though, is very different from that of the *Symposium*, and it is perhaps appropriate to Socrates' theme of eros as 'divine madness' and divine inspiration. Socrates is taken out of his usual surroundings, the city, and put in the open country where 'he breaks out in admiration of the trees and grass, the fragrance of the flowering shrubs, and the shrill music of the cicadas. The place too is consecrated to Achelous and the nymphs. Socrates gradually falls under its inspiration and speaks in lyrical language, which as the astonished Phaedrus notes, is very unlike his usual manner.'[3] Guthrie speaks of 'the magical air of unreality which is shed over this ideal summer's day'.[4] And as Cornford further notes, 'Plato could not have indicated more clearly that this poetic and inspired Socrates was not known to his habitual companions.'

Thus the theme, the characters, and the setting all seem appropriate to Plato's middle dialogues and to the treatment of eros as mediating between the sensible world and the divine world of Platonic Forms. Here we shall concentrate on Socrates' two speeches.

Pleasure, Rationality and Eros as Human Madness

Let us begin with the issues of pleasure and rationality, which Vlastos has brought to our attention.

> Had I been able to work more intensively on the *Phaedrus* in this essay I would have taken a crack at the extraordinary fact that here eros is

> not only described, but *defined*, as *mania* by our ultra-rationalist, Plato, and is associated as *mania* in the closest terms with philosophy no less than with the mystic cults ... This convergence of *mania* and *nous* in love does not seem to intrigue commentators. Few of them notice the paradox at all or, if they do, they seem bent on explaining it away ....[5]

This is not a puzzle of Vlastos' own making. We can see that he is on the right track by the following passage from the *Republic*:

> But tell me this – can there by any communion between temperance and extravagant pleasure? How could there be, he said, since such pleasure puts a man besides himself no less than pain? Or between it and virtue generally? By no means. But is there between pleasure and insolence (*hybris*) and license? Most assuredly. Do you know of greater or keener pleasures than those associated with Aphrodite? I don't, he said, nor yet of any more insane (or mad). But is not the right love (eros) a temperate and harmonious love of the orderly and the beautiful? It is indeed, he said. Then nothing of madness, nothing akin to license, must be allowed to come near right love. (403ab)

Let us expand on Vlastos' themes and take a crack at the puzzle ourselves.

Plato is certainly an ultra-rationalist in his theory of eros in the *Symposium*. What does this mean? Very roughly speaking, let us say that rationality in cognition consists in maximizing the truth or at least the probabilities for it. Belief is rational if one has reasons or evidence for the truth of what one believes; knowledge, it would seem, is rational by definition, if at least by definition one must have reasons or evidence for the truth of what one claims to know. And let us say, very roughly speaking, that rationality in conduct or in ethics is maximizing the good, at least if one is a teleologist, which Plato probably was. A desire is rational if it is a desire for what one rationally believes or knows is the good, or a part of it or a means to it. And conduct is rational insofar as it is motivated by rational desire. If we accept these very rough explanations of rationality for the moment, and they are Platonic enough, we can see at once that Platonic eros in the *Symposium* is rationalistic. Generic eros is *defined* as the desire for the good to be one's own forever. And eros proper, the desire to beget on a beautiful object for the sake of our own immortality, being a part of generic eros, is just as rationalistic. We saw that the theory of the Form of the Good makes being immortal a good making characteristic and immortality a good. In desiring to beget offspring on a beautiful object for the sake of our own immortality, we desire a means to a good or part of it. Thus this desire too is rational. What is more, eros in the *Symposium* is completely rationalistic or ultra-rationalistic: for no competing motivation to the desire for the good is recognized at all as a part or aspect of eros. And this is extraordinary indeed. It is commonly recognized that eros often brings intense – perhaps the most intense – pleasure, and the desire for such pleasure a motivation for love. Freud assigns pleasure as the aim of love. And for Plato himself the most common candidate for a competing motivation to the desire for the good is the desire for pleasure. Yet, his theory in the *Symposium* leaves pleasure entirely out of account.

In the *Phaedrus* Plato attempts to remedy this defect and make up for this omission. The issues of pleasure and rationality are faced clearly enough in Socrates' definition of eros in his first speech:

> Let us first agree on a definition of love, its nature and its power: Now everyone sees that love is a desire; and we know too that non-lovers also desire the beautiful. How then are we to distinguish the lover from the non-lover? We must observe that in each one of us there are two ruling and leading principles, which we follow whithersoever they lead; one is the innate desire for pleasures, the other the acquired opinion which strives for the best. These two sometimes agree within us and are sometimes in strife; and sometimes one and sometimes the other has the greater power. Now when opinion leads through reason toward the best and is more powerful, its power is called self-restraint, but when desire irrationally drags us towards pleasures and rules within us, its rule is called excess (*hybris*). Now excess has many names, for it has many members and many forms; and whichever of these forms is most marked gives its own name, neither beautiful nor honorable, to him who possess it. For example, if the desire for food prevails over the higher reason and the other desires, it is called gluttony ... So I say that the desire which overcomes the rational opinion that strives toward the right, and which is led away toward the pleasure of beauty and again is strongly forced by the desires that are kindred to itself toward bodily beauty, when it gains the victory, takes its name from that very force, and is called eros. (237d-238d)

Here eros seems to be defined as irrational and overpowering desire for the pleasures of bodily beauty! Notice that Plato is not saying that desire for pleasure is always irrational: it is irrational only when it is in conflict with reason's opinion as to what is best (and the attendant desire for what is best). Moreover, the definition makes references only to desires for the pleasures of beauty and the 'kindred' pleasures of 'bodily beauty' – to sexual pleasures. Within these limits, however, eros is still defined as irrational desire, desire contrary to what is best, for the pleasures of bodily beauty. A far cry this from Platonic eros in the *Symposium*, even the lowest kind, among animals and between man and woman, which strives for immortality, a rational striving for the good! Indeed, eros in Socrates' first speech has been reduced to a kind of weakness, moral weakness or weakness of character, a gluttony for sexual pleasures! If Plato is trying to remedy the ultra-rationalism of the *Symposium*, he has now gone to the other extreme and made eros ultra-irrational.

Socrates proceeds to describe the lover of this kind: old and ugly, jealous and possessive, he cares for nothing but his pleasure, degrades his beloved and reduces him in body, soul, and spirit. When his passion dies and sense and reason replace eros and madness (*mania*) (241a), he drops the beloved and forgets all his oaths and promises. The conclusion is that a beloved is better off with a non-lover than a lover of this kind.

Eros as Divine Madness

> And when Love speaks, the voices of all the gods
> Make heaven drowsy with the harmony.
>
> Shakespeare

Now Socrates repudiates this speech as well as the earlier speech of Phaedrus, and at one point says that they contain 'nothing sound or true' (242e). A bit later though he says that someone listening to these speeches would imagine that 'he was listening to people brought up among low sailors, who had never seen a generous love' (243c). This seems to concede that the eros Socrates defined in his first speech does occur; the definition is false because not all eros is like that. In a second speech Socrates undertakes to give a fuller, sound, and true account of eros.

He begins by giving an *a priori* argument against his first definition:

> If eros is, as indeed he is, a god or something divine, he can do nothing evil; but the two speeches said that he was evil. So they erred about Eros. (242e)

His next major point is about madness or *mania*:

> And I must say that this saying is not true, which teaches that when a lover is at hand the non-lover should be more favored, because the

> lover is insane (or mad) and the other sane. For if it were a simple fact that madness is an evil, the saying would be true; but in reality the greatest of goods come to us through madness, when it is sent as a gift from the gods ... Therefore let us not be afraid on that point, and let no one disturb and frighten us by saying that the reasonable friend should be preferred to him who is in a frenzy. Let him show in addition that eros is not sent from heaven for the advantage of the lover and the beloved alike, and we will grant him the prize of victory. We on our part must prove that such madness is given by the gods for our greatest happiness. (244a, 245b)

The message here is clear enough: not all madness is evil; the madness sent by the gods, who are good and can do no evil, is the source of the greatest goods and the greatest happiness. Eros is a species of this divinely given madness (the others being prophecy, augury and art), while, presumably, the eros of Socrates' first speech is human madness and the lowest kind of eros.

Socrates continues with a very long speech that leaves us dizzy, breathless, mystified, exhausted, and even mad. He weaves into it religion, myth, fantasy, metaphor, simile, allegory, the immortality and tripartite division of the soul, the theory of recollection, and even the theory of Forms – a formidable mixture of poetry, religion, and philosophy. It has to be read to be believed or doubted. Perhaps this is what happens when one comes under the spell of divine madness! What can we make of it?

Its main elements are as follows. First, Socrates argues that all soul is immortal: our souls exist before they entered our bodies and continue to exist after death. Then he likens the soul 'to the composite nature of a pair of winged horses and a charioteer' (246a), and describes the soul's previous existence in the heavens. The horses of the gods are both good, and the divine charioteers have an easy time traveling upwards around the heavens. In human souls one of the horses is noble and good but the other of the opposite character; human charioteers have to struggle to drive upwards, some of them lose their wings, fall to the earth and inhabit bodies. The nature of the wings is to soar upwards; they partake of the nature of the divine, which is 'beauty, wisdom, goodness and all such qualities', qualities by which the wings of the soul are nourished and grow.[6] (246e) Zeus leads a huge procession of souls around the heavens. The souls of the gods are able to get to the top and behold 'absolute justice, temperance and knowledge'. But the human souls do not behold these realities completely. Because their horses are unruly they see some things but not others. Depending on how much they behold in the heavens and how much they recollect of the eternal realities when here on earth, they become different kinds of people, varying from the best kind, the philosopher, to the worst, the tyrant who is ruled by the bad horse. Thus our lives on this earth are largely determined by how much our souls in a previous existence 'saw' of the world of Platonic Forms, and how much we recollect of this previous knowledge. It is to this 'story' that Socrates appeals to explain and understand eros. Let us see how he does it.

One problem with Socrates' speech is that it makes eros a species of divine madness but it does not tell us what madness is, human or divine. But one of our problems is about this notion: why did Plato define eros as madness in the *Phaedrus*, when in the *Symposium* he defines eros as ultra-rationalistic, and in the *Republic* tells us that the right eros has nothing to do with madness?

Our hypothesis is that in the *Phaedrus* Plato is trying in part to remedy a defect of his own theory of eros in the *Symposium*: in the latter work his definition and description of eros does not bring in and account for the passion, intensity, and even frenzy that can characterize eros: passion and frenzy presumably caused by the intensity of sexual desires and pleasures. He attempts to do this by characterizing eros as *mania*, madness or frenzy, bringing in with this notion the intensity and passion of sexual pleasures and desires. But presumably he wishes to remedy the defect of the *Symposium* theory without contradicting that theory, especially the part that eros is rational, a striving for good. To accomplish all this, he (1) makes the distinction between human and divine madness, (2) brings in the immortality and tripartite division of the soul, and (3) makes use of the theory of Forms and the theory of recollection. The first distinction and the theology that goes with it enable him to claim that divinely given madness is not irrational. The division of the soul – a soul now composed of rational and passionate elements – enables him to account for the passionate aspect of eros and the inner conflict eros can cause. The theory of Forms and its epistemology enable him to interpret the popular, mythical notions of divinity in terms of Forms, to reinstate eros as love of beauty, and to account for love as both human and divine. And the theory of recollection enables him to explain the attraction of beauty on this earth by reference to the attraction of the Form Beauty in our previous existence. Let us discuss these points in turn.

1 As noted, Plato does not define or explain *mania* – madness – for us. We have to gather for ourselves the elements he builds into this concept. Now in his first speech Socrates tells us that eros is desire, but not simply desire for beauty since non-lovers also desire beauty.

He goes on to characterize eros as a species of *hybris*, excess or lack of self-control. *Hybris* in turn is characterized as overpowering desire for the pleasures of food, drink, or sex, resulting in conduct contrary to reason's judgment of what is best. Eros then is defined as overpowering desire for the sexual pleasures of bodily beauty resulting in conduct contrary to reason's judgment of what is best. And both *hybris* and its species *eros* are contrasted to *sophrosyne* – temperance or self-control. In this passage Socrates does not use the term *mania*, but a bit later (241a) he characterizes this love as eros and *mania*. We might be tempted here to think that Plato is identifying *mania* with *hybris*, or with that species of *hybris* which is eros. The passage we quoted from the *Republic* gives essentially the same analysis of eros but *mania* is explicitly used – so our temptation seems reinforced. But this certainly cannot be correct for the *Phaedrus*: for such identification would make *mania* always irrational – contrary to reason's judgment of what is best – whereas Socrates goes on to say, in his second speech that divinely given madness is not evil but the cause of the greatest goods, and so not contrary to reason or irrational. In the *Phaedrus* therefore Plato could not have identified *hybris* with *mania*, but at most *hybris* with human madness. But if *hybris* or erotic *hybris* is a species of madness – divine madness being the other species – what is the genus madness? How did Plato think of it? We can only offer an educated guess – that he thought of madness, at least erotic madness, as intense, passionate, and even irresistible desire for the pleasures of beauty, but not only for the *sexual* pleasures of *bodily* beauty. I think we shall find this guess confirmed in Plato's descriptions of the divinely mad lovers – 'the god-maddened lovers of the *Phaedrus*', as Guthrie aptly calls them.[7] For the moment we may notice that our hypothesis allows that madness is not always irrational, contrary to reason's judgment of what is best. The cases of love Plato seems to be considering in the *Phaedrus* – and in the *Republic* passage – are homosexual boy-love; and the best kind of lover, the divinely mad lover, does not indulge in intercourse which Plato considers contrary to what is best. As we shall see, this lover is able to control himself because of his association with the divine.

The distinction between human and divine madness is brought in to demarcate the cases between rational and irrational erotic madness. Socrates makes elaborate use of the mythology of the Greek gods, but I think this part of his story is all allegory. He is not referring literally to the gods of Greek mythology. After all, Plato had in front of him Euripides' *Madness of Hercules* in which Hera, one of the divinities of Socrates' speech, implants in Hercules a madness that is as destructive as one can imagine. As for Eros, another of Socrates' gods, it is described by Sophocles as 'invincible Eros' who 'distracts men's minds to wickedness and harm' (*Antigone* 781–92). No, Socrates' gods are immortal souls that are completely good, souls that have never inhabited bodies and are thus uncorrupted by animality, souls that know a reality that is 'colorless, shapeless, and intangible'; that is, the Forms (247c). Plato's divine madness is a source only of good not because the gods of Greek mythology were completely good, but because Plato redefines the divine as everlasting disembodied soul which has knowledge, always, of the eternal Platonic Forms.

2 Human souls, on the other hand, are not always free of body: they have difficulty following the gods and knowing the divine Forms, they fall to earth and inhabit bodies, forget their knowledge and have to try to recollect it through the earthly shadows of the Forms (248ff). As we saw, in the famous simile of the charioteer, Socrates likens the soul to a charioteer with two horses. The charioteer is reason, the part of the soul that is capable of knowledge of the Forms; one horse is spirit, the source of anger and indignation and the ally of reason; the other horse is desire, the source in humans of the appetites for food, drink and sex. (The simile of the charioteer presumably points to some tripartite division of the soul similar to that of *Republic* Book IV, and somewhat similar to Freud's Ego, Id, and Superego.) All the horses of divine souls are good with their wings whole, and their charioteers can stay in the world of Forms. But in human souls the steed of appetite, unruly and powerful, is bent on the pleasures of animality, and drags the soul to earth, whilst the charioteer has a mighty struggle to control it and lead it upwards again. Thus human souls contain both divinity and animality: all souls being immortal, the divine part of human souls, reason, had some contact, more or less, with the Forms, and had experienced the pleasures of contemplating divine beauty; the animal part, appetite, has the pleasures of bodily beauty as its object, the earthly shadow of divine beauty. Depending on how fully a human soul had 'seen' divine Beauty and how far it recollects it now when it encounters its earthly shadows, the resulting love can be rational or irrational madness. Thus, the passion and intensity of erotic madness is accounted for both by the power and intensity of bodily appetite at the sight of bodily beauty and by the intensity of reason when it encounters the incomparably greater splendor of divine Beauty. Reason has its own passion, its own 'madness'.

3 In an extended passage Socrates describes the best and worst kinds of love, divine and human erotic madness, using the theory of Forms, degrees of recollecting the Forms, and the evils of the body to account for the differences:

> All my discourse so far has been about the fourth kind of madness, which causes him to be regarded as mad, who, when he sees the beauty on earth, remembering the true beauty, feels his wings growing and longs to stretch them for an upward flight, but cannot do so, and like a bird, gazes upward and neglects the things below. My discourse has shown that this, of all inspirations, is the best and of the highest origin to him who has it or who shares in it, and that he who loves the beautiful, partaking in this madness, is called a lover ... every soul of man has by the law of nature beheld the realities ... but it is not easy for all souls to gain from earthly things a recollection of these realities, either for those which had but a brief view of them at that earlier time, or for those which, after falling to earth, were so unfortunate as to have forgotten the holy sights they once saw ... Beauty ... shone in brilliance among these visions; and since we came to earth we found it shining most clearly through the clearest of our senses; for sight is the sharpest of the physical senses, though wisdom is not even seen by it, for wisdom would arouse terrible love, if such a clear image of it were granted as would come through sight, and the same is true of the other beautiful realities; but beauty alone has this privilege, and therefore it is the most clearly seen and lovable. Now he who is not newly initiated, or has been corrupted, does not quickly rise from this world to the other world and to absolute beauty when he sees its namesake here, and he does not revere it when he looks upon it, but gives himself up to pleasure and like a beast proceeds to lust and begetting; he makes license his companion and is not afraid or ashamed to pursue pleasure in violation of nature. But he who is newly initiated, who beheld many of these realities, when he sees a god-like face or form which is a good image of beauty, shudders at first, and something of the old awe comes over him, then, as he gazes, he reveres the beautiful one as a god, and if he did not fear to be thought stark mad, he would offer sacrifices to his beloved as to an idol or god. (249d-251c)

This is a remarkable passage. It answers many questions that the *Symposium* left unanswered about the rationality of eros, about the terrible passions it arouses, and the role of beauty in eros. The worst kind of lover Socrates describes seems to be very much like the lover of his first speech, the lover of human and irrational madness. But even this lover seems now to be put in a new perspective: the perspective of the immortality and the tripartite division of the soul, of the theory of Forms and the epistemology of recollection.

Even this lover, when he sees bodily beauty, recollects the divine Beauty he once saw: he is attracted to bodily beauty perhaps because he was once attracted to divine Beauty and now perceives its earthly manifestations through the sharpest of the senses, sight, which can arouse terrible passion. But he has not 'seen' divine Beauty recently or fully, or has been corrupted by the body he inhabits, and so when he sees bodily beauty he is not able to turn to divine Beauty and revere it but gives himself to bodily pleasure. The origin of this madness is perhaps divine, but the link to divine Beauty is too weak, and this 'fallen' madness looks very much like the human madness of Socrates' first speech. In saying that the pleasures this lover takes are 'contrary to nature' Socrates implies that this madness is irrational; though he does not explain what he means by this phrase, Socrates is probably referring to the sexual pleasures of homosexual boy-love, pleasures that serve no good purpose either by the theory of the *Symposium* or the *Phaedrus*, pleasures that are not a means to creation of offspring or the betterment of the lover or beloved.[9]

At the other end of the spectrum, we have the lover whose love is truly divine madness. He has seen more of divine beauty and more recently, he has an adequate recollection of it, and has not been corrupted by the body. When he sees a god-like face on earth or a body that is a good image of divine Beauty, he is 'stricken with amazement', 'shudders at first', 'with sweat and unwonted heat'. He is passionately attracted to it because of his attraction to divine Beauty and because its earthly manifestation comes to him through the sharp sense of sight, 'as the effluence of beauty enters him through the eyes'. He too has an unruly horse, the steed of sexual appetite, and he too has to struggle to control it. But because his memory of divine Beauty is recent and vivid and because he has not been corrupted through previous bodily experience, he is able to control himself: he prizes the bodily beauty of the boy because it is a good image of divine Beauty, and he is able to turn upward to the world of Forms and turn his love for the boy into a love for Beauty itself. He is the philosopher who cares for the betterment of the soul. Of such lovers Socrates says:

> If now the better elements of the mind, which lead to a well ordered life and to philosophy, prevail, they live a life of happiness here on earth, self-controlled and orderly, holding in subjection that which causes evil in the soul and giving freedom to that which makes for virtue; and when this life is ended they are light and winged, for they have conquered in one of the three truly Olympic contests. Neither

> human wisdom nor divine inspiration can confer upon man any greater blessing than this. (256b)

This lover is still passionate, but his real passion is for the divine Beauty itself and only secondarily for his beloved: just as his beloved is seen as an image of Beauty itself, so his passion for his beloved is an earthly, bodily reflection of his passion for Beauty. His passion for Beauty itself is divine, the passion of reason;[10] his passion for his beloved human, the passion of appetite. His love is madness because it is passionate – with its double object it engages both reason and the appetites of the soul. But his madness is rational because with the aid of his divine vision and passion he can control his human passion.

We can now also see why Plato thinks that beauty is constitutive of (specific) eros and why eros of beauty arouses such terrible passion. Of all the most valuable things there are, Goodness, Beauty, Justice, Temperance, Wisdom, and so on, Beauty is the only one whose earthly shadows can be literally perceived, and perceived by the 'sharpest' and 'clearest' of the physical senses, sight. We cannot literally (sense) perceive a man or woman's wisdom or justice or temperance or goodness. But we can literally (sense) perceive their physical beauty – of all of these only beauty can be physical. Beauty has, therefore, a double power, to engage both the body and the soul, and to arouse physical passion, as well as the passion of reason. Eros has, therefore, a double power: its origin may be the passion of reason for the Form Beauty; but on this earth this passion is powerfully re-enforced by the sight of bodily beauty. Erotic lovers on this earth are never free of physical passion, never free of potential inner conflict, often on the edge of irrationality. In his relations with Charmides and Alcebiades even Socrates, that Platonic paragon of rationality and self-control, is sometimes on the edge of it.

The *Phaedrus* and the *Symposium*

The best lover looks very much like the philosopher lover at the top of the ladder of love in the *Symposium*. But there is, I think, a crucial difference: at the top of the ladder the philosopher has only the Form Beauty as the object of his love; he has given up, it seems, all earthly attachments and regards the beauty of the flesh as 'mortal trash'. But the best lover in the *Phaedrus* never severs himself completely from passionate attachment to the beauty of human form, and indeed, it seems, of a particular beautiful person. He prizes a particularly beautiful person for being a particularly good image of Beauty, but he prizes a particular person nevertheless, and he is passionately attached to him, so much so that he has to fight for control. Thus unlike the *Symposium*, eros in the *Phaedrus* remains at an interpersonal level, at least for souls on this earth. And this coheres well with our hypothesis that in the *Phaedrus* Plato is trying to capture – or perhaps recapture – and account for the passion and intensity of erotic love. He sees perhaps that (specific) eros cannot be totally divorced from the human body, the source of sexuality and the instrument of powerful visual attraction.

Was this the error of the ladder of love in the *Symposium*? In the upper parts of the ladder the connection with sexuality seems totally lost, and sight, the most powerful instrument of attraction is rendered totally useless. How can one have eros, intense sexual feeling for an abstract entity one cannot even see? And if it isn't sexual feeling how can it be eros? In the *Phaedrus* Plato tries to remedy these defects. By explicitly recognizing passionate sexuality as an element of the human soul and by seeing that the object of this sexuality is the beauty of human form, he seems to give a more realistic account of passionate love: he keeps eros to an interpersonal level – the human–human case is now central – and he gives passion and pleasure its due. But he still places eros within the context of his speculative metaphysics: the immortality of the soul, the theory of Forms and recollection. Through the immortality of soul and the theory of recollection he is perhaps trying to account for the attraction of earthly beauty. Through the theory of Forms he is trying to rank different cases of eros as in the *Symposium*, though a new element is now added to the ranking, whether the lover can control his sexual appetite for pleasure. The human soul is seen as both human and divine: human insofar as it inhabits a body and is subject to lure of bodily beauty and pleasure; divine insofar as it knows the Forms and is able to see human beauty as an image of divine beauty. And just as the soul is both human and divine so is eros.

There are other differences between the *Symposium* and the *Phaedrus*, some easier to understand than others. For example, in the latter work where Plato stays at the interpersonal level, he pays more attention to the question of selection of the beloved:

> Now each one chooses his love from the ranks of the beautiful according to his character, and he fashions him and adorns him like a statue, as though he were his god, to honour and worship him. The

> followers of Zeus desire that the soul of him whom they love be like Zeus; so they seek for one of philosophical and lordly nature, and when they find him and love him, they do all they can to give him such a character. (252de)

Here Zeus is, I think, a symbol not for the god of Greek mythology, but for the divine soul that knows the Forms most fully and permanently. In the chariot ride through the heavens human souls that follow Zeus got a better glimpse of the Forms than human souls that follow the other gods, and so in this life they prize philosophy above all else and become philosophers. They choose, among the ranks of the beautiful, 'according to their character' someone whom 'they love to be like Zeus'. This explanation of selection is more specific than that of the *Symposium*: in that work the principle of selection is beauty, but we are not told how a lover selects from among many beautiful objects. But it is also ambiguous: it is not clear whether the model for selection is likeness to the lover's own character or likeness to Zeus who is already loved. The former would seem incompatible with the deficiency model of desire, according to which we desire and love not something like ourselves but something we lack. The latter explanation would be compatible with it, since Zeus presumably has philosophic features the lover lacks, or has them to a greater degree than the lover. This is very close to one kind of explanation Freud gives of of selection, when the lover selects according to his 'ego-ideal'.

It is noteworthy here that Plato's hypothesis about the pre-existence of the soul and recollection enable him to give historical, developmental, or genetic explanations of the attraction of earthly beauty and the selection of the beloved: that is, explanations that make essential reference to the past of the lover. This is the hallmark of all of Freud's explanations about love; though in his case the reference is to the early years of the individual, infancy and childhood, not to the pre-existence of the soul. Moreover, Freud thought that his views about the early years of the individual were empirical hypotheses that could be confirmed or disconfirmed by experience, whereas Plato's hypotheses clearly belong to speculative metaphysics. But the important insight that to understand love we must study the past of the lover, and even the past of the human race, as in Aristophanes' speech, is one that sometimes Plato shares with Freud.

The passage on selection and the passage describing the best Platonic lover (251ab) also indicate that Plato is aware, more than he showed in the *Symposium*, of overestimation being a feature of some cases of love. To be sure, as Vlastos points out (ibid., p. 29), the best Platonic lover is not in danger of confusing his human idol with the Form Beauty, the most beautiful object there is or can be. But it is not necessary for overestimation that we think that our beloved is the most beautiful thing there is. The passage – 'he reveres the beautiful one as a god, and if he did not fear to be thought stark mad, he would offer sacrifices to his beloved as to an idol or a god' indicates overestimation clearly enough. It is understandable that in a work that emphasizes the passionate side of love Plato would notice overestimation. For it is presumably the passion in love that is partly responsible for it – at least so Plato has Phaedrus tell us in an earlier passage where overestimation is recognized: 'For lovers praise your words and acts beyond measure, ... partly because their own judgment is obscured by their passion' (233b).

Finally, we must notice an important difference that is more difficult to account for. In the *Phaedrus* we hear nothing of personal immortality and the creation of offspring, integral parts of eros proper in the *Symposium*. Instead of personal immortality on earth that few humans achieve through eros, we now have the immortality of all souls. The reward for the best kind of eros is not personal immortality on earth, but a soul that is 'light and winged' in the other life – presumably such a soul is not burdened with the corruptions of a bad bodily existence and it can soar to the world of Forms. Perhaps Plato now thinks that both personal immortality in this earth and a light and winged existence in the after life are rewards of eros – certainly the better kind. But what of the creation of offspring, the creativity of eros so prominent in the *Symposium*? Not only do we hear nothing of it in the *Phaedrus*, but art and artistic creativity are said to be a species of divine madness but not erotic madness – the latter is a different species (244a–245b, 249d). Perhaps Plato saw, with good reason, that not all eros is creative of biological or any other offspring, and that not all creativity is erotic.

Philosophic Eros in the *Phaedo* and the *Republic*

These two dialogues are usually grouped with the *Symposium* and the *Phaedrus*, perhaps forming the core of Plato's middle period with its characteristic theories of Forms, of the immortality of the soul, recollection, and the tripartite division of the soul.[11] We do not have *explicit* theories of eros in the *Phaedo* and the *Republic*: the concept is not taken up separately, defined and elaborated, as it is in the *Symposium* and the *Phaedrus*. However, there are a number of the *Symposium* and the *Phaedrus*. However, there are a number of significant passages in which erotic language is applied to the philosopher and some notion of eros is used to elucidate the philosophic life and distinguish it from other kinds of lives.[12] Though we do not know the exact chronological order of our four dialogues, it is plausible to suppose that there is some philosophical continuity and consistency among them, and that the erotic passages of the *Phaedo* and the *Republic* 'reflect' the theories of eros of the *Symposium* and the *Phaedrus*, either anticipating them or perhaps applying them. Thus our hypothesis is that there is something more going on in these erotic passages than 'sexual metaphor' or simile, as Dover supposes.[13] In particular, I think that the distinction between generic and specific eros, drawn in the *Symposium*, and the expansion of specific eros, ranging all the way from eros of a beautiful body to the Form Beauty itself, can perhaps be employed to understand the relevant passages in the *Phaedo* and the *Republic*.

The dramatic setting in the *Phaedo* is very different from the noisy celebrations of the *Symposium* and the idyllic country scene of the *Phaedrus*. It is Socrates' last day on this earth, and his friends, fearful and sad, go to jail to visit him for the last time. Appropriately, the conversation turns to Socrates' avocation, philosophy, and the possibility that his soul will continue to exist after death. Socrates displays remarkable calm, courage, and even cheer, because he believes not only that the soul is immortal, but also that the body with all its demands and needs, its pleasures and pains, is a hindrance to philosophy. A soul free of body can best pursue philosophy, the love of wisdom, and can best attain knowledge of eternal realities.

The philosopher, says Socrates, does not care about the pleasures of food, drink and sexual intercourse, nor thinks much about the cares of the body (64d). The body is a hindrance to the acquisition of wisdom: not only are the senses deceptive, but we cannot with them – but only with reason – apprehend such realities as (the Forms) Justice and Beauty and Goodness (65–6).

> The body fills us with loves [erōtōn] and desires and fears ... so that it really and truly makes it impossible for us to think at all ... if we are to think of anything clearly we must be free of the body and behold the realities with the soul alone. And then, as our argument shows, when we are dead, we are likely to possess the wisdom we desire and claim to be enamored of [erastai], but not while we are alive. (66c, 66de, tr. Fowler)

The philosophers would be foolish to fear death, the separation of soul from body, in which they can hope to finally attain what they loved (erōn) all along, namely wisdom (67e). Shall he who really loves wisdom (phroneseōs ... erōn) and has a firm belief that he can find it nowhere than in the other world grieve when he dies and not be glad to go there? (68a).

Moreover, only the philosopher, the lover of wisdom, will have 'genuine virtue', which is found only with wisdom: ' ... courage and self-restraint and justice, and in short true virtue exists only with wisdom, whether pleasures and fears and other things of that sort are added or taken away' (69b). Without wisdom, in the body lovers, we will find only imitations of virtue (what are later at 82ab called 'demotic' or 'political' virtues), where in courage one fear is controlled because of another, and in temperance one pleasure is restrained because of another (69ab).

Relying on the distinction between philosophic and demotic virtue and on the erotic description of the philosopher as a lover and not just a man of wisdom, Kahn has argued that here we have a new version of the 'unity of virtue'. There is no reason to believe that the demotic virtues will always be found together. But in the philosopher the union of wisdom and eros, passion for the Forms, 'represents the dynamic causal principle for *bringing about* the other virtues, since it drains off psychic energy from the other desires (for pleasure, for wealth, and mere survival), and thus eliminates or overcomes the animal drives that could lead a man either to vice or the vulgar virtue.'[14]

It is certainly striking that in the *Phaedo* we find the application of erotic terms to the philosopher as well as to 'body lovers', and thus we have the expansion of the concept that is characteristic of the *Symposium* and the *Phaedrus*. It is also striking that the philosopher is thought of not just as a man of superior but cold and purely intellectual knowledge of the Forms, but also as a man with eros, a passion for that knowledge and its objects. And this too is characteristic of our two dialogues. What is unclear is whether the theories of eros of the *Symposium* and the *Phaedrus* are presupposed or merely anticipated in the *Phaedo* – probably the latter. We have no distinction between specific and generic eros, and the Form Beauty is not assigned any special role in the eros of the philosopher. But the close chronological grouping of our four dialogues, and the commonality of Platonic doctrines of the middle period, give us reason to believe that Plato's application of erotic terms to the philosopher in the *Phaedo* is not just a passing fancy or merely 'sexual metaphor'. Perhaps the erotic passages of the *Phaedo* are the first signal that Plato thought of the Forms, the cornerstones of his philosophy of the middle dialogues, not only as the objects of wisdom and knowledge but also as objects of attraction, ideal exemplars which engage our passions as well as our reason.

The expansion of the concept of eros, reaching all the way to the Forms, and the characterization of the philosopher as a 'lover' is found even more explicitly in the *Republic*. This is of course a much richer and more complex work, containing several new theories, including the theory of social justice and the ideal city, the tripartite division of the soul and the definitions of the individual virtues, and the theory of the Form of the Good. But Plato does not take up the concept of eros explicitly, define it, and show the bearing of his new theories on it. Instead, we find erotic terms applied both to sexual desire and to the passion of the philosopher, perhaps in close similarity to the view of the *Phaedrus*.

We quoted earlier *Republic* 403a, where Plato says that right eros has nothing to do with sexual desires and pleasures, the most intense of all pleasures. To this we may now add that at 439d, where the tripartite division of the soul is argued, eros in the sense of sexual desire is apparently assigned to the appetitive element of the soul. And in Bk. IX (573ff, and especially 573d, 574de, 578a), the tyrannical man is characterized as one whose soul is tyrannized by eros, again in the sense of sexual desire originating in the appetitive element of his soul. This man is the very opposite of the philosopher in both virtue and happiness (576d), the most vicious and wretched. Apparently the tyrant is a sex maniac. Just why Plato thinks of the tyrannical soul in this way is not entirely clear: perhaps because he thinks of sexual desire as originating in the worst part of the soul and as being the most intense and uncontrollable; so a soul ruled by such desires is literally tyrannized, just as a city is enslaved by a tyrant; and it is the worst soul because it is enslaved by its worst element. In any case, the low esteem in which Plato holds sexual eros in the *Republic* could hardly be made more clear: sexual desires originate in the worst part of the soul; they are the most lawless of all desires (571ff), and when they rule the soul they produce the worst and most wretched kind of man. In the *Republic* Plato does not tell us explicitly what the connection is between this sexual eros, whose aim seems to be nothing but sexual pleasure, and the right eros of the earlier passage or the eros of the philosopher in the passages we are about to consider. But the views of the *Phaedrus*, on the best and the worst kind of lover and the connection between the eros of the eyes and the eros of reason, seems to fit best with what Plato says about eros in the *Republic*.

The passages about philosophic eros occur mainly in Books V & VI, after Socrates propounded the famous paradox of the philosopher-king, in response to Glaucon's question, whether the ideal city is possible of realization and if so how. Socrates says that it is possible if philosophers become kings or kings and rulers become philosophers; without such a union of political power and philosophic intelligence 'there can be no cessation of troubles ... for our states ... nor for the human race' (473d).

This remarkable paradox demands that the philosopher be defined and distinguished from other men. Socrates begins this enterprise by suggesting that when someone loves something (*philein ti*) he loves not just part of it but all of it. He gives several illustrations. A lover (*erotikō*) of beautiful youths loves all kinds of physical beauty in them – that is how he reacts to beautiful youths (474d). Lovers of wine (*philoinous*) love all wine, and lovers of honor (*philotimous*) go after every honor. Socrates concludes that when a man desires something he desires the whole kind or class. So the philosopher, the lover of wisdom, desires all wisdom and goes after every lesson gladly. To indicate what kind of wisdom he has in mind, Socrates now introduces the Forms Beauty itself, Goodness itself, Justice itself, and distinguishes them from their sensible participants, such as (in the case of beauty) beautiful sounds, colors and shapes. The philosophers are not those who apprehend and delight only in such beautiful colors and sounds, but those who are able to apprehend and delight in the Forms themselves, distinguishing them from their sensible participants. In a famous passage Socrates goes on to distinguish knowledge or wisdom from opinion, and assign only the Forms as the objects of such knowledge. He concludes that those who love (*philein*) beautiful sounds and colors and do not know Beauty and the other Forms should be called 'doxophilists' (lovers of opinion), while those who know and delight in the Forms are entitled to be called philosophers.

In this passage Socrates has not actually applied the language of eros to the philosophers, but he has rather drawn a parallel between the erotic lover's love of beautiful youths and the philosopher's love of wisdom: just as the former love all the physical beauty of youths, so the latter love all of wisdom and its objects.

In the next passage, however, Socrates does apply erotic terms to the philosophers. They ought to be the rulers of the state since they know the ideal entities, such as Beauty, Justice and Goodness, and have the ideal patterns in their own souls; provided that they are not deficient in experience and virtue, which, Socrates proceeds to argue, they will not be. It is a trait of the philosophic nature to be always in love with the lesson (*mathematos ge aei erōsin*) which reveals to it eternal reality (the Forms – 485b). A man of such a nature, will desire all of wisdom, as the previous illustrations about the lover of beautiful youths and wine and honor show. And a man who is in love with all of wisdom will love truth and hate falsehood, since there is nothing more akin to wisdom than truth. Moreover, Socrates continues:

> when in a man the desires incline strongly to any one thing, they are weakened for other things. It is as if the stream has been diverted into another channel .... So when a man's desires have been taught to flow in the channel of learning and all that sort of thing, they will be concerned, I presume, with the pleasures of the soul in itself, and will be indifferent to those of which the body is the instrument, if the man is a true and not a sham philosopher. (485de, tr. Shorey)

Such a man, Socrates concludes, will be temperate and not greedy for wealth or what wealth can buy, nor small-minded; being habituated to think of all time and all reality, he will think little of human life and death being terrible, and so he will be courageous; and being temperate and great-minded and courageous, he cannot fail to be also just.

This is an interesting passage for several reasons. Kahn has drawn our attention to the fact that Plato here seems to be deducing the other virtues from eros of wisdom: it is not a deduction just from knowledge or wisdom, but from the philosopher's passion for knowledge and its objects, the Forms, together with the idea of the 'channeling of desires'.[15] The last seems to be a new idea, not found in previous dialogues, so far as I know.[16] It seems remarkably similar to Freud's 'hydraulics' model of the mind, in which 'psychic energy' can flow from one channel to another, strengthening the flow of energy in one direction and weakening it in others. Both ideas presuppose that the quantity of 'psychic energy' available to an individual is limited, so that if more flows in one direction, less will flow in another, as the stream metaphor that Plato uses indeed suggests. This idea explains why Plato thinks that the philosopher will be able to be temperate and courageous and just, if he has been educated to love wisdom and the Forms. The desires which usually lead to the opposite of these virtues, for food, drink and sex, for life, for property and wealth, will be weakened, the energy for them 'drained off', so that there will be little if any psychic conflict. Thus the eros for wisdom and the Forms and the re-channeling of desires make possible the unity of the virtues in the philosopher and, we might add, the unity and harmony of the philosophic soul.

Moreover, this passage throws some light on the 'transference of passion' in the ladder of eros, if we are allowed to interpret the *Symposium* on the basis of the *Republic*. As we saw in the *Symposium*, the lover begins with an exclusive attachment to one beautiful body, and by changes in perception and understanding he is led to new beautiful objects and new attachments, till at the top he apprehends the Form Beauty and becomes attached to it. How are we to understand this change of emotional attachments? Does he give up the old attachments and come to be exclusively in love with Beauty itself? The channeling of desires passage in the *Republic* suggests that corresponding to the changes of intellectual perspective and the new valuations that take place as the lover goes up the ladder, there is a weakening of the old attachments and a concentration of 'psychic energy' on the new ones. And this not just because of the changes in intellectual perspective and understanding, but also because the amount of emotional energy is limited; and as more flows to the new objects less goes to the old ones.

But what kind of eros is this that the philosopher has for wisdom and the Forms in the *Republic*? If we are allowed to use the *Symposium*, especially its distinction between specific and generic eros, the answer would seem to be that it is generic eros, the desire for the Good. The relation between Beauty and Goodness is still unclear in the *Republic*. But the philosophic ladder that Plato constructs in this work, represented statically by the Divided Line and dynamically by the Allegory of the Cave, has the Form of the Good at the top. It is to this Form that the philosopher must ultimately ascend, and his 'greatest lesson' is to apprehend and understand the Form of the Good, 'by which just things and all the rest become useful and beneficial' (505a). Without such knowledge the philosopher is not fit to be king or ruler of the state: for without knowledge of the Good he will not understand adequately just and beautiful things and their relation to the Good (506a). Finally, 'the objects of knowledge [i.e. the Forms] not only receive from the presence of the Good their being known, but their very existence and essence is derived to them from it, though the Good itself is not essence but still transcends essence in dignity and surpassing power' (509b, tr. Shorey).

In one of these passages at least (506a) Beauty seems to be subordinated to Goodness, and in the final passage we have just quoted, which seems to be quite general, all the Forms besides the Form of the Good are said to receive their 'existence and essence' from the Form of the Good. As we indicated in chapter 2, we take this to mean that all the other Forms have their ideal attributes, that is what makes them Forms, by virtue of participating in the Form of the Good. The Form of the Good is the formal cause of all the other Forms. Moreover, Plato has told us earlier in the the same passages that the Good is

> that which every soul pursues and for its sake does all that it does, with an intuition of its reality, and yet baffled and unable to apprehend its nature adequately … . (505e, tr. Shorey)

So the Form of the Good, however dimly apprehended, is the ultimate object of all our desires and the final cause of all that we do. The philosopher, who ascending through 'dialectic' does succeed in apprehending the Form of the Good, has finally reached the ultimate object of his desires. Since the passages we examined earlier, in which erotic terms are applied to the philosopher, occur in the same book, whose object is to define the philosopher and describe the philosophic education and life which fits him to be ruler, it would seem that the eros of the philosopher is his desire for the Good. It would appear that every soul has this desire, a point in agreement with the *Symposium*. What presumably distinguishes the philosopher is his 'nature', his predisposition to intellectual pursuits and 'eternal reality'; and his education which directs him to the world of Forms and channels his desires toward the Forms and ultimately to the Form of the Good, thereby weakening his bodily and earthly desires for the transient goods of sexual pleasures, property and honors. It is this unique combination of nature and education, of knowledge and passion, reason and eros, that makes him at once a competent and incorrupt ruler, a philosopher-king.

Notes

1 These phenomena are well described in Carson, A., *Eros: The Bittersweet* see especially, pp. 3–10 and 154–8.

2 For the controversies over dating see Guthrie, W.K.C., HGP, vol. IV, pp. 396–7, and Hackforth, *Plato's Phaedrus*, pp. 3–7.

3 Cornford, F.M., *Principium Sapientiae*. p. 66.

4 Guthrie, ibid., p. 397. For the purposes, themes, setting and characters, see also Hackforth, ibid., pp. 8–18.

5 Vlastos, G., 'The Individual as Object of Love in Plato', *Platonic Studies*, p. 27, n. 80. Greek terms transliterated: *mania* roughly means madness, and *nous* mind or reason.
6 On the role of wings in poetry, the opposite of what Plato assigns them, see Carson, ibid., pp. 155ff.
7 Guthrie's HGP, vol. IV, p. 419.
8 The tripartite division of the soul in the *Phaedrus* poses many problems, especially the implication that disembodied souls have appetite and spirit. For a review see Hackforth, Plato's *Phaedrus*, pp. 75–7. For a comparison of the tripartite division in *Republic* and Freud's division, see Kenny, *The Anatomy of the Soul* pp. 11–14; see also below ch. 7, sections I and II.
9 Dover notes that in *Laws* 636c Plato condemns homosexual intercourse and pleasures as 'contrary to nature', and contrasts this to 'the mood of compromise or tolerance such as he [Plato] shows for the pair who "lapse" in the *Phaedrus*'. GH. p. 165. Apparently he failed to notice that in fact Plato uses the very same phrase to characterize the pleasures of the pair who 'lapse' in the *Phaedrus* 251a2: *para phusin*, contrary to nature. For what this phrase might mean, see Vlastos, *Platonic Studies* 2nd. edn, p. 25, n. 76, and pp. 424–5.
10 I take this phrase from an unpublished paper by M.F. Burnyeat, 'The Passion of Reason in Plato's *Phaedrus*'. Though Burnyeat's concerns are different, his views complement well, I think, the interpretation in this chapter.
11 See Ross, D., *Plato's Theory of Ideas*, p. 2, and Guthrie, HGP, vol. IV, pp. 325, 396–7.
12 I am indebted to Prof. Charles Kahn and to his article 'Plato on the Unity of the Virtues', *Facets of Plato's Philosophy*, ed. W.H. Werkmeister, for pointing out the significance and uses of the erotic passages of the *Phaedo* and the *Republic*.
13 Dover, GH, pp. 43, 156, 157.
14 Ibid., p. 27. Actually Kahn says that 'wisdom' does all this, rather than the union of wisdom and eros; and later in the same page he says that 'Wisdom is defined in the *Phaedo* as a philosophic eros or passion for reality, i.e., for the Forms'. I have been unable to find in the *Phaedo* a text for this definition. In the texts I quoted philosophers are said to be *erastai* of wisdom or to *eran* wisdom or to have *eros* for wisdom, all of which discourage the idea that wisdom *is* eros for the Forms. In the *Symposium* too wisdom appears as an object of eros, on the ground that wisdom is among the most beautiful things (204b).
15 Ibid., pp. 27ff.
16 Shorey thinks that Plato is expressing a similar idea in *Laws* 643d, though this is not perhaps entirely clear – Plato, The *Republic*, tr. P. Shorey, vol. II, p. 8, n. a. In any case Plato does not elaborate the idea beyond the metaphor of the stream, so it is not clear how much we can make of it.

4

Plato on Friendship and Familial Love

Introduction

We saw that the Greeks of Plato's time had no single word for all kinds of love. They used 'eros' for erotic love and 'philia' for familial love and the love of friendship. The question arises whether, despite this linguistic division of the concept, Plato had, or can be plausibly interpreted to have had, a unified theory for all kinds of love. Plato does not explicitly say; but he does discuss friendship in the *Lysis*, and both friendship and familial love briefly in the *Republic*. And we saw that in the *Symposium* he uses the wider notion of generic eros, the desire for the good to be one's own forever, and treats erotic love as a species of it. Our question can now be made more specific: Did Plato think that all kinds of love fall under the desire for the good? If he did, he can be thought to have had a unified theory of love. The desire for the good would be taken as fundamental, present in all human beings, and erotic love, friendship, and familial love would all be thought of as specific forms of it. In this chapter we will argue briefly that in all probability Plato thought of love in this way.[1]

Friendship in the *Lysis*: Like to Like and Opposite to Opposite

> Nothing is there more friendly to a man than a friend in need.
>
> Plautus

The *Lysis* is a difficult dialogue to interpret and there is extreme division of opinion about it.[2] There are a number of reasons for this. Several hypotheses are proposed about what a friend is, but none escapes objection from Socrates; so, as in other 'aporetic' Socratic dialogues, it is difficult to know what Plato's view is. The best we can do perhaps is to speak of 'the favorite hypothesis'. Moreover, unlike Aristotle, Plato in the *Lysis* does not suppose that friendship must be mutual; so he does not confine friendship to a relation between people, and he is willing to speak of health, for example, as a friend (219A). Indeed, his favorite hypothesis is that the good is 'the first friend', or 'the real friend' (219c, 220d). The question Socrates investigates is not 'What is friendship?'; rather, he begins with 'How does one person become a friend to another?' (212a) and ends up with 'What is a friend?' (223b). In addition, these latter questions are thought to be ambiguous: the Greek word for friend, 'philos', means friend when used as a noun, but as an adjective it is usually passive and means something like 'loved', 'liked' or 'dear'. And Socrates does not seem sensitive to these ambiguities.[3] Finally, it should be noted that while 'friendship' and 'friend' are the standard translations for *philia* and *philos*, the cognate verb, *philein*, can mean 'to like', 'to love', 'to feel affection for', and indeed it can range all the way 'from parental love to the love of a glutton for dinner'.[4]

Despite these uncertainties and complications, the *Lysis* provides considerable evidence that Plato thought of friendship as a species of the desire for the good; that the desire for a friend arises out of deficiency or imperfection, and thus satisfies the deficiency model of the *Symposium*; and that it is also egoistic. Let us look at some of the discussion that reveals this evidence.

In the *Lysis* Socrates relates a conversation he had in a wrestling school with two young boys, Menexenus and Lysis. He meets Hippothales outside the school and he is invited inside to see the handsome youths and share in conversation, their usual pastime. It turns out that Hippothales is madly in love with Lysis and goes around like a madman singing his praises. Socrates points out to him that this is not the way to treat one's favorite, for unqualified praises puff him up, make him haughty and difficult to capture. He proposes to engage Lysis in conversation, to demonstrate to Hippothales how to treat a youth one is in love with. It so happens that the young boy is not entrusted with anything in his father's house, not even his own conduct, but has to go around under the supervision of a 'tutor', a slave. Lysis thinks that this is because he is not yet of age. But Socrates takes him through a series of examples, some serious some amusing, and gets him to admit that he is not given control or responsibility for anything because he has not yet acquired the skill or wisdom to run a chariot or conduct the affairs of the household or even his own person (210b). In fact, Lysis is driven to admit that he has no wisdom about anything, and being without much 'mind' he can't very well think himself 'megalomind' (being *aphrōn* he can't very well be *megalophrōn!*).

Having been humbled, Lysis wishes Socrates to administer the same medicine to his friend of the same age, Menexenus, a 'keen disputant' who always refutes Lysis. Here Socrates changes the subject. The first conversation was an exhibition on how a lover should treat his favorite, a direct lesson to Lysis, the favorite, and an indirect one to Hippothales, the lover. But now Socrates says to Menexenus that he admires how he and Lysis are already such good friends, and wants to know from him how one can gain such a great possession, a good friend. This is the new subject, and Lysis and Menexenus are supposed to exemplify it, for they are friends, not lovers.

But Socrates is not interested in the specific, biographical question, how Menexenus came to be a friend to Lysis, but in the general, theoretical question, how one becomes a friend to another, and even the more abstract question, what is a friend. Some of the hypotheses he tries out, as answers to these questions, are natural and understandable, and quite similar to hypotheses we might try out today: two people are friends if they love each other; or if they are similar in characters and so, we might say, 'compatible'; or if they have different but 'complementary' characters, so that they serve each other's needs. And the difficulties that Socrates brings up seem to me also understandable, in view of certain 'facts' about friendship and about the wide and complex uses of the Greek terms 'philia' and 'philos'.[5] As an initial Socratic exploration of the concept, the *Lysis* seems to me as much a 'success' as many other Socratic dialogues of definition. Let us look briefly at this Socratic investigation.

Socrates begins with the most plausible hypothesis: that people become friends by coming to love (philein). When one person loves another, he asks, who becomes friend to whom, the one who loves or the one who is loved or both? The answer given is that they are both friends to each other. But this cannot be correct, Socrates points out, because one's love may not be returned, and he may even be hated in return. When one loves another and is hated in return, they cannot be mutual friends, for hatred makes for enmity, not friendship.[6] So perhaps the remaining possibility is correct: two people are mutual friends when they mutually love each other. But plausible as that may seem to us, for the Greeks it was difficult to accept, for they spoke of 'friends-of-horses', 'friends-of-wine', and 'friends-of-wisdom' (literally philo-sophers), and clearly wisdom and wine cannot be said to love back! So unless 'friend of' (or rather 'philos') is ambiguous, a possibility Socrates does not recognize or allow for, mutual love cannot be the correct general analysis of being a friend.[7] In any case, we might add, in the Greek the analysis borders on the circular and the uninformative, for the word used for friend is 'philos' and for loving 'philein'. In English the corresponding situation would be something like trying to define 'a friend to' by 'has a friendly feeling for' which would certainly be circular and uninformative.

In the next two hypotheses Socrates tries to define a friend by appeal to a person's character, the notions of a good and a bad man. This too is plausible, for it seems part of the core meaning of being a friend that a friend causes no injury (to the one he is a friend to or a friend of), whereas an enemy tries to do just that; and a good man, on Socrates' view, causes no injury whereas a bad man does just that.[8]

Socrates begins by appealing to Homer who said, 'Yea, ever like and like together God doth draw' (214a). So perhaps 'like must needs be always friend to like?'. Part of this, Socrates argues, cannot be correct, for two people may be like in both being wicked or bad men. But bad men injure each other and the injurer and the injured cannot be friends. Perhaps then friends are those who are alike in both being good men. This is also objected to on the ground that a good man, insofar as he is good, is sufficient unto himself; if so, he has no need of anything; if so, he does not love anything. And 'he who loves not is no friend' (215b). So two good men cannot be friends since neither is in need of the other. Whether or not this argument is sound, it gives clear evidence of the deficiency and egoistic model being applied to friendship: Unless one has a need for something, he will not value it, love it, and will be no friend to it, nor consider it a friend. It also implies that unless one loves something he is no friend to it.

The next hypothesis considered is that perhaps opposites are friends. This is speedily refuted on the ground that friendship and enmity, the good and the bad, the just and the unjust are all opposites but cannot be friends.

What is Neither Good nor Bad is Friend to the Good

Out of these refutations now emerges what I have called the favored hypothesis in the *Lysis*: 'It may rather be something neither good nor bad that will prove after all to be what we call friend of the good.' (216C). At this point Socrates refers to the ancient proverb, 'the beautiful is friendly (dear)', and to his own belief that 'the good is beautiful'. He then constructs an argument for the hypothesis:

There are three kinds of things, the good, the bad, and that which is neither good nor bad.

The good is not friend to the good, nor the bad friend to the bad, nor the good to the bad (by previous agreements that neither alike nor opposite things are friends).

Hence, either what is neither good nor bad is friend to what is neither good nor bad, or else to the good. (These are the remaining possibilities.)

But what is neither good nor bad is no friend to what is neither good nor bad (by previous agreement that things alike are not friends).

Therefore, only what is neither good nor bad is friend to the good (216c-217a).

Socrates now illustrates the hypothesis and adds some important elements to it. A body in health is in no need of a doctor; and because of its health, which is a good thing, it is no friend to the doctor. But a body diseased is a friend to medicine or the doctor, a good thing, because of its disease, a bad thing. So, the body, which itself is neither good nor bad, is a friend to the good because of the presence of the bad. But for this to be the case the body must not be completely corrupted by disease so as to be beyond help. A better illustration for this point is the soul. A completely ignorant soul, one which had no knowledge even of its own ignorance, would not love wisdom. But one which was ignorant but was at least aware of its ignorance (the familiar Socratic 'wisdom') would love wisdom. So such a soul, which is itself neither good nor bad, would be a friend to something good (wisdom) because of the presence of something bad (ignorance). Socrates concludes that 'in the soul and the body and everywhere, that which is neither good nor bad is friend to the good because of the presence of the bad' (218c).

This is what I called the 'favored hypothesis' about what a friend is in the *Lysis*. It can be easily seen that it satisfies the deficiency and egoistic models and embodies desire for the good; and it can thus be seen as a species of the generic eros of the *Symposium*. And as in the *Symposium* eros, generic or specific, was not confined to relations among humans, so here being a friend is similarly expanded: it can be a relation to an inanimate object. Generally, to be a friend to something is to recognize it as a good of which one is in need because of the presence in him of something bad.

Socrates goes on to mention some misgivings he has about this hypothesis and eventually abandons it. For one thing, sometimes we are a friend to something for the sake of something else; a sick man is a friend to a doctor for the sake of his health. We prize such things as medicines, silver and gold, for the sake of something else. But this cannot go on forever: there must be something for the sake of which we prize everything else, but do not prize it for the sake of other things. And this, he says, must be the 'first' or 'original' or 'real' friend, the other things we are friends to being like shadows of it. 'Then the real friend is a friend for the sake of nothing else that is a friend' (220b). And that is 'the good', whatever it turns out to be. Real, or the most real friendship, then, is to be defined in terms of a non-instrumental good by relation to which all the other goods are instrumentally good. Similar remarks could be made about generic eros in the *Symposium*, and also about specific eros: the real specific eros, Plato might say, is the eros for Beauty itself, not for things that are beautiful by relation to it. So far this is not necessarily an objection to the hypothesis: we can have, we might say, a 'ladder of friendship'; the friend of gold and silver is lower on the ladder than the friend of wisdom, and so on.

But now Socrates finds the hypothesis puzzling, especially the part that says 'it is because of the bad that the good is loved' (220b). He finds this puzzling on the face of it, especially since he does not distinguish sharply enough between 'because of it' and 'for the sake of it' (220e). Of course it seems absurd to suppose that we love the good for the sake of the bad. However, the original statement was that we desire and love the good because it will cure us of the bad present in us. But Socrates finds a puzzle even in this correct statement: he takes it to imply that if the bad (or evil) did not exist the good would be of no use and so not loved. Can it be the nature of the good, he asks, 'to be loved because of the bad, by us who are midway between the good and the bad, whereas the good for its own sake is of no use at all?' (220d). He now speculates about what would be the case if bad or evil were abolished. He concludes correctly that certain desires such as hunger and thirst, which are by themselves neither good nor bad, would still exist, since if evil were abolished that is no reason to think that things not evil would also be abolished. For us to desire and love the good, it is not necessary that something bad or evil is present in us, but only that we lack or are deficient of the good. And this is the view of the deficiency model used in the *Symposium*: it is not positive evil, but only lack of goodness or beauty that is required for love and desire for beauty and goodness.

Thus, the phrase 'because of the bad' is dropped from the favored hypothesis. Being a friend consists in desiring and loving some good we lack and are in need of. And the best and most ideal friendship is where we desire and love not instrumental goods but the good itself.

But once more Socrates finds fresh difficulties. For no apparent reason he drops the good and concentrates on desire and deficiency as 'the cause of' friendship. Perhaps the desiring subject is a friend to what he desires, and since he desires something he is deficient in, he is a friend of that in which he is deficient. And one becomes deficient when something is taken away from him. So perhaps, he says, it is what belongs to one (to oikeion) that is the object of eros and friendship and desire. And two people are friends when they 'belong' to each other.

Since Socrates has dropped the good from the hypothesis, he is in a sense right to look for a new characterization of the deficient and the objects of desire. For without reference to the good, the concept of deficiency is wide open, and we could even say that when evil is taken away from one, one lacks that evil or is deficient of it. Moreover, the concept Socrates puts in place of the good, to *oikeion*, has some plausibility since it is the very notion we would use to characterize the objects of familial love; and *philia* spans familial love as well as friendship. In familial love, we love literally our *oikeioi*, those of our home, our father, mother, children and so on. In addition, the notion that what we love is our own, not necessarily the good, is a deep rooted one: it was the notion that in the *Symposium* Aristophanes used to characterize eros: eros is desire for what once was a part of ourselves. And Freud himself uses that notion in his study of narcissism. Even Plato makes use of it, as we shall see, in the *Republic*.

Here, though, the literal notion of *oikeioi*, one's blood relatives, is of not much use, for the subject is friendship, and friends obviously extend beyond blood relatives. So Socrates searches for some way to characterize 'what belongs to one', but in vain. If we say 'the belonging' is the same as 'the like' we run into our previous difficulties: bad men will be friends, which is not correct since they injure each other; and good men will be friends, which violates the deficiency model (222b). And if we say that 'the good belongs to everyone, while the bad is alien' (222c), so that 'the good and the belonging are the same, we cannot avoid making the good a friend only of the good' (222cd). And this was also previously rejected.

Socrates says he has become quite dizzy by all this, the discussion is interrupted by the boys' tutors, and the dialogue ends with Socrates remarking that though they believe they are friends, they still don't know 'what a friend is'.

What is the moral of the *Lysis*? And what can we extract from it and attribute to Plato? It is fairly clear that, as in the *Symposium*, the desire for the good and the deficiency and egoistic models of desire dominate the discussion. And as in the case of eros, Plato is not content to think of philia as a relation between humans: as there can be eros of inanimate and abstract objects, indeed the best kind of eros, so in the *Lysis* he speaks of the best kind of philia as being a relation to the good. But it is also clear that Plato had a harder time with philia in the *Lysis* than with eros in the *Symposium* and the *Phaedrus*. We can speculate that perhaps one of the main reasons for this is a rather fundamental difference between eros and friendship: eros need never be mutual; one can love erotically without ever being loved back, and so eros is susceptible to analysis by a one-way relation such as desiring. Plato habitually refers to the terms of the eros relation as 'lover' and 'beloved'; and the 'beloved' could be an inanimate or abstract object. But it is at least difficult to think of friendship as not being mutual and as not holding between people. This was perhaps masked from Plato's clear view by the fact that *philia* was also used for familial love, which like eros need not be mutual; and also by Plato's tendency to think that the same word always means the same thing.

Aristotle saw through the mask and in his analysis of friendship concentrated on a mutual relation between people. Instead, Plato concentrates on the question, 'What is a friend?' But the mutuality of friendship keeps breaking through the discussion. Thus at one place he characterizes someone who needs and desires the good as a friend of the good. But he also calls the good a friend. But surely the good is not a friend to us in the same sense: the good is not in need of us nor does it desire and love us. Presumably the good qualifies as a 'friend' in the first place because it can never harm but only benefit us.

At the same time Plato is by no means blind to friendships as mutual relations between people. Socrates ends the discussion with the remark that 'we are friends to each other'; and he is clearly bothered by the fact that he cannot account for the case of two good people being friends. Surely if any people can be friends, good people can. The point is clearly affirmed in *Phaedrus* (255b): 'evil can never be friend to evil, nor good fail to be friend to good'. Here we can speculate that the problem lies in applying the deficiency model of desire to *philein*, to love; and perhaps in too strong a concept of a good person. To be mutual friends two people must love (*philei*) each other. But to love each other, each must lack or be deficient in some good he can expect to 'receive' from the other: one or another of the virtues. But if they are both good men they already have all the virtues; at least on the Socratic view of the unity of virtues, that if a man has one virtue he has them all. Though this view is not appealed to, it would account for the difficulties encountered in the case of friendship between two good men. It remains to be seen whether these difficulties are overcome in the *Republic*.

Friendship and Familial Love in The *Republic*

> Nor can spirits ever be divided that
> love and live in the same divine principle;
> the root and record of their friendship.
>
> William Penn

The *Republic* contains no definition or extended discussion of eros or friendship or familial love. However, Plato makes a very important use of friendship and familial love. As Vlastos has noted, 'The ideal society of The *Republic* is a political community held together by bonds of fraternal love.'[9] This fraternal love or civic friendship is philia, conceived by Plato now in a new way, as a blend or even identity between familial love and friendship. But what kind of blend or identity? Is he assimilating familial love to friendship, or friendship to familial love, or both to something else?

It is easier for us to distinguish between familial love and friendship than it must have been for Plato: not only can we imagine parents and children, brothers and sisters not being friends, and friends not being members of the same family, but we also have different words for these relations, whereas Plato had one and the same word. In a remarkable passage early in the *Lysis* (210cd) Socrates tells Lysis that his father would not love him, nor would anyone else, in so far as he is useless: but if he became wise, useful and good, all would be his friend and *oikeioi* (family). What is remarkable here is the idea that seems to be excluded; that is, that a father would not love his son simply because he is his son, an extension of himself. The object of familial love, it seems, is the good, just as it is in the case of friendship. A father, like everyone else, loves the good, and if his son is good, he and everyone else will love him and be a friend to him. In the *Lysis*, it would appear, both familial love and friendship are species of the desire for the good. But is this the view of the *Republic*?

Earlier on in the *Lysis* (207c) we find an idea that Plato takes quite seriously in the *Republic*: that friends have things in common. It is repeated at the end of the *Phaedrus* (279c). And in the *Symposium* (204c) we find an indirect application of it: soul lovers will have a greater community and a surer friendship (than biological lovers) because they share a more beautiful and immortal offspring. This becomes the central idea in the *Republic*: the essence of philia, friendship and familial love, is having all things in common, sharing everything.

The proverb that friends have things in common is first appealed to at 423-424, when questions about the unity of the city are discussed. It is briefly applied to the possession of wives and children. It is then taken up again in Book V, when major reforms are proposed for the upper two classes, the guardians and the rulers. Socrates is reminded of the proverb and his earlier application of it to the family, and is asked to say more about it (449c). After discussing the equality of women, he comes back to the topic and makes three bold proposals: First of all, the guardians and rulers shall have 'houses and meals in common, and no private possessions of that kind (property)' (458cd). Secondly, 'women shall all be common to all these men, and ... none shall co-habit with any privately; and ... the children shall be common, and ... no parent shall know its own offspring nor any child its parent'. (457cd) As a result no guardian could 'think or speak of his co-guardian as an outsider' (the opposite of *oikeion*); 'for no matter whom he meets, he will feel that he is meeting a brother, a sister, a mother, a son, a daughter, or the offspring or forebearers of these' (463c). So far we have the abolition of private property and the private family, and have in their place one big family with common property; everyone and everything will be everyone's own. They will all be friends and of one's own home (oikeioi). The justification for these proposals is that there is no greater evil for a city 'than the thing that distracts it and makes it many instead of one, or a greater good than that which binds it together and makes it one' (462ab). Private property and family would make the guardian and rulers apply the words 'mine' and 'not mine' to different things; common family and property to the same things; the former makes for division and conflict, the latter for unity.

But even these reforms do not go far enough. In the third place, 'it is the community of pleasures and pain that binds', and 'the individualization (privatization) of those feelings is a dissolvent, when some grieve exceedingly and others rejoice at the same happenings to the city and its inhabitants' (462bc). So the guardians and the rulers must have not only property and family but even feelings in common. And the ultimate model of that is not the family, but the individual:

> That city, then, is best ordered in which the greatest number use the expression 'mine' and 'not mine' of the same things in the same way. And the city whose state is most like that of an individual man. (462c)

An individual man's members are all his own, and when there is pain or pleasure in one of them, he as a whole is pleased or pained, even though the pleasure or pain is in a part of him.[10]

> That is the kind of state, then, I presume, that, when anyone of the citizens suffers ought of good or evil, will be most likely to speak of the part that suffers as its own and will share the pleasure or pain as a whole. Inevitably, he said, if it is well governed. (462de)

The city will be best governed when everyone, if possible, but certainly the guardians and rulers, has property and family in common; and more important yet, takes pleasures and pains in the very same things. And we can easily add that, for Plato, they will not take pleasures and pains in the same things, unless they all think the same things good and the same things evil, and unless they all love and hate the same things. The saying that friends have things in common has been taken literally, applied ruthlessly to all things, and made the fundamental emotional tie that holds citizens together and assures the unity of the city.[11]

Friendship as Sharing Knowledge and Desire for the Good

Since Plato does not define *philia* in the *Republic*, what he does with it is not entirely clear and unambiguous. In the pre-*Republic* dialogues, certainly in the *Lysis* and the *Symposium*, it looks very much as if he held the view that one does not love (philei) something unless he considers it something good that he lacks and is in need of himself. And this is the fundamental proposition he uses to understand philia; and even to understand eros, though in this case beauty is brought in and assigned a special role. But in the *Republic* he is concerned with a much broader range of social, political, and ethical problems: specifically with an essentially social concept, justice, and the possibility and stability of an ideally just society. He thinks that a necessary condition for such a society is that the ruling classes, the guardians and the rulers, identify their interests and the interest of the city. Thus earlier in the third book, in considering the selection and education of the guardians, he says:

> But one would be most likely to be careful of that which he loved. ... And again, one would be most likely to love that whose interests he supposed to coincide with his own, and thought that when it prospered he too would prosper, and if not, the contrary. (412d)

So the guardians must be educated and trained to think that their interest and the interest of the city always coincide or are the same. Now the first two reforms we considered above, the community of property and family, seemed designed to assure that this condition will actually prevail. Each guardian will not have separate property of his own and not another's. What is not clear here is what fundamental proposition Plato is relying on. It is possible that he is not relying on the proposition that one loves what he considers something good that he is in need of, but rather that one loves what he considers his own – his own possessions and family. So it may be that he is relying on familial love, taken as fundamental and primitive. One tends to love his own: therefore, if we make all possessions each guardian's own, and all members of the community each guardian's own family (oikeioi) each guardian will love the whole community and will not see any separation between his interest and those of the community. At any rate, here Plato does not put the restriction on familial love that he put in the *Lysis*, that is, that a father would not love his son unless he thought his son were good and useful.

This is consistent with Plato's new psychology in the *Republic*, the tripartite division of the soul into reason, spirit and appetite. This new psychology has implications for the Socratic fundamental proposition that we all desire what we consider something good that we lack and are in need of, and ultimately the good. The new psychology says that sometimes we desire or love something because, and only because, our reason judges it to be a good or the good. These are rational desires or the desires and loves of reason. They correspond to the passion of reason in the *Phaedrus*, the passion for the Form Beauty in a previous existence. This is the Platonic rendering of the Socratic fundamental proposition. But other times we come to think that something is good because we *already* have a desire or love for it, a desire or love that arises antecedently of knowledge or belief, out of somatic sources (hunger, thirst, sexual appetite), or perhaps social circumstances such as possessions and family. Here we desire, love or become attracted prior to reason. These desires and loves are not necessarily irrational. They are, to begin with, non-rational; they become irrational if they persist and are followed if and when we come to know that their objects are not good. Reason has its desires and loves, which are for goodness and beauty. But the other parts of the soul also have their desires and loves, for pleasures or honor for example, and their objects may or may not be beautiful or good. It is possible that Plato thought of familial love as such a non-rational attachment, and in his 'extended family' proposal he is trying to make use of this primitive love to assure an identity of 'love of one's own' and 'love of one's country'.

But can it be that for Plato this is all there is to philia? I think not. The desire for the good, in its new Platonic version, is brought in after all. We can see this from several elements throughout the *Republic*. For one thing, earlier in the first book Socrates proposed a Socratic-looking description of friend and enemy: A friend is a good man, a man who is useful and beneficial, an enemy a bad man, one who injures and harms (334-5). There is no reason to suppose that this is ever retracted. On the contrary, the guardians and rulers, for whom Socrates proposes the three major reforms considered in the last section, are supposed to be people who already satisfy the principle of social and individual justice: they are good citizens in that each is doing the social task for which he is best suited by nature and education; and they are good men and women in the sense that in their souls each part is doing its own proper work – reason rules the rest of the soul with the help of the spirit. Moreover, the rulers are men of knowledge, men capable of knowing the Platonic Forms and above all the Form of the Good. Their desires are the desires of reason, and they tell and teach the others what is good and bad. It is within this broader social and ethical context that the three major reforms are to be understood. Thus when we consider the third and most radical proposal, that guardians and rulers have identical feelings of pleasures and pains, this is to be understood in a particular way: they all take pleasure in the promotion of good, what the rulers have determined on the basis of reason to be good; and they take pains in the occurrence of evil. The pleasures and pains they share are the pleasures and pains of reason, the pleasures and pains of good and evil. Philia, real friendship, is this sharing: sharing not only possessions and family, but sharing the very same goods and evils in their knowledge, their beliefs and their feelings. In the sharing of possessions and family Plato may be taking advantage of and using the idea of 'loving one's own'. But in the broader ethical context of the *Republic* and in the third proposal, it is clear, I think, that philia consists in sharing knowledge or true beliefs about good and evil, and hence feelings and emotions.

The deficiency model and the difficulties of the *Lysis* no longer stand in the way. To have philia is not to love each other in a direct way, nor just to love the Good, but to share knowledge or belief and love of the Good, and thus to have the same loves and hates for the same goods and evils. Good men can certainly do that. We become friends by sharing this love for the Good.[12]

Notes

1 Traditionally there has been lively controversy about the distinction and relation between eros and philia in Plato, and correspondingly about the relation of the themes of the *Lysis* and the *Symposium*. Guthrie (HGP, vol. IV, pp. 137–143) reviews the controversy, which ranges from Friedlander's view that eros and philia in Plato are the same to Willanowitz's that they are fundamentally different emotions. (For some related controversies, see Bolotin, D., *Plato's Dialogue on Friendship*, pp. 201–225.) Guthrie offers good evidence that they are not the same. The difficult question is how they are related. The strategy we use here is to take seriously the *Symposium* distinction between generic and specific eros and think of philia as another species (besides eros proper) of desire for the good.

2 Guthrie reviews briefly some extremely different estimates of the merit of our dialogue, ranging all the way from Cornford's 'an obscure and fumbling essay' to Edith Hamilton's 'it has no superior among the dialogues ... as an illustration of the Socratic method'. Guthrie himself thinks 'it is not a success', 'completely at the mercy of ambiguities of the Greek word for it [philia]', the whole thing inflicted on boys under age still liable to parental whipping. HGP, vol. IV, pp. 143–4 and notes.

3 For pointing out the ambiguities, see, e.g. Guthrie, HGP, vol. IV, pp. 136–7, and most recently Bolotin, *Plato's Dialogue* p. 55, n. 26. But Bolotin does not agree with Guthrie that the conversation is 'completely at the mercy' of these ambiguities. Similarly, David Glidden finds 'no philosophical lapse in Plato's use of case or voice involving *philos*', and in fact finds Plato clarifying the active/passive sense of *philos* at 212b–213d, where Socrates seems to distinguish between *philōn* and *philoumenos*. 'The *Lysis* on Loving One's Own', *Classical Quarterly*, vol. 31, no. 1, 1981, pp. 40–1 and notes. Perhaps so. The fact remains though that Socrates does not explicitly acknowledge any ambiguity in his questions or in his arguments: there is no explicit evidence that at different times in the discussion different concepts are being defined, and this is in line with all the 'Socratic' dialogues of definition. It may be, however, that Socrates handles the Greek terms far more successfully than Guthrie seems to

think, so that there is still substantial plausibility and philosophical interest in Socrates' arguments.

4 Guthrie, ibid., pp. 136–7.

5 Some of the main facts he appeals to, as we shall see, are that a friend does not cause injury to the person he is a friend to, and that friendship and enmity are opposites. Some of the 'linguistic' facts in the background are that one can speak of a philos of wine or wisdom, and that philia covers familial love as well as friendship.

6 Socrates' argument is more complex because in answer to his question, 'When one loves another who becomes a friend: is the friend the one who loves of the one who is loved or the one who is loved of the one who loves?' he takes up separately the two possibilities mentioned in his question after he has disposed of the possibility that in such a case both are friends of each other. It is here that the active/passive ambiguity and the existence of the Greek compounds 'friend-of-horses', 'friend-of-wisdom' etc. make the arguments difficult to follow.

7 It is important to note, though, that Socrates does not take these refutations to imply that one can be a friend without loving: at least in a subsequent argument he uses the premise 'And one who does not love (phelein) is no friend' (215b) to refute a hypothesis; and in the 'favored hypothesis' the friend of the good is said to desire the good.

8 This is why, when Socrates considers the next hypothesis, that those who are 'like' are friends, he considers only being alike in terms of both being good men or bad men. He seems to assume that being alike in other respects, for example good birth wealth, is not relevant. While this may not be entirely true and seems to be modified in Book V of the *Republic* (as we shall see), it is plausible since there seems to be a necessary connection between being a good man and being a friend: they both by definition cause benefit (and similarly with bad men and enemies:they both by definition cause harm). At least this seems to be assumed in Socrates' conversation with Polemarchus in Book I of the *Republic,* which may be 'Socratic'.

9 Vlastos, G., 'The Individual as Object of Love in Plato', *Platonic Studies*, p. 11, and n. 28 and 29 for references in Plato in which *philia* and its cognates range over friendship and familial love.

10 This remarkable passage perhaps provides some evidence that in his theory of social justice Plato was a (non-hedonistic) utilitarian, at least if we accept Rawls' view that utilitarianism does not take seriously the distinction between persons. *A Theory of Justice*, pp. 26–7 and 186–7.

11 We find the same idea in *Politicus* 311b and in *Laws* 739–40, though in the latter Plato recognizes the limits of its application.

12 Prof. Vlastos has criticized Plato's conception of philia in the *Republic* on the ground that it does not allow for tolerance of differences in

'valuational response', in emotional and aesthetic preferences, and above all for 'personal freedom at its deepest level – the freedom to feel whatever it be one wants to feel', *Platonic Studies*, pp. 18–19. I believe that this criticism has validity, but I think its target is complex. What makes this criticism relevant is the fact that in the *Republic* Plato turns philia into a political ideal , one which the ideal city would be justified in enforcing through censored and mandatory education (for feelings and valuation) and other sanctions (for property and family). As a private ideal, Plato's concept of philia in the *Republic* is not necessarily subject to the same criticisms. It may be that persons with the same evaluative and emotional responses are among those most capable of the closest and most enduring friendships. Disagreements and differences among such friends may result in attempts to resolve them or they may end the friendships; but such friendships would not imply force or restriction of personal freedom.

5

Freud's New Theory of Sexuality

Love's mysteries in souls do grow,
But yet the body is his book.

John Donne

Introduction

Some twenty-three centuries separate Plato and Freud. In this vast interval several new theories of love were developed in western culture.[1] These theories are outside the scope of this book, but we may briefly note a few relevant facts which seem well attested in the literature.

To begin with, Plato's grand theory of love became influential enough to assure its author of immortality, the appropriate Platonic reward for his love of philosophy. Plato was particularly successful in implanting in the western mind the idea that love is always of beauty or goodness, that love has nothing to do with what is perceived or thought to be evil or ugly.[2] Even when love is passionate and mad it is not irrational: its object being beauty or goodness or an image thereof, it is always more or less choiceworthy. The idea of a ladder of love, constructed according to degrees of goodness or beauty of the object, and of a possible ascent from animal to a god-like love, is a natural corollary and it proved equally influential.[3]

In one important respect, though, Plato's theory did not prevail. In the *Symposium*, as we saw, Plato made a move towards a unified theory of love: he claimed that eros, or erotic love, is a species of desire for the good, which he called generic eros. Friendship would be another species of desire for the good; and we saw evidence that even familial love was conceived by him as a species of desire for the good. Thus we have in Plato a thesis that we may well call 'the Unity of Love': every kind of love is a species of desire for the good. The Greek language did not favor this thesis, for it had no single word for this generic love. Perhaps partly because of this, Plato's unified theory did not prevail, and it is hardly even recognized by the commentators. Aristotle kept erotic love, familial love and friendship separated, and he even liberated the highest type of friendship from Plato's deficiency and egoistic models.[4] In the Gospels and St. Paul *agape*, a word that Plato never used, came to signify God's love for man, man's love of God and love of neighbor. When we look, for example, at the famous passage in which St. Paul describes this kind of love (*Corinthians* I, 13), it is difficult to find any similarity to Platonic Eros, or even Platonic Philia: there is no hint that this love arises out of deficiency, it is anything but egoistic, and its object need not be beautiful or good; God is indeed the supreme good, but one's neighbor might be ugly, deformed and even evil.[5] Like ancient Greek, the Latin language had no single word for all kinds of love. St. Augustine and the medieval philosophers attempted various grand syntheses of Platonic or NeoPlatonic Eros and Christian Agape, the *Caritas* syntheses which Nygren so well traces. But these syntheses fell apart with the Reformation, and in any case these writers have a different word for sexual love which does not fall under *caritas*.[6]

Possibly, Dante can be viewed as having made a daring and remarkable move toward reconciling erotic and Christian love: he put his love for Beatrice, a love not entirely desexualized, in the same scale as the love of God. In the *Divine Comedy* the figure of Beatrice leads him through the Purgatory into Paradise and to the Beatific Vision.[7] But this view did not prevail either. In the renaissance Romantic love and Christian agape are once more separate and unrelated.[8]

In any case, by the time Freud became interested in the study of love, early in the twentieth century, the concept remained quite fragmented: familial love, friendship, romantic love, and Christian 'charity' were all regarded as separate concepts with nothing evident to relate or unite them. But unlike Greek and Latin, German and English do have a single generic word for all these different concepts, 'liebe' and 'love', a fact that did not fail to impress Freud.[9] For this and other more fundamental reasons, Freud became the second great systematic thinker to try for a unified theory of love, a new and controversial theory.

The new hypothesis, put forward in *Group Psychology and The Analysis of the Ego*, is that all these kinds of love, unrelated as they may seem, are really sexual in origin. Normal erotic or 'romantic love' consists of sexual desire and the tender feelings of affection; but this affection consists of older sexual impulses that have been inhibited in their aim. The affection of friendship and familial love is also aim-inhibited sexuality. And the devotion to abstract entities and aesthetic ideals is sublimation, sexual energy that has been diverted away from its original sexual aims. This thesis depends on

Freud's 'expanded concept of sexuality' and his new answers to the question, 'What is sexual?', to which we shall soon turn.

Apart from questions of unity, the concept of love has remained puzzling and mysterious, especially the concepts of courtly and romantic love, the successors to Plato's eros proper. In his psychoanalytic practice Freud became extensively acquainted with the love lives of his patients: their recollections, under hypnosis or free association, and their dreams revealed an amazing array of puzzling phenomena: perversions, inversions, psychic impotence, seemingly irrational choices for far younger or older beloveds and hints of incestuous attachments. How are all these 'abnormalities' to be understood and explained? And what is their relation to 'normal love'? Moreover, is normal romantic love really any less puzzling? Consider Romeo and Juliet, a classic case of romantic love. When Romeo first sees Juliet he is or thinks he is in love with Rosaline. Within the space of a few minutes he falls in love with Juliet – 'love at first sight'. We have a case of 'instant selection' and 'instant idealization', and the feeling is perfectly mutual. Moreover, this love proves to be real and powerful: within a few hours Romeo proposes marriage, proves that he cannot live without Juliet, and she reciprocates to the fullest. How are we to understand all this? A Platonist or neo-Platonist might say that Romeo saw Juliet as the embodiment of beauty and goodness. He was already in love with Beauty and Goodness, and now through sight, the powerful instrument of visual attraction, his love is directed toward this particular beauty. This explains the choice, while the powerful passion aroused explains the idealization. We could reasonably extract this explanation from the *Symposium* and the *Phaedrus*. But does it really dispel the mystery? It seems far too general and abstract to do so. After all, Romeo saw many other beauties and did not fall in love with them, and many other handsome lads saw Juliet and did not fall in love with her. Why did this particular gentleman fall in love with this particular beauty? We could ask this question about Dante and Beatrice and countless lesser cases of 'normal' romantic love. When we make our question about love so specific, it is difficult to escape the idea that to answer it we must know more about Romeo and Juliet, about their lives and their personalities. But what about their lives and personalities would help us answer the question of choice, and understand the fact of idealization – the hallmark of romantic love? Here too Freud gave revolutionary and controversial answers to these questions: the love choices we make at puberty and adulthood are modeled after much earlier sexual and love choices we make in infancy and childhood, usually within the family circle; idealization too has its origin in these earlier attachments. As in the case of Freud's new unification thesis about love, here too these new ideas were made possible and were entirely based on his new theory of sexuality and his new views on psycho-sexual development. Therefore, to understand Freud's new theory of love we must first look briefly at his expanded concept of sexuality and his views on the development of the sexual instinct.

The Old and the New Concepts of Sexuality

When Freud came to expound his new theory of sexuality in *The Three Essays on The Theory of Sexuality* he was already in possession of his new theory of mind, of the unconscious, repression and resistance, mental conflict and defence.[10] His interest in sexuality was aroused by the increasing frequency of sexual factors in the aetiology of the neuroses.[11] The theory he expounded in the *Three Essays* was as new and revolutionary as his theory of the mind. In the opening page he sets forth what he regarded as the dominant view of sexuality – the received view for thousands of years – a view, he thought, full of errors and inaccuracies. The paragraph is worth quoting in full:

> Popular opinion has quite definite ideas about the nature and characteristics of this sexual instinct. It is generally understood to be absent in childhood, to set in at the time of puberty in connection with the process of coming to maturity and to be revealed in the manifestations of an irresistible attraction exercised by one sex upon the other; while its aim is presumed to be sexual union, or at all events actions leading in that direction. We have every reason to believe, however, that these views give a very false picture of the true situation. If we look into them more closely we shall find that they contain a number of errors, inaccuracies and hasty conclusions. (SE vol. VII, p. 135)

This popular view of sexuality is entirely incompatible with the theory of love that Freud later developed. If sexuality is absent in childhood, the love that children indisputably display towards their parents could not possibly be sexual; and the choices we make in romantic love at puberty and beyond could not possibly be modeled after infantile and childhood sexual choices, nor could idealization have its origins in early sexual attachments.

Freud begins his criticism of the popular view by drawing a distinction between the *object* and the *aim* of the sexual instinct, the libido. The sexual object is 'the person from whom the sexual attraction proceeds', the sexual aim 'the act towards which the instinct tends' (ibid, p. 136). The popular view has it that *the* object is a person of the opposite sex and *the* aim sexual union. But observation shows, Freud argues, that numerous deviations occur with respect to both object and aim.

Among deviations with respect to object Freud discusses inversion, or homosexuality where a person of the same sex is taken as object, cases where a child or even an animal is taken as a sexual object; and 'fetishism' where even an inanimate object, a kerchief or a garter, is treated as a sexual object. After discussing several possible explanations of such deviations from the 'normal' sexual object, the major conclusion Freud reaches is that there is no innate connection between the sexual instinct and any object; as he puts it, 'the sexual instinct and the sexual object are merely soldered together ... it seems probable that the sexual instinct is in the first instance independent of its object' (Ibid, p. 148). And 'what is essential and constant in the sexual instinct' is not the object but something else. This conclusion points to the first error of the popular view. Contrary to it, human beings have to *find* an object more or less suitable for sexual satisfaction; finding an object is something we *learn*. And if such learning occurs during the early years, in infancy and childhood, this conclusion opens the way to developmental explanations of selection of sexual and love objects in puberty and adulthood.

Going next to deviations with respect to sexual aim, Freud notes that even in the most 'normal' sexual process, the union of the genitals, there are involved other activities, such as touching and looking, which are regarded as preliminary sexual aims, and other areas of the body besides the genitals which are sources of sexual excitement, such as the mouth in kissing. These other activities and areas are pleasurable in themselves and they also intensify the excitation of the union of genitals. Under certain conditions these other activities and areas of the body – the erogenous zones – can take the significance of 'perversions'.

'Perversions are sexual activities which either (a) extend, in an anatomical sense, beyond the regions of the body designed for sexual union, or (b) linger over the intermediate relation to the sexual object [preliminary aims] which should normally be traversed rapidly toward the final sexual aim' (Ibid., p. 150). The crucial point to note here is that these activities can be perversions not because of their content, but when they become detached from the normal aims and the genitals. In extreme cases, where the perversions become pathological, they are marked by 'exclusiveness and fixation' (ibid., p. 161). In scopophilia for example, a person becomes fixated on looking at the genitals of another person, instead of using such looking as a stage toward sexual union; and this activity takes the place of normal sexual activity, sexual union, in *all* circumstances. Once more, it is not in its content that this activity is perverse, but in its unusual relations to the normal. In their less severe form the activities that can become perversions 'are rarely absent from the sexual life of healthy people' (ibid., p. 160).

From his discussion of the perversions Freud draws two major conclusions: first of all, the sexual instinct 'has to struggle against certain mental forces which act as resistances', cultural and ethical ideals and shame and disgust, which result in repression of the normal sexual aim (ibid., p. 162). And, secondly, 'that perhaps the sexual instinct itself may be no simple thing but put together from components which have come apart again in the perversions' (ibid., p. 162). And this points to a second error in the popular view of sexuality, that the sexual instinct has just one aim, sexual union, and that 'sexual' means the same as 'genital'.

What is Sexual?

In his discussion of the sexual aberrations, deviation of object or aim, Freud has already expanded the popular concept of sexuality. The sexual instinct is mobile with respect to object; one kind of object can be 'displaced' by another. Consequently, neither a person of the opposite sex nor any other object can serve to distinguish the sexual instinct from any other. Furthermore, though sexual union is undoubtedly a sexual aim, there are other aims and activities that are sexual: touching, looking, curiosity, cruelty, and even masochism. In addition, even though the genitals are undoubtedly a sexual organ and source of sexual excitation and sexual pleasure, there are other organs and areas of the body that are sexual: the mouth, the anus, the eyes and the whole skin. Are there, then, any bounds to sexuality? How are we to distinguish the sexual instinct from other instincts, in particular from the self-preservative or 'ego instincts', such as hunger?

An instinct, Freud tells us, may be understood as 'the psychical representative of an endosomatic continuous source of stimulation, as contrasted with a 'stimulus', which is set up by *single* excitations from without' (ibid., p. 168). And the principle of individuation for instincts is as follows:

> What distinguishes instincts from one another and endows them with specific qualities is their relation to their somatic sources and to their aims. The source of an instinct is a process of excitation in an organ and the immediate aim of the instinct lies in the removal of this organic stimulus. (Ibid., p. 168)

An increase in the quantity of excitation is felt as unpleasure, and the removal of the organic stimulus as pleasure; the latter is the 'immediate aim' of every instinct, to be distinguished from 'intermediate aims' such as eating in the case of hunger or making love in the case of the libido.. We have here in effect a statement of the famous Pleasure Principle: that the course of mental events is 'invariably set in motion by an unpleasurable tension and it takes a direction such that the final outcome coincides with the lowering of that tension – that is, with an avoidance of unpleasure or the production of pleasure' (SE vol. XVIII, pp. 3ff).

Freud postulates that 'excitations of two kinds arise from the somatic organs, based upon differences of a chemical nature. One of these kinds of excitation we describe as specifically sexual, and we speak of the organ concerned as the "erotogenic zone" of the sexual component instinct arising from it' (ibid., p. 168).

Now if we knew the chemical difference between the two kinds of excitation, we would be able to tell when an excitation is sexual, hence when a source of an instinct is sexual; and also whether the immediate aim, which is the removal of such an excitation, and the pleasure felt from such removal, is sexual. But we don't. The principle of individuation tells us that an instinct is sexual if its source and aim are sexual. But how are we to tell whether its sources and aims are sexual?[12]

We may begin with a fundamental point not in dispute between Freud and the popular view of the sexual instinct: the genitals are by definition sexual organs; hence, the excitation that arises from them is a sexual source, the aim of removing such excitation a sexual aim, and the pleasure felt from such removal sexual pleasure. Thus the instinct for the union of genitals is sexual . But how are we to tell that the other component impulses into which Freud has analyzed the sexual instinct are sexual? – the impulse to look, to touch, to find out? The answer is provided by the study of the perversions (and the more controversial case of the 'negative perversions', the neuroses). These other impulses are sexual by virtue of their relation to the undoubtedly sexual impulse to join the genitals. In normal lovemaking, looking, touching, and finding out are *subordinated* to the union of the genitals: they are preliminary aims – 'foreplay' – intensifying and leading to the excitation arising from the union of genitals. In the perversions they are *substitutes* for it. In the perversions other areas and organs of the body, the oral and anal orifices, the eyes and the skin, 'behave in every respect like a portion of the sexual apparatus' (ibid., p. 169). Thus in scopophilia, the compulsive looking at another's genitals, the eyes behave like, that is, ('correspond to'), an erotogenic zone; the person has been fixated on looking, instead of going on to making love, and he has substituted the excitation and pleasure of looking for the excitation and pleasure of making love. Thus this excitation is sexual, and the pleasure of removing it a sexual aim.

So far, we have considered briefly how Freud's study of the perversions (and the neuroses) led him to expose some of the errors of the popular view of sex, and to expand the concept of sexuality, we might say, anatomically: the sexual is not to be confined to the genital; there are other areas and organs of the body that can be sources of sexual satisfaction.

We now come to the last error of the popular view: that the sexual instinct is 'absent in childhood' and sets in at the time of puberty. On the contrary, Freud argued, the sexual manifestations at puberty are a second phase in the development of the instinct. The first phase occurred in infancy and childhood, and was followed by a period of latency. And the particular form that sexual life takes at puberty and beyond, normal or perverse or neurotic, is determined largely by the particular forms of sexual manifestation in those earlier years. Consequently to understand the love lives of adults we must trace back and identify the main phases and forms of psycho-sexual development from infancy on. This expansion of the concept of sexuality, to infancy and childhood, we may call genetic or developmental. It is more controversial, as Freud noted, than the anatomical expansion which seems now to be largely accepted.

Though the literature on children contained occasional remarks about 'precocious sexual activity in small children', Freud remarks that 'not a single author has clearly recognized the regular existence of the sexual instinct in small children' (ibid., p. 175). He thought that this was due partly to 'considerations of propriety', but mainly to the psychological phenomenon of infantile amnesia. We don't remember but others tell us that as children we 'gave evidence of love, jealousy and other passionate feelings' (ibid., p. 174). Our infantile sexual impulses have been repressed, withheld from consciousness, due to certain mental forces such as 'disgust, feelings of shame and the claims of aesthetic and moral ideals' (ibid., pp. 175, 177).

The main manifestation of infantile sexuality that Freud investigates are thumb-sucking and breast feeding in infancy, and masturbation in childhood. He takes thumb-sucking as paradigmatic, revealing the essence of infantile sexuality. Freud cites Lindner as 'clearly recognizing the sexual nature of this activity', but paediatricians and nerve specialists repudiated this view partly due 'to a confusion between "sexual" and "genital"' (ibid., p. 180). Still, this objection raises 'a difficult question', Freud says: 'What is the general characteristic which enables us to recognize the sexual manifestations of children?' (Ibid., p. 180). How can we tell that thumb-sucking or other infant or child activity which does not involve the genitals, like masturbation, is sexual?

Actually, Freud claims, thumb-sucking is the second sexual activity of the child. The first is 'sucking at his mother's breast, or at a substitute for it' (ibid., p. 181). The passage is worth quoting in full:

> The child's lips in our view, behave like an erotogenic zone, and no doubt stimulation by the warm flow of milk is the cause of the pleasurable sensation. The satisfaction of the erotogenic zone is associated, in the first instance, with the satisfaction of the need for nourishment. To begin with, sexual activity attaches itself to functions serving the purpose of self-preservation and does not become independent of them until later. No one who has seen a baby sinking back satiated from the breast and falling asleep with flushed cheeks and a blissful smile can escape the reflection that this picture persists as a prototype of the expression of sexual satisfaction later in life.

In thumb-sucking 'the need for repeating the sexual satisfaction now becomes detached from the need to take nourishment', and becomes an independent sexual aim, with a second erotogenic zone (besides the lips) being created by the child, a part of his own body, the reason for the activity being called 'auto-erotic'.

In these two activities, breast feeding and thumb-sucking, we face anew the difficult Freudian question, 'What is sexual?' Breast feeding is at best an ambiguous case since, as Freud clearly recognizes, it serves the function of nutrition, and so is a manifestation of the other, non-sexual, self-preservative or ego instinct, hunger. Here Freud says that the activity is *also* sexual. Thumb-sucking becomes a crucial case because, as Freud says, here 'there is no question of the purpose of this procedure being the taking of nourishment' (ibid., p. 180). The child seeks a pleasure he remembered from breast feeding which is now obtained independently of feeding since the child persists in thumb-sucking even though he receives no nutrition. The case is still difficult, though, because unlike the cases of adult perverse sexuality, in the infant there is no evident connection between thumb-sucking and the genitals. It is worth noting that as usual Freud is not dogmatic about this. He says that thumb-sucking shows us 'what constitutes an erotogenic zone. It is a part of the skin or mucous membrane in which stimuli of a certain sort evoke a feeling of pleasure possessing a particular quality.' But he adds that it is 'less certain' that the pleasure of thumb-sucking is sexual (ibid., p. 183).

In any case, on the basis of his discussion of thumb-sucking he answers the difficult question he raised earlier about the nature of an infantile sexual manifestation. Its 'three essential characteristics' are:

> At its origin it attaches itself to one of the vital somatic functions [such as nutrition and elimination]; it has as yet no sexual object, and is thus auto-erotic; and its sexual aim is dominated by an erotogenic zone. (Ibid., p. 182)

This original attachment of the sexual instinct on the self-preservative instinct gives rise to the notorious difficulties of distinguishing between the two at an early age, and it is the reason for calling 'anaclitic' the childhood attachments to the persons who feed or take care of the child. It also gives rise to the difficulty of deciding whether such early attachments are sexual, which is important for Freud's views about love. These difficulties came to a head with the introduction of narcissism later on, and they were perhaps part of the reason why eventually Freud grouped together the self-preservative and sexual instincts under the Greek name 'Eros', and set in opposition to it the newly 'discovered' self-destructive instinct he called 'Thanatos'.[13]

Before closing this section we should note that the difficulties of distinguishing between sexual and self-preservative manifestations at a very early age, roughly one to three, do not necessarily carry over to the next stage of development, roughly the ages three to five. For at this later stage Freud finds what are more clearly sexual activities, such as masturbation, and the curiosity and researches of children about sex differentiation, about how babies are born, and about the sexual activities of the parents (SE, vol. XVI,

p. 325). Since love, the combination of sexual impulses and affection, does not usually appear until this stage, when the work of repression begins, the controversies about infantile sexuality do not perhaps infect Freud's theory of love as much as one might at first suppose. There still remains the difficulty, though, of understanding clearly how early sexual impulses become transformed into affection, an essential part of Freud's theory of love, and a difficulty of which he was aware (SE, vol. XVIII, p. 118).

Psychosexual Development and the First Appearance of Love

> Art thou a woman's son and canst not feel
> What 'tis to love?
>
> Shakespeare

As Strachey reports in his Editor's Note to the *Three Essays*, with the addition of infantile sexuality Freud's new theory of sexuality was complete.[14] If sexual impulses normally operate in infants and young children, the sexual instinct has a long and complicated history. Its appearance at puberty is a reappearance, and the story of its development, its vicissitudes, is what Freud later appeals to to explain the origin of love, the choice of beloved, and the causes of overestimation. It now remains to describe briefly the main stages of psychosexual development.

A unique feature of the development of the sexual instinct is that it is di-phastic: it is interrupted by the period of latency, and so its development comes in two waves, infancy and childhood, and puberty; and the second wave is largely determined by the first. The first wave is divided by Freud into roughly three stages, the oral, the anal and the phallic. We have already discussed the manifestation and the characteristics of infantile sexuality, the first stages. The phallic stage is perhaps the most important for Freud's theory of love. It is marked by the appearance of the Oedipus Complex and the first appearance of love.

The phallic phase still shares the characteristics of infantile sexuality: it is dominated by a new erotogenic zone, the genitals, and the chief sexual activity of this stage, masturbation, is still auto-erotic. At the same time, it begins to acquire some of the characteristics of adult sexual life. Freud tells us that psychosexual development beyond infantile sexuality has two aims: 'first, the abandonment of auto-eroticism, the replacement of the subject's own body by an outside object, and secondly the unification of the various objects of the separate instincts, (the oral, the anal, and the genital) and their replacement by a single object' (SE, vol. XVI, p. 329). In the phallic phase this development takes place to some extent, then it becomes interrupted by the latency period, and reaches completion in puberty.

> The processes of finding an object are fairly compelex and no comprehensive account has hitherto been given of them. For our purposes it may be specially pointed out that when, in the years of childhood before puberty, the process has in some respects reached a conclusion, the object that has been found turns out to be almost identical with the first object of the oral pleasure instinct. Though it is not actually the mother's breast, at least it is the mother. We call the mother the first *love*-object. We speak of love when we bring the mental side of the sexual trends into the foreground and want to force back the underlying physical or 'sensual' instinctual demands or to forget them for the moment. At the time at which the child's mother becomes his love-object the psychical work of repression has already begun in him, which is withdrawing from his knowledge awareness of a part of his sexual aims. To his choice of his mother as a love-object everything becomes attached ... under the name of the 'Oedipus Complex'. (Ibid., p. 329)

According to Freud both direct observation of children and analytic examination of adult neurotics (ibid., p. 332–7) confirm all that the Oedipus legend describes. The child shows exclusive attachment to the parent of the opposite sex, jealousy and resentment of the parent of the same sex, and his behavior toward his parents, or brother or sister substitutes, is unmistakably erotic or sexual.[15] The incest barrier now intervenes and psychical repression begins.

> In all this the fact is entirely overlooked that such an inexorable prohibition of it in law and custom would not be needed if there were any reliable natural barriers against the temptation to incest. The truth is just the opposite. A human being's first choice of object is regularly an incestuous one, aimed, in the case of the male, at his mother or sister; and it calls for the severest prohibitions to deter this persistent infantile tendency from realization. (Ibid., p. 335)

This repression results in the withdrawing from the child's knowledge awareness of a part of his sexual aims – sexual union with a parent of the opposite sex. The sexual instinct becomes 'inhibited in its aim' and turns into affectionate or tender feelings, which later, when directed to new non-incestuous objects, can become a component of 'normal' love.

After the latency period, a kind of interruption in psychosexual development, which Freud found remarkable and thought unique to the human species (ibid., p. 326), the period of puberty sets in. In normal development, where neuroses and the perversions are relatively absent, during the age of puberty the several component sexual instincts of infancy and childhood become organized and unified under the primacy of the genitals; the object of the instinct is now a person of the opposite sex, and the (intermediate) aim is sexual union, an act that serves both the immediate aim of the instinct, sexual pleasure, and also reproduction and perpetuation of the species (SE vol. VII, pp. 207ff). The psychosexual history we have been describing up to puberty, makes normal development of the final stage difficult. Freud describes some of the difficulties and tasks of normal development:

> We learn that at puberty, when the sexual instinct first makes its demands in full strength, the old familiar incestuous objects are taken up again and freshly cathected with libido. The infantile object-choice was only a feeble one, but it was a prelude, pointing the direction for the object choice at puberty. At this point, then, very intense emotional processes come into play, following the direction of the Oedipus complex or reacting against it, processes which however, since their premises have become intolerable, must to a large extent remain apart from consciousness. From this time onwards, the human individual has to devote himself to the great task of detaching himself from his parents, and not until that task is achieved can he cease to be a child and become a member of the social community. For the son this task consists in detaching his libidinal wishes from his mother and employing them for the choice of a real outside love-object, and in reconciling himself with his father if he has remained in opposition to him, or in freeing himself from his pressure if, as a reaction to his infantile rebelliousness, he has become subservient to him. These tasks are set for everyone; and it is remarkable how seldom they are dealt with in an ideal manner – that is, in one which is correct both psychologically and socially. (SE vol. XVI, pp. 336–7)

Freud adds that 'no solution at all is arrived at' by neurotics: the son remains all his life 'bowed beneath his father's authority and he is unable to transfer his libido to an outside sexual object'. In the perversions, on the other hand, a partial solution is arrived at, but one that remains unsatisfactory: the sexual instincts are either never united and organized under the primacy of the gentials and put in the service of reproduction, or fall apart again into the infantile component instincts, both of which may result in deviations with respect to normal object or aim. Presumably, a solution is correct socially – a culture-bound standard – when the incest barrier and the social conventions regarding sexual perversions are respected, and perhaps when sexual psychical energy is at least sometimes put to work for more socially accepted aims than sexual pleasure, as in the case of sublimation. A solution is psychologically correct when the transformations of puberty result in a normal sexual life:

> A normal sexual life is only assured by an exact convergence of the affectionate current and the sensual current both being directed toward the sexual object and sexual aim. (The former, the affectionate current, comprises what remains of the infantile efflorescence of sexuality.) It is like the completion of a tunnel which has been driven through a hill from both directions. (SE vol. VII, p. 207)

Normal Sexuality

But why does Freud think this is 'a normal sexual life'? And is normalcy an ethical standard?

Unlike Plato, Freud did not have an ethical theory, and so in his case it is more difficult to discover his standards for normal sexual life and normal love. In general he seems to appeal to a variety of bio-medical, developmental and cultural factors.

In the present case, when Freud is speaking of an 'ideal' solution to the Oedipus Complex, he seems to be appealing to social, biological and developmental notions. 'Ceasing to be a child' and 'becoming a member of the social community' is achieved by becoming independent of parental authority and detaching libidinal wishes from one or the other of the parents, that is, by solving the problems of the early dependence of the child on the family and the incest barrier. These problems are created by the social institution of the private family, the socio-biological necessity of the incest barrier, and the plain biological fact that human beings are born weak, immature, and dependent. The 'ideal' solution is in part suggested by these socio-biological facts that create the problem.

But a solution is not 'ideal' unless there is also, in the love relations between men and women, at puberty and beyond, a convergence of the affectionate and sensual feelings on the same person. Why? Because (as we shall see in the next chapter) unless there is such convergence, a man can have affection and love for a woman but be 'psychically impotent' with her (he is sexually impotent even though there is no physical impairment); or he can have sexual desire for her but no affection, care, or respect. In the former case the individual obtains no satisfaction, in the latter he has transient and even degrading relationships. But when the two kinds of feelings do converge the individual can obtain satisfaction and can have a lasting and caring relation suitable to family life and the rearing of children. The psychological and physical demands of the individual and the demands of society and civilization are best met when this convergence takes place. Here we have an appeal to psychological, developmental and cultural factors. The case of psychic impotence is treated as a psychical illness and so is the case of the man who has endless sexual relationships but cannot love. And both result from 'fixation' in psychosexual development: 'Every pathological disorder of sexual life is rightly to be regarded as an inhibition in development' (SE vol. VII, p. 208).

But why should a psychosexual development relatively free of fixations be judged to be 'normal', 'ideal' and 'better'? The cultural factors appealed to do not seem to be a secure basis since they can vary with culture and time. The biological factors do not seem sufficient either since 'nature' is insufficiently determinate, as De Sousa points out (pp. 205–7). After all, the child is by nature 'polymorphously perverse'; why should we single out a development that does not encourage some of these 'perversions' and call it ideal? Our earlier discussion of the perversions is of no help here, since the normal was presupposed and perversions were defined by relation to it.

I think Freud's most fundamental answer is given from what we might call a 'medical perspective', in his discussion of the relations of the neuroses to health. (*Introductory Lectures*, SE vol. XVI, pp. 455–7) Here he uses 'normal' and 'healthy' interchangeably. He tells us that, as in the case of the perversions, there is no hard or sharp distinction between health and neuroses: the distinction does not hold at all in dreams but 'only during the day' and 'a healthy person, too, is virtually a neurotic' (ibid., pp. 456–7). Moreover, healthy people are only relatively healthy; they display neurotic symptoms that are trivial and unimportant – Freud calls this 'nervous health'. Then he says:

> The distinction between nervous health and neurosis is thus reduced to a practical question and is decided by the outcome – by whether the subject is left with a sufficient amount of capacity for enjoyment and of

> efficiency. It probably goes back to the relative sizes of the quota of energy that remains free and of that which is bound by repression and is of a quantitative, not of a qualitative nature. (Ibid., p. 457)

The first sentence of this paragraph, I think, gives what Freud regards as the ultimate, fundamental or primitive criteria for neurosis, a diminished capacity for enjoyment and efficiency. These are, I think, the psychological equivalents to the primitive signs or symptoms of physical illness, physical pain or malfunction. The second sentence of the paragraph gives a psychoanalytic diagnosis of the causal factors with which the capacity for enjoyment and of efficiency varies. This coheres well with the ideal of analytic therapy that Freud described two pages earlier:

> Thus our therapeutic work falls into two phases. In the first, all the libido is forced from the symptoms into the transference and concentrated there; in the second, the struggle is waged around this new object and the libido is liberated from it. The change which is decisive for a favorable outcome is the elimination of repression in this renewed conflict, so that the libido cannot withdraw once more from the ego by flight into the unconscious. This is made possible by the alteration of the ego which is accomplished under the influence of the doctor's suggestion. By means of the work of interpretation, which transforms what is unconscious into what is conscious, the ego is enlarged at the cost of this unconscious; by means of instruction, it is made conciliatory towards the libido and inclined to grant it some satisfaction and its repugnance to the claims of the libido is diminished by the possibility of disposing of a portion of it by sublimation. The more closely events in the treatment coincide with this ideal description, the greater will be the success of the psychoanalytic therapy.

Freud is describing here the stages and strategies of psychoanalytic therapy by which the patient's diminished capacity for enjoyment and efficiency may be increased. Freud's aetiological diagnosis of such diminished capacity, the therapy he prescribes, and the theory upon which these rest, are all peculiar to psychoanalysis. But the ultimate or primitive criteria he uses for neurosis or psychosexual disorders are not, and in principle they are not different form the primitive signs of bodily disorder, physical pain and malfunction of parts or organs of the body. Freud starts as a physician would start, from the complaints of the patient. He has a new theory of sexuality which redefines the distinctions and relations between the normal, the neurotic, and the perverse, and a new theory of the aetiology of the neurotic and the perverse, but, so far as I can see, he does not have or propose new ethical standards about what is good or evil, right or wrong. To be sure, when he speaks of the convergence of affectionate and sensuous feelings on the same person as 'normal' or 'healthy' love, and speaks of an 'ideal' solution, he is making or implying a value judgment. But this is because he discovered that 'psychic impotence' is due to lack of such divergence and he assumes that psychic impotence is something bad or evil to be avoided. This assumption is of course a value judgment, but it is not peculiar to psychoanalysis nor particularly new or controversial. It is like the physician's assumption that health is a good, illness an evil. So far as I can see, the new theory of sexuality by itself has no value implications, and Freud was on the right tract when he was generally reluctant to make value judgments on the basis of his theory.[16]

Notes

1 For theories of love between the times of Plato and Freud, see especially Nygren, A., *Agape and Eros*; Singer, I., *The Nature of Love*, vols. I and II, de Rougemont, D., *Love in the Western World*, and Hunt, D.M., *The Natural History of Love*. Nygren is especially good on the history of Christian Agape, while de Rougemont, Singer, and Hunt detail also the traditions of courtly and romantic love.

2 Nygren traces well the history of this idea in Hellenistic and Neo-Platonic philosophy, in St. Augustine and the medieval theologians. Ibid., Part II, chs. 1–4.

3 For the history of the various ladders of love, see Nygren, *Agape and Eros*, especially Part II, chs 2 and 3.

4 Cf. Vlastos, G., 'The Individual as Object of Love in Plato', *Platonic Studies*, pp. 3–6, and Cooper, John M., 'Aristotle on Friendship' *Essays on Aristotle's Ethics*, ed. A. Rorty.

5 See Nygren, *Agape and Eros*, Part I, ch. 1, and ch. 3.

6 For the various *caritas* syntheses see Nygren, *Agape and Eros*, Part II, chs 1–5. Nygren develops in some detail the most influential of these syntheses, that of St. Augustine. It is worth noting that what Augustine synthesized was not so much Platonic eros and Gospel agape, but rather Neo-Platonic Eros and mostly Pauline agape: that is, only the upper reaches of Plato's ladder are involved, and on the Christian side it is our love of God, rather than God's love, that is taken as the model for agape. Caritas includes all these, but not sexual love, such as the love of a woman, which falls under *cupiditas*. Indeed in Augustine there is no greater contrast and conflict in love than that between his cupiditas for his mistress and his caritas for

God. As in Plato, we have no term here under which all love falls; but contrary to Plato, no concept either. In these respects, the situation is perhaps no different in St. Thomas. Cf. for example, *The Confession of St Augustine* , Bk 8, chs 8–12; *Aquinas*, ed. T. Gilbey, pp. 252–7, 325–31; and Nygren, *Agape and Eros*, Part II, chs 1 and 4.

7 For a discussion of Dante's love for Beatrice and the role it plays in *The Divine Comedy* see, e.g. Williams, Charles, *The Figure of Beatrice*, and Walsh, Gerald, *Dante Alighieri*. There is controversy about what kind of love Dante had for Beatrice, and the matter is too complex for us here. But it is difficult to escape the impression from *La Vita Nuova* that Dante was 'in love' with Beatrice, and the impression from the *Confessions* that Augustine would have been astonished at the idea that the woman he was in love with could lead him to God.

8 See Nygren, *Agape and Eros*, Part II, ch. 6, and de Rougemont, D., *Love in the Western World*, Bks II and IV.

9 See SE, vol. XVIII, p. 91; this passage is discussed below, in the beginning of ch. 6.

10 The new theory of the mind is expounded in *The Interpretation of Dreams*, ch. VII. Even the Oedipus Complex is found in this work. For a description of Freud's early models of the mind see Ellenberger, H., *The Discovery of the Unconscious*, pp. 480–500. For a more theoretical account see Rapaport, D., *The Structure of Psychoanalytic Theory*, pp. 39–71.

11 See Strachey's Introduction to the *Three Essays*, and ch.3 of *An Autobiographical Study*.

12 We may note in passing that for Plato the principle of individuation for desires would be importantly different: a desire is sexual if its *object* and/or aim (or function) is sexual. The general principle is stated in *Republic* 477 and applied to distinguish knowledge and belief. For an extended discussion see my 'Hintikka on Knowledge and its Objects in Plato', in *Patterns in Plato's Thought*, ed. J.M.A. Moravcsik, pp. 34–46. We may also note that the very definitions of generic and specific eros are given in terms of objects and aims.

13 Sulloway, F., *Freud: Biologist of the Mind*, Basic Books, NY 1979, gives an extensive bibliography on this controversy, pp. 258–64. For informed discussion of Freud's expanded concept of sexuality, see also Wollheim, R., *Sigmund Freud*, ch. IV; Ellenberger, ibid., pp. 500–510, and Ellis, H., *Psychology of Sex*, ch. III.

14 Strachey notes that Freud committed himself to the hypothesis of infantile sexuality around 1897, when he abandoned his 'seduction theory' and at the same time 'discovered' the Oedipus Complex in his self-analysis. Ellenberger reviews the various other sources from which Freud drew evidence for his new theories; pp. 503–8. It is worth mentioning that in a footnote to the *Three Essays*, added in 1910, Freud notes that when the book had been first published his evidence for infantile sexuality came in part from 'psycho-analytic

research upon adults'. He now adds that the hypothesis is confirmed by analysis of neurotic children during the early years of childhood, and cites in particular the famous Little Hans case (SE, vol. VII, pp. 193–4).

15 For a massive review of 'empirical findings' about this crucial theory of Freud's, the Oedipus Complex, see Greenberg, R.P., and Fischer, S., *The Scientific Credibility of Freud's Theories and Therapy*, ch. 4. The results are mixed. Empirical research confirms most of Freud's Oedipal hypotheses about males, but it throws serious doubts on his Oedipal models of female development. See especially pp. 218–224, and 404–9. In his presidential address to the American Psychological Association, Gardner Lindsay cites impressive biological evidence for the universality of the incest taboo and the presence of incestuous impulses. He finds numerous methodological faults with psychoanalytic theories, but credits Freud with fundamental contributions to our knowledge of sexuality, early experience, and the Oedipus complex. 'Some Remarks Concerning Incest, the Incest Taboo, and Psychoanalytic Theory', *American Psychologist*, 1967, Vol. 22, pp. 1051–59.

16 I have benefited greatly from De Sousa's able and far-ranging essay on 'Norms and the Normal' in *Freud*, ed. R. Wollheim. I have differed somewhat from his view in emphasizing what I have called the 'medical perspective' as being the most fundamental in Freud. De Sousa may be right in thinking that Freud relied on other criteria such as truth, reality, and rationality. But I think that Freud had no particular philosophical theories about these notions. The reality principle is a principle of adaptability to whatever reality there is, and rationality is used in the minimal sense of taking effective means (being efficient) to one's ends.

6

Freud's Theory of Love

Lust, thro' some certain strainers well refined,
Is gentle love, and charms all womankind.

Pope

Introduction

Freud's psychological writings show a growing and consistent interest in the concept and the experience of love. *The Three Essays* (1905) lay some of the important theoretical foundations for the theory of love later developed, though the subject itself is approached only occasionally and indirectly. In 1906 Freud 'announced his intention of writing an essay or book on the "love life of man"' (Jones, *Sigmund Freud*, vol. 2, pp. 297–8). The 'Contributions to the Psychology of Love' was apparently the result. In the first of the three papers under this heading, 'A Special Type of Choice of Object Made by Men' (1910, SE, vol. XI), love is the main subject of investigation for the first time, and a theory of love begins to emerge. Here the phenomena of choice of love object and of idealization are explained, and the distinction between 'normal' and 'abnormal' love is made.

In the opening paragraph of this essay Freud also tells us that 'up to now we have left it to the creative writer' to investigate love, but that he will extend 'a strictly scientific treatment to the field of human love' (1910, SE, vol. XI, p. 165). The recent controversies over the scientific character of Freud's general theories are beyond the scope of this book, but this and other passages show that Freud thought that in his investigation of love he was doing 'science'.

Freud's interest in love continues in the important paper, 'On Narcissism: An Introduction' (1914, SE, vol. XVI). After Freud introduces his new system of instincts in *Beyond the Pleasure Principle* (1920, SE, vol XIX), we have extended discussions on love in *Group Psychology and the Analysis of the Ego* (1921, SE, vol. XVIII), and in *Civilization and its Discontents* (1929, SE, vol. XXI). There are also brief discussions in many other works. So far as I know, there is no systematic and detailed reconstruction of Freud's theory of love, as distinct from his general theory of sexuality. Standard expositions of Freud either do not mention the topic at all or give a brief and cursory treatment.[2] Here we attempt such a reconstruction.

The central thesis of Freud's theory of love is that all love is a derivative of the sexual instincts. The nuclear case is sexual or 'romantic' love, where the love-object is a person of the opposite sex and the aim is sexual union; these are the 'normal' object and (intermediate) aim of the sexual instinct. All other kinds of love including self-love, familial love, friendship, and the love of humanity, love of concrete objects and abstract entities, are formed by displacement of the normal object or by inhibition or by deflection of the normal aim.

The first task of a theory of love is to explain and make understandable the central case of sexual love. Freud tried to do this by describing the main observable characteristics of sexual love – exclusive attachment and overvaluation – and by constructing genetic explanations of these characteristics on the basis of his theories of the libido and the psychosexual development of the individual (the theories we sketched in the last chapter).[3]

The remaining task of a theory of love is to explain and make understandable all the other kinds of love. This is also done on the basis of the theories of the libido and psychosexual development. Freud tried to show that all these other attachments are derived from the sexual instinct and are formed through the mechanisms of object displacement, repression or inhibition of aim, and deflection of the normal sexual aim.[4]

We shall begin this chapter with a fuller statement of Freud's central thesis. Then we shall consider in detail his descriptions and explanations of the central case of sexual love; and finally we shall discuss his account of the remaining kinds of love.

The Central Thesis: All Love is Sexual in Origin

A direct statement of the central thesis, as well as some interesting related claims, occurs in *Group Psychology and The Analysis of The Ego* (1921, SE, vol. XVIII, pp. 90–91). Two paragraphs are worth quoting in full:

> Libido is an expression taken from the theory of the emotions. We call by that name the energy, regarded as a quantitative magnitude (though not at present actually measurable) of those instincts which have to do with all that may be comprised under the word 'love'. The nucleus of what we mean by love naturally consists (and this is what is

> commonly called love, and what the poets sing of) in sexual love with sexual union as its aim. But we do not separate from this – what in any case has a share in the name 'love' – on the one hand, self-love, and on the other, love for parents and children, friendship and love for humanity in general, and also devotion to concrete objects and to abstract ideas. Our justification lies in the fact that psychoanalytic research has taught us that all these tendencies are an expression of the same instinctual impulses; in relations between the sexes these impulses force their way towards sexual union, and in other circumstances they are diverted from their aim or are prevented from reaching it, though always preserving enough of their original nature to keep their identity recognizable (as in such features as the longing for proximity, and self-sacrifice).
>
> We are of opinion, then, that language has carried out an entirely justifiable piece of unification in creating the word 'love' with its numerous uses, and that we cannot do better than take it as the basis of our scientific discussions and expositions as well. By coming to this decision, psychoanalysis has let loose a storm of indignation, as though it had been guilty of an act of outrageous innovation. Yet it has done nothing original in taking love in this 'wider' sense. In its origin, function, and relation to sexual love, the 'Eros' of the philosopher Plato coincides exactly with the love-force, the libido of psychoanalysis, as has been shown in detail by Nachmansohn (1915) and Pfister (1921); and when the Apostle Paul, in his famous epistle to the Corinthians, praises love above all else, he certainly understands it in the same 'wider' sense. But this only shows that men do not always take their great thinkers seriously, even when they profess most to admire them.

Freud expressed essentially the same views about love eight years later in *Civilization and Its Discontents* (SE, vol. XXI, ch. IV), a work in which love receives considerable attention.

In the passages quoted Freud makes three claims of interest to us: (1) the central thesis itself – that all the kinds of love enumerated are 'an expression of the same instinctual impulses', the sexual impulses; (2) the claim that language – in this case presumably the German language – has carried out 'an entirely justifiable piece of unification' in grouping all the attachments mentioned under the word 'liebe'; and that (3) Plato's 'Eros' coincides in important respects with the 'love-force, the libido of psychoanalysis'. The last claim we shall take up in the next chapter. But before we take up the first claim in some detail, which is our main task in this chapter, we need to comment briefly on the linguistic remarks Freud makes.

The piece of unification that the German language carried out is paralleled in the English language: in both languages all the cases

Freud mentioned in the first quote fall under the terms 'liebe' and 'love'. And Freud is saying that psychoanalysis provides a justification of these linguistic facts by its hypothesis that the tender feelings of affection that characterize all cases, besides the nuclear case of sexual love, originate in the sexual instinct. He says this explicitly in another work, discussing the same point: 'The careless way in which language uses the word "love" has its genetic justification.'[5]

So psycho-analysis adopts this wide linguistic use and provides a genetic explanation of it; and thus we might say language provides indirect support for Freud's thesis about love. It should be noted, though, that the genetic explanation is not the only possible one of the linguistic fact. Interestingly enough, another possible explanation would be a non-genetic, Platonic one: all these cases fall under the term 'love' because they have a common nature or essence (for Plato this would be desire for the good). Moreover, the 'storm of indignation' Freud talks about was directed against the psychoanalytic hypothesis about love, not against the wide linguistic use of the term. The hypothesis clearly goes far beyond the linguistic use and seems to have been very much an innovation.[6]

The Main Characteristics of Love: Exclusive Attachment and Overvaluation

It is important to note at the outset that the main characteristics Freud attributes to love remain fairly constant throughout his writings, while his theoretical explanations of these characteristics change and broaden with his important paper on narcissism, written in 1914. Accordingly, in the case of explanations we have to distinguish between pre- and post-narcissistic periods.[7]

In an early paper Freud tells us that 'A combination of exclusive attachment and credulous obedience is in general among the characteristics of love' (SE, vol. VII, p. 296). In subsequent works these two characteristics are amplified and the description of the phenomenon of love filled out.

By exclusive attachment is meant a (libidinal object-cathexis) choice of a single object – usually another person – with a view to sexual gratification (SE, vol. VII, p. 199). The exclusiveness is perhaps manifested by absorption in that person's interests and by jealousy.

The attachment may be only 'sensual', or it may be only 'affectionate', or it may be both. Freud describes the first case thus:

> In one class of cases being in love is nothing more than object-cathexis on the part of the sexual instincts with a view to direct sexual gratification, a cathexis which expires, moreover, when this aim has been reached; this is what is called common, sexual love. But, as we know the libidinal situation rarely remains so simple. It is possible to calculate with certainty upon the revival of the need which has just expired; and this no doubt must have been the first motive for directing a lasting cathexis upon the sexual object and for 'loving' it in the passionless intervals as well. ('Being in Love and Hypnosis' in *Group Psychology and the Analysis of the Ego*, 1921, SE, vol. XVIII, p. 111.)

Whether lasting or not, this is only sensual or 'earthly love'. When the tender feelings of affection and care are also attached to the same object we have a full-blown case of being in love, or as Freud calls it 'normal love' (ibid., pp. 112–13). As he puts it:

> To ensure a fully normal attitude in love, two currents of feelings have to unite – we may describe them as the tender affectionate feelings and the sensual feelings. (SE, vol. XI, p. 180)

On the other hand, when the two currents of feeling are not united on the same object and the attachment is only of the tender and affectionate feelings, we have a case of love referred to in art and literature, Freud says, as unsensual, 'heavenly love'.[8]

This kind of love is also found in the case of psychic impotence that occurs in men, where 'A man will show a sentimental enthusiasm for women whom he deeply respects, but who do not excite him to sexual activities, and he will only be potent with other women whom he does not "love" and thinks little of or even despises'.[9]

In sum, exclusive choice of object or attachment to a person, whether sensual or affectionate or both, is a universal characteristic of love. It is a task of a theory of love to explain and make understandable all three kinds of attachment and choice: how these choices are made, why sometimes the two currents of feelings converge in a single object, and why in other cases – sometimes tragically – they remain separate.

The second characteristic of love, of which 'credulous obedience' is a part, is sexual overvaluation or overestimation:

> In connection with this question of being in love we have always been struck by the phenomenon of sexual overvaluation – the fact that the love object enjoys a certain amount of freedom from criticism, and that all its characteristics are valued more highly than those of people who

> are not loved, or than its own were at a time it itself was not loved. If the sensual impulsions are more or less effectively repressed or set aside, the illusion is produced that the object has come to be sensually loved on account of its spiritual merits, whereas on the contrary these merits may really only have been lent to it by its sensual charm. ('Being in Love and Hypnosis', SE, vol. XVIII, p. 112)

The last sentence explains in part why Freud calls this overvaluation 'sexual'. This characterization and the fact that he speaks of 'being in love' in this passage may lead one to think that Freud attributed overvaluation only to the phenomenon of being in love, as distinct from familial love, the love of friendship, and so on. This is not so: he observed and described, somewhat amusingly, overvaluation in parental love, and apparently he thought that sexual overestimation is characteristic of all types of love.[10]

Freud described overvaluation as early as the *Three Essays* in 1905:

> It is only in the rarest instances that the psychical valuation that is set on the sexual object ... stops short at its genitals. The appreciation extends to the whole body of the sexual object and tends to involve every sensation derived from it. The same overvaluation spreads over into the psychological sphere: the subject becomes, as it were intellectually infatuated (that is, his powers of judgment are weakened) by the mental achievements and perfections of the sexual object and he submits to the latter's judgment with credulity. (SE, vol. VII, p. 150)

Freud also observed overvaluation in the case of transference-love, when in the therapeutic situation there is 'a transference of feelings on to the person of the doctor' though the situation in the treatment does not justify the development of such feelings.[11] In the next paragraph Freud tells us that transference-love, somewhat surprisingly, occurs in the case of male as well as female patients (towards a male doctor):

> There is the same attachment to the doctor, the same overvaluation of his qualities, the same absorption in his interests, the same jealousy of everyone close to him in real life. (Ibid., p. 442)

Freud had clearly observed overvaluation in women in transference love, and this is confirmed in his paper 'Observations on Transference-Love' where he speaks mostly of women patients.[12] This is of interest since earlier he expressed doubts on whether overvaluation occurs in women in love. In the *Three Essays* he says that 'the factor of sexual overvaluation can best be studied in men' since women's erotic life 'is still veiled in an impenetrable obscurity' (SE, vol. VII, p. 151). And in 1912 he wrote that 'as a rule they (women) develop little of the sexual overestimation natural to men'.[13] Despite his observation of overvaluation by women in transference-love, he still wrote in 1920: 'In typical cases women fail to exhibit any sexual overvaluation toward men; but they scarcely ever fail to do so toward their own children.'[14] Apparently then, overvaluation is not on the same footing as exclusive attachment or exclusive choice of object: there can be no love without the latter, whereas overestimation occurs regularly in male love but can be absent in female love. We shall return to this point when we consider explanations of overestimation.

In sum, overvaluation consists in valuing the characteristics of the loved object more than those of people who are not loved, or in valuing them more than at a time when the object was not loved; it results in (presumably unusual) credulity, and this credulity is a source of viewing the loved object as an authority (presumably, again, to an unusual degree). It is a second task of a theory of love to explain and make understandable this overvaluation, as well as, presumably, its frequent absence in the case of women in love.

Freud mentions several other features of love: 'the longing for proximity and self-sacrifice', and 'traits of humility, of the limitation of narcissism, and of self-injury' which, he tells us, 'occur in every case of being in love'.[15] The longing for proximity is easily explainable, at least in the case of sexual love, since only in such proximity can the sexual instinct attain its aim. The other traits mentioned are best understood in relation to Freud's narcissistic characterizations of love, and they will be considered later in that context.

Explanations of the Choice of Love-Object

> Tisn't beauty, so to speak, nor good talk necessarily. It's just It. Some women stay in a man's memory if they once walked down the street.
>
> Kipling

One of the important conclusions that Freud reached in the *Three Essays* is that there is no innate or necessary connection between the sexual instinct and its object: 'the sexual instinct and the sexual object are merely soldered together'. (SE, vol. VII, p. 148). The uniformity of the normal picture, where one chooses a person of the opposite sex, tends to mislead us into thinking that there is an intimate connection between the two and that the choice is solely due to the attraction of the object. But cases that are considered abnormal show us that anything that is suited for satisfaction of the sexual instinct can be taken as an object, ranging from the subject's own body to animals, inanimate objects, and other persons of either sex. Consequently, all choices of object need explanation, even the so-called normal choice: 'Thus from the point of view of psycho-analysis the exclusive sexual interest felt by men for women is also a problem that needs elucidation and is not a self-evident fact based upon an attraction that is ultimately of a chemical nature' (ibid., p. 146, note added in 1915).

The explanations that Freud offers of choice of object are always genetic or developmental.[16] In addition to the present psychological condition of the subject and the perceived attractiveness of the object, the explanation always makes reference to his past states, and also relies on patterns of psychosexual developments as given by the libido theory we sketched in the last chapter. An important fact about the psychosexual development of the process of finding an object is that this process is diphastic, 'that is, that it occurs in two waves. The first of these begins between the ages of two and five and is brought to a halt or a retreat by the latency period; it is characterized by the infantile nature of the sexual aims. The second wave sets in with puberty and determines the final outcome of the sexual life' (ibid., p. 200). The second wave is by no means independent of the first. On the contrary, the finding of an object at puberty moves along the pathways of choice established during the phallic stage. As Freud puts it, 'the finding of an object is in fact a re-finding of it' (ibid., p. 222). Consequently, no choice of love-object in the adult can be understood without reference to the first love-object of the child. This is one meaning of Freud's remark, 'the child is the father of the man'.

The first choice of love-object occurs during the phallic stage when the child comes under the Oedipus Complex and is confronted by the incest barrier. Typically, the first love-object of the child is the parent of the opposite sex or a parent-substitute, a brother or sister or other person who has taken care of the child. As Freud says, 'A human being's first choice of object is regularly an incestuous one, aimed, in the case of the male, at his mother and sister; and it calls for the severest prohibitions to deter this persistent infantile tendency from realization' (SE, vol. XVI, p. 235). The prohibitions result in the repression of the incestuous sexual aims, and the inhibited sexual impulses turn into feelings of tenderness and affection. It is this transformation, due to repression, that makes the parent of the opposite sex the first *love*-object of the child: 'We call the mother the first *love*-object. We speak of love when we bring the mental side of the sexual trends into the foreground and want to force back the underlying physical or 'sensual' instinctual demands or to forget them at the moment. At the same time at which the child's mother becomes his love-object the psychical work of repression has already begun in him, which is withdrawing from his knowledge awareness of a part of his sexual aims' (ibid., p. 329).

The feelings of affection and tenderness for the parent persist throughout childhood. Then, at puberty:

> There supervenes upon this state of things a powerful current of 'sensual' feeling the aims of which can no longer be disguised. It never fails, apparently, to pursue the earlier paths and to invest the objects of the primary infantile choice with currents of libido that are far stronger. But in relation to these objects it is confronted by the obstacle of the incest barrier ... consequently it seeks as soon as possible to pass on from these objects unsuited for real satisfaction to others in the world outside, with whom real sexual life may be carried on. These new objects are still chosen after the pattern (image) of the infantile ones. (SE, vol. XI, p. 181)

Thus, the new love-objects chosen are, as Freud puts it, 'mother surrogates' or 'father surrogates': they bear similarities to the actual father or mother. The similarities may be in physical characteristics, such as face, voice, movements; they may be role-similarities – the older woman who takes care or the father who protects; or they may be situational similarities – the choice may be a replay, as it were, of the family Oedipal situation.

An example of this type of explanation is elaborated by Freud in the paper 'A Special Type of Choice of Object Made by Men' (SE, vol. XI). He begins by giving four conditions that characterize this type of choice, and then offers a detailed explanation of the choice. The first two conditions pertain to the object chosen, the remaining to the lover's behavior. The first is 'the need for an injured third party; its effect is that the person in question never chooses as an object of love a woman who is unattached ... but only one in regard to whom another man has some right of possession ... ' (p. 166). The second condition is that the woman is 'more or less sexually discredited, whose fidelity and loyalty admit of some doubt ... this condition could be called that of "love for a harlot"' (p. 166).

The third is that, contrary to the case of normal love, the highest value is set upon women who are more or less sexually discredited; such women are 'the only ones it is possible to love', and passionate attachments of this type are repeated many times over, 'each an exact replica of the others' in the lives of this type of lover. The last condition is the desire that lovers of this type express 'to rescue' the beloved. The man is convinced that the loved woman has need of him, that without him she would lose all hold on respectability and rapidly sink to a deplorable level (p. 168).

Freud thought that he discovered a single causal source for this syndrome of seemingly unrelated conditions pertaining to the choice of object of neurotics, the same source as that of choices in normal love.

> When we view the various features of the picture presented here – the condition that the woman should belong to another man, her 'light' nature, the high value set upon this last, the thirst for jealousy, the fidelity which is in spite of all compatible with the long chain of repetitions, and the longing to 'save' – any hope of tracing them all back to a single source will seem very remote. And yet penetrating psychoanalytic study of the lives of those concerned yields this quite easily. The choice of an object complying with these peculiar conditions and this strange way of loving her have the same source as the normal attitude in love; they are derived from a fixation of the infantile feelings of tenderness for the mother and represent one of the forms in which this fixation expresses itself. In the normal attitude there remain only a few traces unmistakably betraying the maternal prototype behind the chosen object, for instance the preference young men show for mature women; the detachment of the libido from the mother is accomplished comparatively swiftly. In our type, on the contrary, the libido has dwelt so long in its attachment to the mother, even after puberty, that the maternal characteristics remain stamped on the love-objects chosen later – so long that they all become easily recognizable mother-surrogates (pp. 168–9).

Thus the explanation of this strange type of choice of object is similar to that of choice in normal love; the main difference is that in the case of this type of neurotic love the fixation of the infantile feelings of tenderness for the mother lasts much longer, even after puberty, and the maternal prototype is more strongly stamped on subsequent choices of object.

Freud devoted the rest of the paper to showing the connections between the single source of the choices and the four conditions that characterize this type of choice – how these conditions 'actually derive from the group of feelings relating to the mother' (p. 169). It is easy to show this, he says, in the case of the first condition, the need for an injured party: 'one sees at once that the fact of the mother belonging to the father would come to be an inseparable part of the mother's nature to the child growing up in the family circle, also that the "injured third party" is none other than the father himself' (p. 169). He admits that the second condition, that of the 'loose' character of the woman chosen, seems to stand 'in sharp opposition to a derivation from the mother-complex' since the grown man's conscious mind regards his mother as 'a personification of impeccable moral purity'. Freud replies that while in the conscious mind 'mother' and 'harlot' are contraries in the unconscious they are a united whole; the unconscious association dates back to the child's discovery of parental intercourse when the mother was indulging in forbidden acts and was unfaithful to her son – associations revealed in phantasies of the mother's 'infidelity'. The high value placed on women of this low character, and the endless series of love affairs associated with it, is explained by the fact that one's mother is unique and irreplaceable, and that the satisfaction sought is never found because the surrogates are never the original love-object whose image persists in the unconscious. Finally, the need to rescue is also a derivative of the mother-complex: 'When the child hears that he owes his life to his parents, that his mother gave him life, the feelings of tenderness in him mingle with the longing to be big and independent himself, so that he forms the wish to repay the parents for this gift and requite it by a like value'. As Jones remarks, 'The phantasy of saving … represents in the unconscious the desire to beget a child by the woman; Freud expounded in some detail the connections between these rather distant ideas' (ibid., p. 229).

It may be objected that the explanations Freud has offered for this type of choice of object – characterized by the four conditions – are too strong: since the source of choice in neurotics is the same as that of choice in normal love – the feelings attached to the maternal prototype – why are not all choices of object made by men characterized by these four conditions? Why, for example, is not the need for an injured third party, since it derives from the son-mother-father triangle, characteristic of all choices of object made by men who have been raised in such triangular 'family romances'? Freud raises a similar objection to his explanation of psychic impotence.[17] His answer is twofold: first, these conditions are indeed observed in healthy people as well, though they are not as pronounced and are not always grouped together, and second, the fixations of the infantile feelings for the mother are stronger, and last longer in the case of the neurotics under discussion (ibid., pp. 184ff).

Narcissistic Models of Object-Choice

> And therefore is Love said to be a child,
> Because in choice he is so oft beguil'd.
>
> Shakespeare

The explanations of choice of object we have been considering predate the paper on narcissism (1915), and are of a type called by Freud *anaclitic*, 'based on attachment to early infantile prototypes' (SE, vol. VII, p. 222, note added 1915). In this paper he reaffirms the anaclitic type of choice:

> The sexual instincts are at the outset supported upon the ego-instincts; only later do they become independent of these, and even then we have an indication of their original dependence in the fact that those persons who have to do with the feeding, care, and protection of the child become his earliest sexual objects: that is to say, in the first instance the mother or her substitute. (SE, vol. XIV, p. 81)

Thus the child forms libidinal attachments to those who satisfy his ego or self-preservative instincts.

In the paper on narcissism Freud does not reject this type of explanation of choice of love-object. Rather he comes to think of it as applicable mostly to choice of love-object made by men ('Complete object-love of the anaclitic type is, properly speaking, characteristic of men'), and develops a new kind of genetic explanation, the narcissistic, which he thinks applies especially to women.

> Side by side with this type and source of object-choice, which may be called the anaclitic type, a second type, the existence of which we had not suspected, has been revealed by psycho-analytic investigation. We have found, especially in persons whose libidinal development has suffered some disturbance, as in perverts and homosexuals, that in the choice of their love-objects they have taken as their model not the mother but their own selves. They are plainly seeking themselves as a love-object and their type of object-choice may be termed narcissistic. (Ibid., pp. 87-8)

Before we discuss several examples of narcissistic explanations, we need to take a brief look at the 'hypothesis of narcissism' which is now added to the libido theory.

Freud begins the paper by saying that the word narcissism was taken by P. Nacke 'to denote the attitude of a person who treats his own body in the same way as otherwise the body of a sexual object is treated.[18] That is to say, he experiences sexual pleasure at gazing at, caressing and fondling his body, till complete gratification ensues upon these activities' (p. 73). (Later Freud attributes this conception of narcissism to Havelock Ellis.) Developed to this degree, Freud says, narcissism has the significance of a perversion. The question arises whether some degree of narcissism may not be found in every human being, whether 'a disposition of the libido which must be described as narcissistic might ... claim a place in the regular sexual development of human beings' (p. 73). Freud claims that the study of paraphrenics (schizophrenics or people suffering from dementia praecox) leads to the conclusion, 'that the narcissism which arises when libidinal cathexes are called in away from external objects [in the case of schizophrenics] must be conceived as a secondary form, superimposed upon a primary one that is obscured by manifold influences' (p. 74).

> Thus we form a conception of an original libidinal cathexis of the ego, part of which cathexis is later yielded up to objects, but which fundamentally persists and is related to object-cathexes much as the body of a protoplasmic animalcule is related to the pseudopodia which it puts out. In our researches, taking, as we did, neurotic symptoms for their starting point, this part of the disposition of the libido necessarily remained hidden from us at the outset. We were struck only by the emanations from this libido – the object-cathexes, which can be put forth and drawn back again. We perceive also, broadly speaking, a certain reciprocity between ego-libido and object-libido. The more that is absorbed by the one, the more impoverished does the other become. The highest form of development of which object-libido is capable is seen in the state of being in love, when the subject seems to yield up his whole personality in favour of object-cathexis. (Ibid., pp. 75–6)

Further, we may derive knowledge of narcissism from three other sources, organic disease, hypochondria, and love between the sexes. In organic disease, for example, we see the reciprocity of ego-libido and object-libido. It is known that a person suffering from organic pain relinquishes his interest in the things of the outside world, insofar as they do not concern his suffering.

> Closer observation teaches us that at the same time he withdraws libidinal interest from his love objects: so long as he suffers, he ceases to love. The banality of this fact is no reason why we should be deterred from translating it into terms of the libido theory: We should then say: the sick man withdraws his libidinal cathexes back upon his own ego, and sends them forth when he recovers. (Ibid., p. 82)

The paper on narcissism, thus, introduces an important modification or at least addition to the libido theory. Central to the older theory was the distinction – indeed antithesis – between the ego or self-preservative instincts and the sexual instincts; and also the concept of object-libido, the investment of psycho-sexual energy on external objects, which was the source and origin of love of others. To this is now added the concept of ego-libido, the idea that the ego itself is originally invested with libidinal energy, and that this is the source and origin of narcissistic or self-love. Moreover, narcissism may be primary or secondary: the former is the original infantile investment of the ego with libido, associated though distinct from auto-eroticism; while secondary narcissism arises when there is a withdrawal of libido from external objects and reinvestment of it in the ego. We shall not enter here into the difficulties which the introduction of narcissism produces for the distinction between the ego instincts and the sexual instincts, or the associated disputes between Freud and Jung – these matters are well covered by Jones.[19] It is perhaps sufficient to point out what Jones notes: 'to say there is reason to suppose that ego is strongly invested with libido is clearly not the same thing as to say that it is composed of nothing else' (ibid., p. 303). This point is implicit in Freud's definition of narcissism as 'the libidinal complement to the egoism of the instinct of self-preservation'.[20] Confusion on this point is sometimes produced because the addition of narcissism introduces a new egoistic-altruistic antithesis of ego-libido versus object-libido, on top of the older antithesis between the ego of self-preservative instincts and the sexual instincts (ibid., p. 208).

The incorporation of narcissism into the libido theory enabled Freud to give a broader range of genetic explanations of choice of love-object than he had done before. He gives a schematic classification of all the explanations he now allows as follows:

> We conclude these suggestions with a short survey of the paths leading to object-choice.

> A person may love:
> (1) According to the narcissistic type:
> (a) What he is himself (actually himself).
> (b) What he once was.
> (c) What he would like to be.
> (d) Someone who was once part of himself.
>
> (2) According to the anaclitic type:
> (a) The woman who tends.
> (b) The man who protects.
>
> And those substitutes which succeed them one after another. (SE, vol. XIV, 90)

Case l(a) is illustrated by the 'type most frequently met with in women, which is probably the purest and truest feminine type' (pp. 88–9). The paragraph is worth quoting in full:

> With the development of puberty the maturing of the female sexual organs, which up till then have been in a condition of latency, seems to bring about an intensification of the original narcissism, and this is unfavorable to the development of true object-love with its accompanying sexual over-estimation; there arises in the woman a certain self-sufficiency (especially when there is a ripening into beauty) which compensates her for the social restrictions upon her object-choice. Strictly speaking, such women love only themselves with an intensity comparable to that of the men's love for them. Nor does their need lie in the direction of loving, but of being loved; and that man finds favor with them who fulfills this condition. The importance of this type of woman for the erotic life of mankind must be recognized as very great. Such women have the greatest fascination for men, not only for aesthetic reasons, since as a rule they are the most beautiful, but also because of certain psychological constellations. It seems very evident that one person's narcissism has a great attraction for those others who have renounced part of their own narcissim and are seeking after object-love ... The great charm of the narcissistic woman has, however, its reverse side; a large part of the dissatisfaction of the lover, of his doubts of the woman's love, of his complaints of her enigmatic nature, have their roots in this incongruity between the types of object-choice. (Ibid., pp. 88–9)

Case 1(d) is briefly described by Freud as follows:

> Even for women whose attitude towards the man is cool and narcissistic there is a way which leads to complete object-love. In the child to whom they give birth, a part of their own body comes to them

> as an object other than themselves, upon which they can lavish out of their narcissism complete object-love. (p. 89)

This case illustrates not only how object-love can develop from self-love – how ego-libido can flow into object-libido – but also how one kind of parental love is a derivative of the sexual instinct.

Case 1(b) is also briefly described by Freud in the same paragraph:

> Other women again do not need to wait for a child in order to take the step in development from (secondary) narcissism to object-love. Before puberty they have had feelings of a likeness to men and have developed to some extent on masculine lines; after this tendency has been cut short when feminine maturity is reached they still retain the capacity of longing for a masculine ideal which is really a survival of the boyish nature that they themselves once owned. (p. 89)

It should be noted that in the first case 1(a) we have only self-love – such women, as Freud says, love only themselves. In the last two cases, on the other hand, we have object-love developing out of self-love: in the last case, 1(b), the woman herself at her masculine-boyish phase becomes the model or prototype for choice of love-object, and such choices presumably can be repeated on the same model; while in case 1(d) the woman loves her child not after the model of herself, but through association with (being a part of) her own body, and here the child itself may become the model for love of younger men by older women.

Freud thinks that the anaclitic type of choice is more characteristic of men and the narcissistic of women, but he does not claim that this division is universal. He admits that there are 'countless women who love according to the masculine type ... ' (p. 89). Nor are human beings to be divided into two sharply differentiated groups according to the two main types of object-choice:

> We rather assume that both kinds of object-choice are open to each individual, though he may show a preference for one or the other. We say that the human being has originally two sexual objects: himself and the woman who tends him, and thereby we postulate a primary narcissism in everyone, which may in the long run manifest itself as dominating his love-choice. (p. 88)

Throughout Freud's remarks on object-choice 'he' is to be read as 'he/she', and he assures us explicitly that his 'description of the feminine form of erotic life' is not meant 'to depreciate women'.

The remaining case of narcissistic choice, 1(c), where a person may love what he would like to be, is more complex and introduces the concept of 'ideal ego', the forerunner of the super-ego.

Freud observes that in normal adults 'their former megalomania has been subdued and ... the mental characteristics from which we have inferred their infantile narcissism have vanished. What has become of their ego-libido?' (p. 90). He rejects the answer that 'the whole of it has passed over into object-cathexes', and suggests instead that some of the ego-libido is directed towards the person's ideal ego:

> We have learned that libidinal impulses are fated to undergo pathogenic repression if they come into conflict with the subject's cultural and ethical ideas ... [ideas which] he recognizes ... as constituting a standard for himself and acknowledges the claims they make on him ... The very impressions, experiencs, impulses and desires that one man indulges or at least consciously elaborates in his mind will be rejected with the utmost indignation by another, or stifled at once even before they enter the consciousness. The difference between the two ... can easily be expressed in terms of the libido-theory. We may say that the one man has set up an *ideal* in himself by which he measures his actual ego, while the other is without the formation of an ideal . From the point of view of the ego this formation of an ideal would be the condition of repression.
>
> To this ideal ego is now directed the self-love which the real ego enjoyed in childhood. The narcissism seems now to be displaced onto this new ideal ego, which, like the infantile ego, deems itself the possessor of all perfections. As always where the libido is concerned, here again man has shown himself incapable of giving up a gratification he has once enjoyed. He is not willing to forego his narcissistic perfection in his childhood; and if, as he develops, he is disturbed by the admonition of others and his own critical judgment is awakened, he seeks to recover the early perfection, thus wrested from him, in the form of an ego-ideal. That which he projects ahead of him as his ideal is merely his substitute for the lost narcissism of his childhood – the time when he was his own ideal. (pp. 93-4)

This, once more, is self-love, secondary narcissism deriving from infantile, primary narcissism, and displaced on one's ideal ego. It may happen, however, that this narcissistic gratification encounters actual hindrances, and in such a case:

> ... a person loves ... someone who possesses excellence which he never had (cf. supra, (c)). The parallel formula to that given above runs thus: whoever possesses an excellence which the ego lacks for the

> attainment of its ideal, becomes loved. This expedient is of special importance for the neurotic, whose ego is depleted by his excessive object cathexis and who on that account is unable to attain to his ego ideal. He then seeks a way back to narcissism from his prodigal expenditure of libido upon objects, by choosing a sexual ideal after the narcissistic type which shall possess the excellences to which he cannot attain. This is the cure by love, which he generally prefers to cure by analysis. (p. 101)

Finally, we may note that later in the *Ego and the Id* (1923), where Freud proposed his new division of the mind into the id, the ego, and the super-ego, he revised his views about primary narcissism. He now holds that 'at the very beginning, all the libido is accumulated in the id … [which] sends part of this libido out into erotic object-cathexes, whereupon the ego, now grown stronger, tries to get hold of this object-libido and to force itself on the id as a love object. The narcissism of the ego is thus a secondary one, which has been withdrawn from objects.'[21] And in an earlier chapter Freud described charmingly this process by which the ego tries to master the id:

> When the ego assumes the features of the object it is forcing itself, so to speak, upon the id as a love-object and is trying to make good the id's loss by saying: "Look, you can love me too – I am so like the object." (SE, vol. XIX, ch. 3)

Freud's Explanations of Overestimation

> For Love can beauties spy
> In what seem faults to every common eye.
>
> John Gay

Before the introduction of narcissism Freud noticed overestimation or overvaluation and tried to explain it within the context of his theory of anaclitic love.

In the *Three Essays* the term is introduced without explanation and the phenomenon is associated with extension of the sexual object from the genitals to other regions of the body and to the psychological sphere:

> It is only in the rarest instances that the psychical valuation that is set on the sexual object, as being the goal of the sexual instinct, stops short of the genitals. The appreciation extends to the whole body of the

> sexual object and tends to involve every sensation derived from it. The same overvaluation spreads into the psychological sphere: the subject becomes, as it were, intellectually infatuated (that is his powers of judgment are weakened) by the mental achievements and perfections of the sexual object and submits to the latter's judgments with credulity. (SE, vol. VII, p. 150)

The suggestion here seems to be that psychic valuation is set on the sexual object, because it is suited to the aim of the instinct, – the object is valued because it is wanted. It is perhaps not entirely clear or evident why this should result in overestimation. The last time the subject is mentioned in the *Three Essays*, an increase in overvaluation in men is attributed to resistance or increase in resistance on the part of the woman – a correlation that is usually thought to prevail in the cases of courtly and romantic love where excesses of overvaluation were associated with the unattainability of the women. (See, e.g., Hunt, M.M., *The Natural History of Love*, ch. V.) So far we have perhaps hints at explanations.

In the essays, 'A Special Type of Choice of Object Made by Men' and 'Degradation in Erotic Life', a pre-narcissistic Freudian explanation of overvaluation begins to emerge. It should be remembered that both essays deal only with male love, which is typically characterized by overvaluation, and that in both only anaclitic explanations of choice of object are given. Within these confines we should expect that overvaluation will somehow derive from the male child's original feelings for the mother. This is indeed what we find. In the only mention of overvaluation in the first essay Freud writes:

> The feature of overestimation by which the loved one becomes the unique, the irreplaceable one, fits just as readily into the infantile set of ideas, for no one possesses more than one mother, and the relation to her rests on an experience which is assured beyond all doubt and can never be repeated again. (SE, vol. XI, p. 169)

As might be expected, the second essay is more informative since degradation of the sexual object is the opposite of overvaluation of it. The essay deals with explanations of psychic impotence, 'the refusal on the part of the sexual organs to execute the sexual act, although both before and after the attempt they show themselves intact and competent to do so, and although a strong mental inclination to carry out the act is present'.

Freud summarized the explanation he offers for psychical impotence as follows:

> We have reduced psychical impotence to a disunion between the tender and the sensual currents of erotic feeling, and have explained this inhibition in development itself as an effect of strong fixations in childhood and of frustration in reality later, after the incest-barrier has intervened. (Ibid., 184)

When the fixation is extremely strong 'the whole current of sensual feeling in a young man may remain attached in the unconscious to incestuous objects', and the result is total impotence. In less severe conditions some of the sensual feeling at puberty finds some outlet in reality, but the sexual object chosen must have no association with feelings of tenderness:

> The sensual feeling that has remained active seeks only objects evoking no reminder of the incestuous persons forbidden to it; the impression made by someone who seems deserving of high estimation leads, not to a sexual excitation, but to feelings of tenderness which remain erotically ineffectual. The erotic life of such people remains disassociated, divided between two channels, the same two that are personified in art as heavenly and earthly (or animal) love. Where such men love they have no desire and where they desire they cannot love. In order to keep their sensuality out of contact with the objects they love, they seek out objects whom they need not love ... The principal means of protection used by men against this complaint [psychical impotence] consists in lowering the sexual object in their own estimation, while reserving for the incestuous object and for those who represent it the overestimation normally felt for the sexual object. (Ibid., pp. 182–3)

What makes possible this lowering of estimation of the sexual object is the disunion of the sensual feelings and the tender feelings which derive from the infantile sensual feelings for the mother. This suggests clearly that the overestimation of the sexual object that prevails in normal cases derives from the tender feelings, the aim-inhibited infantile sensual feelings for the mother. This is confirmed by Freud's remarks on normal development in the same paper. In the child's mind the mother occupies a unique and irreplaceable role – she is already overvalued. In normal development, at puberty the new and powerful sensual feelings find an external object in whom the normal sexual aim may be attained:

> These new objects are still chosen after the pattern (imago) of the infantile ones; in time, however, they attract to themselves the tender feeling that has been anchored to those others. A man shall leave

> father and mother – according to the Biblical concept – and cleave to his wife; then are tenderness and sensuality united. The greatest intensity of sensual passion will bring with it the highest mental estimation of the object (the normal overestimation of the sexual object characteristic of men). (Ibid., p. 181)

The last sentence should not mislead us into thinking that overestimation derives from the new sensual feelings developed at puberty. The view is that it derives from the feelings of tenderness, but once tenderness and sensuality are united, in the normal case, overestimation will vary with intensity of the sensual feelings.

In the paper on narcissism Freud offers a new explanation of overvaluation. It seems that the new explanation is to replace the old one we have been considering, for it is given in the very case of male anaclitic love where the older explanation was meant to apply:

> Complete object-love of the anaclitic type is, properly speaking, characteristic of the man. It displays the marked sexual overestimation which is doubtless derived from the original narcissism of the child, now transferred to the sexual object. This sexual overestimation is the origin of the peculiar state of being in love, a state suggestive of neurotic compulsion, which is thus traceable to an impoverishment of the ego in respect of libido in favour of the love-object. (SE, vol. XIV, p. 88)

This is a surprising statement. It occurs in the very same page where Freud gives a pre-narcissistic, anaclitic type of explanation for the choice of object for the very same case, male love. He has told us that in this case the male takes the mother, not his own self, as a model for the choice of love-object. In such a case we would expect that the overestimation would derive from the original sensual feelings, now turned into tender feelings by repression, for the mother. Instead he tells us that the overestimation derives from the original narcissism of the child: in that original narcissism the infantile ego 'deems itself the possessor of all perfections' (p. 94), that is, it is overestimated; when ego-libido flows into an external object, the overestimation of the ego flows over into the object, and the sexual object itself becomes overestimated. This is the new explanation of overestimation. Freud is thus combining a non-narcissistic explanation of choice of object with a narcissistic explanation of overestimation in the very same case. It is not entirely clear that this is consistent: presumably it is if it is theoretically possible for overestimation to derive from two sources at once.[22] Nor is there any sign in the paper that Freud was aware of any possible difficulty here.

In any case, it is clear that in the rest of the paper Freud now prefers the narcissistic explanation of overestimation. This is clear in a change he makes in his description or definition of the state of being in love. In the beginninig of the paper he tells us that 'the highest form of development of which object-libido is capable is seen in the state of being in love, when the subject seems to yield up his whole personality in favor of object-cathexis ... ' (p. 33) This seems compatible with both pre-narcissistic, anaclitic, and narcissistic conceptions of love. But at the end of the paper he tells us, 'the state of being in love consists in a flowing-over of ego-libido to the object'. This conception of love seems entirely narcissistic. Idealization is also given a narcissistic explanation in *Group Psychology* (SE, vol. XVIII, pp. 112–13).

Though Freud does not explicitly say so, it is possible that in the paper on narcissism we have a new view of the origin of love; we have not only the addition of the concept of female narcissistic love, where both the choice of object and over-estimation are given narcissistic explanations, but also a reconceiving of male anaclitic love. The new conception would be that the original attachment of the male child to the mother is already 'a flowing-over of ego-libido to the object' (*An Outline of Psychoanalysis*, 1940,SE, vol. XXIII, p. 150). On this view the first love-object would not be the mother but the infantile ego itself, and all love would flow from self-love. But the uniqueness of the mother would still presumably make her a dominant model for subsequent anaclitic choices of love-object. This interpretation has the advantage of reducing possible inconsistency and assuring considerable continuity in Freud's views on love.

Narcissistic and Egoistic Love

It is not entirely clear, however, that Freud saw or worked out all the complications and implications of the new conception of love resulting from the hypothesis of narcissism – one of the reasons perhaps why Jones called the essay on narcissism 'disturbing'.[23] An interesting complication comes to light if we raise the controversial issue whether love, on Freud's view, is essentially egoistic or essentially altruistic or perhaps neither. The pre-narcissistic theory of the sexual instinct would suggest that love is essentially egoistic, since a love object is selected with a view to the lover's own gratification, which is the immediate aim of the instinct. Now one would suppose, at first glance, that the addition of narcissism would reinforce this egoistic conception of love. For narcissism, self-love, might be thought to be egoistic by definition. Indeed Freud tells us:

> Narcissism and egoism are indeed one and the same: the word 'narcissism' is only employed to emphasize that this egoism is a libidinal phenomenon as well; or, to put it another way, narcissism may be described as the libidinal complement of egoism. (SE, vol. IV, 223)

That is, narcissism is sexual egoism. Now if all sexual love of others flows out of this sexual self-love, is not all sexual love of others essentially egoistic? The answer is not entirely clear in Freud's writings. We saw that in *Group Psychology*, a work in which Freud subscribes to the hypothesis of narcissism, he told us that being in love is characterized by 'self-sacrifice', 'humility', 'limitation of narcissism', and 'self-injury'. And in the paper on narcissism he told us that in the state of being in love the lover 'seems to yield up his whole personality in favor of object-cathexis', that 'the lover is humble'; and that while being loved raises self-regard, loving lowers the self-regard of the lover. Is this consistent with love being regarded as essentially egoistic?

In the *Introductory Lectures* Freud discusses briefly the relations among the four concepts involved here: egoism, narcissism, altruism, and object-love (SE, vol. XVI, pp. 417–18). Narcissism, he says, is the libidinal complement of egoism. 'When we speak of egoism, we have in view only the individual's *advantage*; when we talk of narcissism we are also taking his individual satisfaction into account'. One can be absolutely egoistic and also maintain powerful object-cathexis, when the ego needs libidinal satisfaction from the object and sees to it that there is no damage to the ego. One can also be egoistic and excessively narcissistic, when one has very little need of an object for direct or indirect sexual satisfaction. In these cases, he says, egoism 'is what is self-evident and constant, while narcissism is the variable element'. Here Freud is distinguishing egoism from narcissism on the basis of the fundamental distinction between sexual or libidinal and self-preservative instincts to which he still holds, as he makes clear in the following pages (p. 420). Egoism refers to the advantage or interest of the individual; narcissism more narrowly to his sexual satisfaction which may or may not be to his advantage in a given case. But egoism is compatible with both narcissism or ego-libido, and object-libido or love of others. Now the opposite of egoism, altruism, he says, 'does not, as a concept, coincide with object-cathexis, but is distinguishable from it by the absence of longings for sexual satisfaction' (p. 410). So, presumably, when we act with a view only to the advantage of another and we have no sexual longing for him/her we have a case of non-libidinal altruism. But, Freud continues:

> When someone is completely in love, however, altruism converges with libidinal object-cathexis. As a rule the sexual object attracts a portion of the ego's narcissism to itself, and this becomes noticable as what is known as the 'sexual overvaluation' of the object. If in addition there is an altruistic transposition of egoism on to the sexual object, the object becomes supremely powerful; it has, as it were, absorbed the ego. (p. 418)

So we can have a case of being 'completely in love' in which the love is altruistic: ego-libido flows (completely?) into object-libido, the lover puts the beloved in the place of his own ego, and out of narcissism we get altruistic love. This is the lover who is characterized by 'self-sacrifice', 'humility', and 'self-injury'. But what of the 'longings for sexual satisfaction' which must be present in this case? Are they not egoistic? Freud does not explain what he means by 'an altruistic transposition of egoism on to the sexual object'. Perhaps he means that by putting the beloved in the place of the lover's ego, the lover has put the interests, the advantage of the beloved in the place of his own advantage, and that this would apply even to his own sexual longing for the beloved: he puts the sexual satisfaction of the beloved in place of his own. How this is possible is not clear. Be that as it may, it is difficult to see how Freud's earlier theory of anaclitic love could acknowledge or account for such a case of altruistic love, any more than Plato's theory of love would. Freud's altruistic love, flowing out of narcissism, seems to come close, surprisingly, to the Biblical notion of loving others as one loves oneself, though Freud found the commandment to love one's neighbor puzzling.[24]

Familial Love, Friendship, and Sublimation

> The might of one fair face sublimes my love,
> That it hath weaned my soul from low desires.
>
> Michelangelo

With the exception of filial love, which is part of the libido theory and the Oedipus complex, Freud made no sustained effort to substantiate his claim that all these kinds of love are sexual in origin. There is some discussion of parental and sibling love and the love of friendship. Freud gave considerably more thought to sublimation, but even here his discussion seems rather fragmentary.

In Freud's early theory of the Libido and the Oedipus complex there is a fundamental asymmetry between parental and filial love. The theory contains an account of the sexual origin of filial love, of the anaclitic or attachment type of choice of the mother as the first love object of the child. This theory is based on the fact that the mother takes care of the ego or self-preservative needs of the child, the proposition that the components of the sexual instincts are first attached, through the erotogenous zones, to the self-preservative instincts, and the hypothesis that the child thus forms his first libidinal attachment to the mother. But there are no similar facts to support a similar hypothesis about parental love: the child does not take care of the mother or the father. How then can parental love be sexual in origin? The account we just alluded to, of course, gives Freud's pre-narcissistic view of the origin of love, and in this account there seems no way to answer our question. It is no accident, therefore, that Freud's main discussion of parental love occurs in the paper on narcissism where a new origin, primary narcissism, is postulated for some kinds of love. Freud tells us:

> The primary narcissism of children ... is less easy to grasp by direct observation than to confirm by inference from elsewhere. If we look at the attitude of affectionate parents toward their children, we have to recognize that it is a revival and reproduction of their own narcissism, which they have long since abandoned. The trustworthy pointer constituted by overvaluation, which we have already recognized as a narcissistic stigma in the case of object-choice, dominates, as we all know, their emotional attitude. Thus they are under a compulsion to ascribe every perfection to the child – which sober observation would find no occasion to do – and to conceal and forget all his shortcomings. Moreover, they are inclined to suspend in the child's favor the operations of all the cultural acquisitions which their own narcissism has been forced to respect ... The child shall fulfil those wishful dreams of the parents which they never carried out – the boy shall become a great man, a hero in his father's place, and the girl shall marry a prince as a tardy compensation for the mother. At the most touchy point in the narcissistic system, the immortality of the ego, which is so hard pressed by reality, security is achieved by taking refuge in the child. Parental love, which is so moving and at bottom so childish, is nothing but the parents' narcissism born again, which is

transformed into object-love, unmistakably reveals its former nature. (SE, vol. XIV, pp. 90–91)

This narcissistic explantion of parental love does not seem as convincing as the anaclitic explanation of filial love, at least insofar as it is supposed to show that the origin of parental love is sexual. Perhaps the main reason for this is that the anaclitic explanation is solidly based on the indisputable existence of erotogenous zones, the fact that these serve both self-preservation and sexual gratification, and the fact that the parents take care of the self-preservative needs of the child. But there seem to be no comparable, clear cut facts to support the view that the original primary narcissism of the parents is sexual. Later in *The Ego and the Id*, as we saw, the original narcissism of anyone, including parents, would be viewed as a secondary one: the ego takes over the features of the objects of the erotic cathexes of the id; this love for the ego would then be sexual in the sense of being a sublimation of these original erotic cathexes of the id. But in the paper on narcissism this explanation is not available. Moreover, the apparent breakdown of the original distinction between the sexual and self-preservative instincts, which narcissism seemed to bring with it and which is officially adopted later in *Beyond the Pleasure Principle*, clouds the issue and points to possibilities of alternative explanations of parental love. Perhaps, as Plato thought, the parent cares for the child because he sees it as a means to his own immortality; or as a modern psychobiologist might have it, offspring is seen as one's representative in future generations. In these conceptions it is self-preservation or continued existence, not sexuality, that is being appealed to; and in Plato's case the explanation is teleological, not genetic.

Of the love of friendship we hear very little beyond the bare claim that it is aim-inhibited sexuality. Freud claims that aim-inhibited instincts always preserve a few of their original sexual aims and are thus recognizable as sexual in origin: 'even an affectionate devotee, even a friend or an admirer, desires the physical proximity and sight of the person who is now loved in the "Pauline" sense' (SE vol. XVIII, pp. 138–9). He also points out that in the case of directly sexual feelings there is a loss of energy every time there is satisfaction, whereas aim-inhibited instincts 'are not capable of really complete satisfaction' and are thus 'especially adapted to create permanent ties' such as friendship.[25] These are interesting remarks, but there is no full treatment of the topic. How friendships are formed, how selection is made, what makes for better and worse friendships – these questions are not raised.

Sublimation covers the remaining case of love, devotion to concrete objects and abstract ideas, and it corresponds to love in the upper parts of Plato's ladder, to which we shall compare it in the next chapter. Freud consistently described sublimation as a diversion or deflection of the normal aims of the sexual instinct or components of it. Some of the sexual energy whose source is the erogenous zones becomes diverted from sexual aims to artistic or scientific aims which are more valued – more sublime – than the sexual ones. In the *Three Essays* he tells us:

> Historians of civilization appear to be at one in assuming that powerful components are acquired for every kind of cultural achievement by this diversion of sexual instinctual forces from sexual aims and their direction to new ones – a process which deserves the name of 'sublimation'. (SE, vol. VII, p. 178)

In the paper on narcissism:

> Sublimation is a process that concerns object-libido and consists in the instinct's directing itself towards an aim other than, and remote from, that of sexual satisfaction; in this process the accent falls upon deflection from sexuality. (SE, vol. XIV, p. 94)

And in *The Ego and the Id*:

> The transformation of object-libido into narcissistic libido which thus [by the ego identifying with the objects of the erotic object-cathexis of the id] takes place obviously implies an abandonment of sexual aims, a desexualization – a kind of sublimation, therefore. Indeed, the question arises ... whether this is not the universal road to sublimation, whether all sublimation does not take place through the mediation of the ego. (SE, vol. XIX, p. 20)

In an extensive review of the literature, H.B. Levey writes that Freud was clear that sublimation is an unconscious process, that in sublimation the instinct escapes repression, that it is an alternative to perversion and neuroses, and that sublimation is an important source of the highest artistic, scientific and cultural achievements (Levey, pp. 239–249). But, Levey claims, he was equally unclear about the mechanisms and causes of sublimation: reaction formations, the period of latency, inhibitions, unusually strong sexual constitutions, and identification are all cited as factors at one time or another, but no clear theory emerges. Freud himself tells us about unresolved problems: in 1905 he wrote that 'the inner causes of sublimation are quite unknown to us' (SE, vol. VII, p. 239); in 1921 he wrote that 'there is some difficulty in giving a description of such a diversion of aim which will conform to the requirements of metapsychology' (SE, vol. XVIII, p. 138); and in 1929 he implied something similar.[26]

Perhaps the most interesting and concrete application of the concept of sublimation is to be found in Freud's lengthy psychobiography of Leonardo Da Vinci. In this fascinating and controversial study Freud tells us that Da Vinci's devotion to his art and his 'love of truth and his thirst for knowledge' were sublimations of his infantile sexual curiosity and sexual researches. His early artistic work, his scientific investigations in his middle life, and his return to painting were the result of three successive sublimations of his infantile sexual curiosity and erotic attachment to his mother (SE, vol. XI, pp. 130–4). Freud goes into considerable detail, emphasizing various factors of Da Vinci's childhood: the early absence of the father, the passionate attachment to the mother, 'the intensity of his infantile sexual researches', the fact that 'the instinct to look and the instinct to know were those most strongly excited', and a fixation on 'the erotogenic zone of the mouth'. A 'powerful wave of repression' ended this stage, resulting in the avoidance of 'every crudely sensual activity' and a sexually abstinent life. Then,

> When the excitations of puberty came in their flood upon the boy, it did not, however, make him ill by forcing him to develop substitute structures of a costly and harmful kind. Owing to his very early inclination towards sexual curiosity the greater portion of the needs his sexual instinct could be sublimated into a general urge to know, and thus evaded repression. (Ibid., p. 132)

Some of his early works, 'the heads of laughing women and beautiful boys' were 'representations of his sexual objects'. After the second sublimation that resulted in his scientific discoveries, he underwent a new transformation that led to his last great artistic works:

> At the summit of his life, when he was in his early fifties – a time when in men the libido not infrequently makes a further energetic advance – a new transformation came over him. Still deeper layers of the contents of his mind became active once more; but this further regression was to the benefit of his art, which was in the process of becoming stunted. He met the woman who awakened his memory of his mother's happy smile of sensual rapture; and, influenced by this revived memory, he recovered the stimulus that guided him at the

> beginning of his artistic endeavors, at the time when he modeled the smiling woman. He painted the Mona Lisa, the 'St. Anne with Two Others' and the series of mysterious pictures which are characterized by the enigmatic smile. (Ibid., pp. 133–4)

Freud was careful to point out that he was not trying to explain Da Vinci's artistic and scientific genius but only 'the inhibitions in Leonardo's sexual life and in his artistic activity' (ibid., p. 131). And he claimed anything but certainty for the fascinating results of his study, because, as he admitted, we do not know enough about Da Vinci's life or about the mechanisms of sublimation.

Freud's study is of interest to us because it is the main example of a detailed and concrete application of the notion of sublimation, and also because Leonardo's devotion to art and science would presumably be placed somewhere in the upper reaches of Plato's ladder of love. But it is not clear that the study resolved any of the difficulties and questions about the causes and mechanisms of sublimation. In his 1939 study Levey at least concluded that though Freud's 'concept contributed highly valuable generalizations in the description of sublimation as a vicissitude of non-repressed instinct, as an unconscious process, and one helpful in preventing neurosis' these generalizations 'have remained untested and unverified' (ibid., p. 269). He also claims that post-Freudian literature did not clear up the confusions nor did it provide confirmation.[27]

Love, Happiness, and Civilization

In the last work in which Freud makes extended remarks about love, *Civilization and its Discontents* (1930, SE vol. XXI), he discusses explicitly the relation of love to individual happiness, and the role of love in the development of civilization. His view on the *nature* of love seems to be substantially the same as that of *Group Psychology*. But his remarks here are worth considering, not only for the sake of completeness, but especially because he is now discussing very large questions about love, which cannot fail to interest any student of human affairs, whether philosopher, artist, or scientist.

In chapter II Freud raises the questions, 'What do men show themselves by their behaviour to be the purpose and intention of their lives? What do they denand of life and wish to achieve in it?' (SE, vol. XXI, p. 76). He answers that they strive for happiness, and says that this endeavour has a negative and a positive aim, the absence of pain and unpleasure, and the experiencing of strong feelings of pleasure.[28] Freud then discusses the various 'techniques in the art of living' by which men try to attain either one or both of these aims.

One technique is 'the way of life which makes love the centre of everything, which looks for all satisfaction in loving and in being loved' (ibid., p. 81). This technique has 'a most remarkable combination of characteristic features':

> it locates satisfaction in internal mental processes, making use ... of the displaceability of the libido ..., but it does not turn away from the external world; on the contrary, it clings to the objects belonging to that world and obtains happiness in an emotional relationship to them. Nor is it content to aim at an avoidance of unpleasure – a goal, as we might say, of weary resignation; it passes this by without heed and holds fast to the original, passionate striving for a positive fulfilment of happiness. And perhaps it comes nearer to this goal than any other method ... . A psychical attitude of this sort comes naturally to all of us; one of the forms in which love manifests itself – sexual love – has given us our most intense experience of an overwhelming sensation of pleasure and has thus furnished us with a pattern for our search for happiness. (Ibid., p. 81)

Indeed, no human being would abandon this path to happiness, the path of love, for any other, were it not for the 'weak side' of this technique:

> ... we are never so defenceless against suffering as when we love, never so helplessly unhappy as when we have lost our loved object or its love. (Ibid., p. 81)

Fear of loss of *love*, Freud tells us later, is the origin of the sense of guilt and of the notion of what is bad (ibid., p. 124). Loss of the *object* deprives the lover of the satisfactions of love. But loss of *love* (of being loved) is worse: it deprives the person of protection and may even expose him/her to the aggressions of the former lover (ibid., p. 124). Worse still, 'in love relations not being loved lowers the self-regarding feelings, while being loved raises them'; so loss of love means loss of self-regard.[29]

Freud goes on to remark briefly on another form of love, besides sexual love, the case in which 'happiness in life is predominantly sought in the enjoyment of beauty'. The aesthetic path to happiness offers little protection against the threat of suffering, he says, but it can compensate for a great deal:

> The enjoyment of Beauty has a peculiar, mildly intoxicating quality of feeling. Beauty has no obvious use; nor is there any clear cultural necessity for it. Yet civilization could not do without it. The science of aesthetics ... has been unable to give any explanation of the origin and nature of beauty ... . Psychoanalysis, unfortunately, has scarcely anything to say about beauty either. All that seems certain is its derivation from the field of sexual feeling. The love of beauty seems a perfect example of an impulse inhibited in its aim. Beauty and attraction are originally attributes of the sexual object. (Ibid., pp. 82–3)

When Freud returns to the topic, he discusses a third form the path of love can take, by which a small minority can find happiness:

> These people make themselves independent of their object's acquiescence by displacing what they mainly value from being loved on to loving; they protect themselves against the loss of the object by directing their love, not to single objects but to all men alike; and they avoid the uncertainties and disappointments of genital love by turning away from its sexual aims and transforming the instinct into an impulse with an *inhibited aim*. What they bring about in themselves in this way is a state of evenly suspended, steadfast, affectionate feeling, which has little external resemblance any more to the stormy agitations of genital love, from which it is nevertheless derived. (Ibid., p. 102)

This is the way of life enjoined by the second commandment, to love thy neighbor as thyself. It gives up the most intense pleasures we can experience, those of sexual love, but it avoids the dreaded 'loss of love', and gains inner peace. Freud cites St. Francis of Assisi as one who 'went furthest in thus exploiting love for the benefit of an inner feeling of happiness' (ibid., p. 102).

In chapter IV Freud discusses the question, 'to what influences the development of civilization owes its origin, how it arose, and by what its course has been determined' (ibid., p. 98). Here he takes up our topic again and tells us that love is 'one of the foundations of civilization,' the other being the necessity for work:

> ... the power of love ... made the man unwilling to be deprived of his sexual object – the woman – and made the woman unwilling to be deprived of the part of herself which had been separated from her – her child. Eros and Ananke [Love and Necessity] have become the parents of human civilization too. (Ibid., p. 101)

Love in its uninhibited form, sexual love, leads to the formation of the family; aim-inhibited love, parental and sibling, strengthens familial bonds; and the aim-inhibited love of friendship creates even wider bonds since it escapes some of the limitations of sexual love such as exclusiveness. In all these forms love 'continues to carry on its function of binding together considerable numbers of people, and it does so in a more intensive fashion than can be affected through the interest of work in common' (ibid., p. 102). And later Freud goes even further: 'civilization is a process in the service of Eros, whose purpose is to combine single human individuals, and after that families, then races, peoples and nations, into one great unity, the unity of mankind' (ibid., p. 122).

In view of all this one might well suppose that eros and civilization are natural allies in the pursuit of individual happiness. But this is not so. Love and civilization come into many conflicts, an old theme in Freud's thought, as Jones points out.[30] To begin with, the love that binds together the family excludes outsiders and makes it hard for family members to enter the outside world, whereas civilization endeavors to form larger units. There is an antithesis between civilization and sexuality in that sexual love is a relationship between two individuals in which a third is 'superfluous or disturbing' (ibid., p. 108). Moreover, women come to oppose the interests of civilization, or rather the demands it makes on men, since they take away energy and love which men would otherwise devote to women and children. On its side, civilzation imposes numerous restrictions on the erotic life of the individual, beginning with the barrier against incestuous choice of object, 'perhaps the most drastic mutilation which man's erotic life has in all time experienced'. (ibid., p. 104). To this may be added the prohibitions to auto-eroticism, pre-genital impulses, perversions, confinement to one sex and even to one mate.

Freud concludes that 'one is probably justified in assuming that its [the sexual life of civilized man] importance as a source of feeling of happiness, and therefore in the fulfilment of our aim in life, has sensibly diminished' (ibid., p. 105). He even speculates, in a long footnote, that apart from the pressures of civilization, there is 'something in the nature of the function itself which denies us full satisfaction'; and he cites a bisexual disposition,[31] ambivalence in erotic relationships;[32] and above all man's assumption of an erect posture and his depreciation of his sense of smell, which may have brought about 'organic repression' of his whole sexuality. And this too is an old theme in Freud's thought.[32]

In *Civilization and its Discontents* we see clearly Freud's conception of the role and importance of love in human life. Eros, which since *Beyond the Pleasure Principle* is seen as comprising both the sexual and self-preservative instincts, of course serves the function of reproduction and the preservation of the species. But its role and importance go far beyond this. Uninhibited sexual love leads humans into couples; the aim-inhibited love of parents and children and siblings into larger and stabler families; and the aim-inhibited love of friendships aids the formation of societies. Even the ideals of religion draw upon such aim-inhibited love. And sublimated love, which frees sexual energy for psychic and intellectual work, is responsible for some of the greatest achievements in art, science and culture. Finally, uninhibited and unsublimated sexual love gives us our most intense feelings of pleasure, and provides us with the prototype of happiness which men show by their behavior to be the aim of their lives. Due to the constitution of the human body such bliss is only periodically possible.[34] Due to the effects of evolution sexuality falls victim to organic repression and becomes inhibited, further reducing the intensity and frequency of the former bliss. And due to the demands of civilization, the original incestuous aims of the infant and the child cannot be satisfied, the development of the sexual instincts is interrupted, and substitute objects have to be found which can never give complete satisfaction. The results of all this divide themselves among normal love lives, perversions and inversions, ideals and sublimations, neuroses and even psychoses. Whether in bliss, achievement, or misery, truly love moves the world.[35]

Hitschmann calls *Civilization and its Discontents* Freud's 'deeply pessimistic book', while Jones says that about the future of society 'Freud always wrote in a vain of tempered optimism'.[36] Without necessarily disputing these judgments, we must add here that Freud recognized that some of the demands and restrictions of civilization are culture-bound and can be changed. And in his psychoanalytic practice he certainly assumed that the disorders that result from all these restrictions can be cured.

Notes

1 For a recent informed discussion and bibliography see Grundbaum, A., 'Freud's Theory', Presidential Address in APA Proceedings, Sept. 1983, and *The Foundations of Psychoanalysis, A Philosophical Critique.* Greenberg and Fischer, *The Scientific Credibility of Freud's Theories and Therapy,* found it amusing that there is a 'stereotyped conviction' that Freud's thinking is not amenable to scientific appraisal, when in fact, as they found in their massive study, the research data pertinent to Freud's theories far exceeds the data available for the personality or

developmental theories of Piaget, Witkin, Allport and Eysenck. They were unable to find any other 'systematic psychological theory that has been as frequently evaluated scientifically as have Freud's concepts' (p. 396). Unfortunately, they cite no research on Freud's ideas about love, except rather indirectly, in so far as there is considerable confirmation about Freud's Oedipal models of male development.

2 See, e.g. Hall, C.S., *A Primer of Freudian Psychology*; Hall, C.S. and Lindsay, G., *Theories of Personality*, Wiley, N.Y. 1970; and Fine, R., *Freud: A Critical Evaluation of his Theories*. In his monumental work, *The Life and Work of Sigmund Freud*, Ernest Jones indexes the subject, but there is no separate or unified treatment of the topic. The same is true of the massive and important studies by Ellenberger, H., *The Discovery of the Unconscious*, and Sulloway. Some of the main critics of Freud's views on love, such as Fromm, E., *The Art of Loving;* Maslow, A.H., 'Love in Healthy People', in *The Practice of Love*, ed. A. Montague; May, R., *Love and Will*, W.W. Norton, N.Y. 1969; and Reik, T., *Of Love and Lust*, criticize without first expounding or reconstructing Freud's theory in any significant detail. There is of course considerable post-Freudian literature on 'object-relations' and on narcissism, but this is beyond the scope of this book. Edward Hitschmann's paper 'Freud's Conception of Love' *International Journal of Psychoanalysis*, vol. 33, is a useful informal lecture that mentions several features of Freud's theory and relates some relevant anecdotes.

3 These tasks are undertaken the first time Freud approaches the subject systematically in *Contributions to the Psychology of Love* (1910, SE, vol. XI).

4 These tasks, among others, are undertaken in the paper on Narcissism, in *Group Psychology and the Analysis of the Ego*, (SE, vol. XVIII) and in *Civilization and its Discontents*, (SE, vol. XXI).

5 *Civilization and its Discontents*, 1929, SE, vol. XXI, p.102. The 'careless way' refers to using the word 'love' not only for sexual love but also for parental and sibling and filial and other kinds of affection. The 'genetic justification' is that this affection is 'aim-inhibited love', and 'Love with an inhibited aim was in fact originally fully sensual love, and it is so still in man's unconscious' ibid., pp. 101–2.

6 It is worth remembering here that the linguistic facts Freud describes have no analogue in ancient Greek, something Freud presumably was aware of since he knew Ancient Greek and had in fact translated *Oedipus Rex* in his Gymnasium days. Perhaps what he means about St. Paul is that he meant *agape* in the 'wider sense' of affection. But sexual love or eros as the Greeks understood it would not fall under this Pauline agape, at least not according to Nygren's interpretation or any other interpretation I know of. And it is difficult to escape the

impression that St. Paul would have been shocked to hear that agape is aim-inhibited sexual impulse.

7 In the next chapter we shall note also the change from the old to the new system of instincts in *Beyond the Pleasure Principle*, (SE, vol. XVIII) which is relevant to our comparisons with Plato.

8 SE, vol. XI, p. 183, and 'Being in Love and Hypnosis', SE, vol. XVIII, p. 112

9 Ibid., p. 112; Freud treats psychic impotence in several places; the case is of interest to us since it displays in bold light the disunion and non-convergence of the two currents of feeling that make up normal love.

10 'On Narcissism: An Introduction', SE, vol. XIV, p. 91.

11 *Introductory Lectures on Psycho-Analysis*, 1916–17, SE, vol. XVI, p. 442.

12 SE, vol. XII, 1915, pp. 159–71.

13 'The Tendency to Debasement in Love', SE, vol. XI, p. 186.

14 *Three Essays*, SE, vol. VII, p. 151, n. 2 added in 1920.

15 *Group Psychology*, SE, vol. XVIII, pp. 91, 113.

16 For a discussion of genetic explanations in Freud see Jerome Neu, 'Genetic Explanation in *Totem and Taboo*', *Freud: A Collection of Critical Essays*, ed. R. Wollheim.

17 'The Tendency to Debasement in Love', SE, vol. XI, p. 184.

18 Cf. also SE, vol. XII, pp. 60–61.

19 Ibid., pp. 302–306.

20 'On Narcissism', SE, vol. XIV, pp. 73–4.

21 In Appendix B of *The Ego and the Id*, Strachey traces in some detail the changes in Freud's views on primary and secondary narcissism from 1909 to 1940.

22 This perhaps could be thought of as a case of over-determination, which Freud generally allows.

23 Ibid., pp. 302–303.

24 *In Civilization and its Discontents*, Freud objects to the Biblical 'ideal demand', 'Thou shalt love thy neighbour as thyself.' His objection, however, is not to the notion of loving another as oneself, but rather to the universality of the object, since one's neighbour is supposed to be every man. SE, vol. XXI, pp. 109–10.

25 The same view of friendship is also taken later in *Civilization and its Discontents*, SE, vol. XXI, e.g. p. 109.

26 *Civilization and its Discontents*, SE, vol. XXI, p. 79: 'A satisfaction of this kind, such as the artist's joy in creating, in giving his phantasies body, or a scientist's solving problems or discovering truths, has a special quality which we shall certainly one day be able to characterize in metapsychological terms.' A metapsychological description of mental events and processes would be one that took into account the 'economic', the 'topographical' and the 'dynamic' factors. See 'The Unconscious', SE, vol. XIV, pp. 173 and 181, and *Beyond the Pleasure Principle*, SE, vol. XVII, p. 7. It is not always clear

which of these factors Freud found problematic in the case of sublimation. In the metapsychological study, *The Ego and the Id*, SE, vol. XIX, 1923, ch. iv, sublimation is discussed again, but the unclarities remain, according to Freud himself, as the opening quote of this note shows.

27 I do not know how true are Levey's claims about post-Freudian literature on sublimation, or about the hypotheses about sublimation remaining 'untested and unverified', up to 1939 when Levey's study appeared. But we note that in their massive review of empirical research testing Freud's hypotheses Greenberg and Fischer (1977) are silent on sublimation.

28 This conception of happiness, which appears to be entirely hedonistic, Freud apparently derives from his pleasure principle. Thus in the very next paragraph he says that 'what decides the purpose of life is simply the programme of the pleasure principle'. And in the next chapter he refers to 'the programme of becoming happy, which the pleasure principle imposes on us' (ibid., 83). See also Ernest Jones, ibid., vol. 3, p. 340. In *Beyond the Pleasure Principle* Freud states that principle as follows: ' ... the course taken by mental events ... is invariably set in motion by an unpleasurable tension, and ... it takes a direction such that its final outcome coincides with a lowering of that tension – that is, with an avoidance of unpleasure or the production of pleasure.' SE, vol. XVIII, p. 7. See also Strachey's note on the associated principle of constancy (ibid., p. 9, n. 2).

29 'On Narcissism: An Introduction,' SE, vol. XIV, p. 98.

30 Ibid., vol. 3, pp. 236–9. See also Strachey's introduction, SE, vol. XXI, p.60.

31 This too is an old theme in Freud. See, e.g. Jones, vol.2, p. 281.

32 'The change of *content* of an instinct into its opposite is observed in a single instance only – the transformation of *love into hate*. Since it is particularly common to find these directed simultaneously towards the same object, their co-existence furnishes the most important example of ambivalence of feelings.' 'Instincts and their Vicissitudes', SE, vol. XIV, p. 133. For the causes of this, see ibid., p. 139; and for the history of the concept in Freud, see Strachey's n. 2, Ibid., p. 131. The first extended discussion of ambivalence appears in the 'Rat Man' case, SE, vol. X, pp. 175 ff. See also the interesting discussion of ambivalence in *The Ego and the Id*, SE, vol. XIX, ch. iv; here, to avoid understanding ambivalence as 'a direct transformation of love into hate', which would contradict the qualitative distinction between Eros and the death instinct, Freud postulates 'a displaceable energy, which, neutral in itself, can be added to a qualitatively differentiated erotic or destructive impulse'.

33 See *Civilization and its Discontents*, SE, vol. XXI, Strachey's introduction, pp. 60–1, Freud's n. 1 on p. 99 and also his note 3 on pp. 105–7.

34 Ibid., pp. 76–77. 'When any situation that is desired by the pleasure principle is prolonged, it only produces a feeling of mild contentment. We are so made that we can derive intense enjoyment only from a contrast ... '.

35 Freud actually quotes a similar phrase from Schiller, 'hunger and love are what moves the world'. *Civilization and its Discontents*, SE, vol. XXI, p. 117.

36 Hitschmann, ibid., p. 427; Jones, ibid., vol. 3, p. 348, quotes several passages from *Civilization and its Discontents*, noting that the last sentence of the book, added later, is not as hopeful.

7

The Two Theories of Love Compared

The love of beauty seems a perfect example of an impulse inhibited in its aim.

Freud

Introduction

We now have the two theories of love before us, hopefully reconstructed with a sufficient degree of clarity, fidelity and completeness, to make comparisons interesting and fruitful. In making such comparisons we cannot proceed mechanically but must remain sensitive to two fundamental points. One is the tremendous historical distance that separates Plato and Freud. Between the fourth century BC and our twentieth century, great and complex changes of course took place in the western culture. To mention only a few of the most relevant: we have the emergence of the Judeo-Christian tradition with its central theme of agape; the various syntheses between eros and agape from Augustine to Aquinas; the traditions of courtly and romantic love in art and literature; and perhaps above all, the emergence of modern science, especially medicine and biology, the sciences in which Freud was trained and educated. These developments are beyond the scope of this book, but this of course is not to say that they make no difference to our comparison and we must remain sensitive to them.

The second point, perhaps partly a consequence of the first, is that our two theories may not be exactly comparable: they may not deal with exactly the same range of phenomena or answer the very same set of questions. Our own set of questions in the first chapter may be useful in indicating roughly the scope and aims of a theory of love, but Plato and Freud did not raise or equally emphasize all these questions. Moreover, both writers had many other theories besides their theories of love, from which they drew support – what we might call for our purposes 'background theories'; and these of course were very different. For all these reasons, we cannot proceed simply to determine whether Plato and Freud said the same or different things about love, but must remain sensitive to differences in historical times and in wider concerns and outlook.

As we remarked in the first chapter, Freud himself makes some comparisons between his theory of love and Plato's eros. Our first task is to discuss these comparisons. But we shall also compare the two theories independently of Freud's remarks. Along the way we shall take note of some passages, especially from the *Republic*, which have been hailed as remarkable anticipations of Freud. And finally, we shall discuss some general differences between Plato and Freud, which hopefully make the differences in their conceptions of love understandable.

Freud's Own Comparisons to Plato

In the fourth edition of the *Three Essays* (1920) Freud notes that 'the purely psychological theses and findings of psycho-analysis on the unconscious, repression, conflict as a cause of illness, the advantage accruing from illness, the mechanisms of the formation of symptoms, etc., have come to enjoy increasing recognition ... '. But, he continues, another part of psychoanalytic theory, 'its insistence on the importance of sexuality in all human achievements and the attempt that it makes at enlarging the concept of sexuality', have not gained general acceptance. He calls the charge of 'pan-sexualism', the idea that psychoanalysis explains everything by sex, 'senseless'. And he is correct: whether in his earlier theory of instincts, where the sexual are contrasted to the self-preservative instincts, or the later theory in which Eros is contrasted to the death instinct, Freud always postulated at least two basic or irreducible instincts. He never explained everything by sex.[1] And he ends the preface by saying:

> And as for the 'stretching' of the concept of sexuality which has been necessitated by the analysis of children and what are called perverts, anyone who looks down with contempt upon psychoanalysis from a superior vantage-point should remember how closely the enlarged sexuality of psychoanalysis coincides with the Eros of the divine Plato. (SE, vol. VII, p. 134)

A year later in a similar context he makes a broader and more exact claim of comparison with Plato. Here he is defending what I called in the last chapter Freud's central claim about love: that the nucleus of love is sexual love with sexual union as its aim, but that self-love, love for parents and children, friendship, the love of humanity, and devotion to concrete objects and abstract entities, are not to be separated from sexual love because all these tendencies are an expression of the same instinctual impulses, the sexual instincts (*Group Psychology and the Analysis of the Ego*, 1921 SE vol. XVIII, p. 90–91). Noting that this view of psychoanalysis 'has let loose a storm of indignation', he proceeds to claim that 'in its origin, function, and relation to sexual love, the "Eros" of the philosopher Plato coincides exactly with the love-force, the libido of psychoanalysis, as has been shown in detail by Nachmanshon (1915) and Pfister (1921)' (ibid., p. 91).

In these passages Freud claims that his view is similar to Plato's with respect to (1) his expanded concept of sexuality; (2) the function of Eros; and (3) the origin of Eros.

These are certainly important claims. They concern important questions about love. And though there is no guarantee that these views about love are true if our two writers agree on them, such agreement would still be impressive, because they reached their views on love in very different cultures and times and on the basis of different data and assumptions.

Are Freud's comparative claims then true? This turns out to be a complex and difficult question.

In the next two sections we shall discuss comparisons (2) and (3); and later we shall take up that part of (1) which deals with sublimation. But before we proceed further we need to discuss a number of preliminary points.

Freud makes other references to Plato, and we have plenty of evidence that he read Plato's *Symposium* and was particularly interested in the myth Plato put in the mouth of Aristophanes.[2] And we shall return to these other references. But in the passages we quoted above Freud was clearly relying on the articles by Nachmansohn and Pfister. The first question that arises is whether the three claims of comparison Freud makes were indeed 'shown in detail' by these writers. To this more modest question we can give a negative answer. It is no hyperbole to say that Freud did himself no favour by relying on these papers.[3]

After discussing Freud's reasons for expanding the concept of sexuality and some disputes with Jung, Nachmansohn gives 'a description of the Platonic doctrine of Eros' and claims that it 'exhibits a striking resemblance to the psychoanalytic theory of libido'. One problem is that many of his descriptions of Plato's view are grossly inaccurate or without foundation. It would be tedious to go into all of them, but the following quotes should suffice:

> Plato knows no love aside from this love [Sensual Eros, Spiritual Eros, Philosophical Eros, Mystical Eros]. Eros and love, be it the love of parents for their children *and vice versa,* be it the love of a man for a woman, be it the love of art and science, be it the love for god, are identical. Only the object changes, not the love.
> ... all the expansions which Freud, to the disgust of so many academics, had made upon the customary interpretation of the libido are to be found already existing in the founder of the academy. Plato, just like Freud, sees the essence of love in the instinct for the preservation of the species and the psychic functions which are connected with it. The Greek thinker also *extends the Eros to the children,* and sees in the parental love of children and *vice versa* the same Eros which holds sway between two mature people of different sex. (Nachmansohn, tr. Craig Decker, p. 82, my italics)[4]

Nachmasohn takes no note whatsoever of the distinction between generic and specific eros, none of the distinction between eros and philia; and he even attibutes to Plato the notion of infantile sexuality! For this remarkable view he produces not one scrap of evidence. Apart from problems of accuracy, Nachmansohn makes no explicit comparisons with respect to function and origin. There is indeed a grain of truth in his comparisons about the expansion of the concepts of love and eros: in both Plato and Freud eros and love have both sexual and non-sexual manifestations; though even here Nachmansohn simply *assumes* that the non-sexual manifestations of Platonic Eros in the ladder of love are sublimations, whereas this is controversial and has to be argued, as we shall see later in this chapter.[5]

In 'The Resistances to Psychoanalysis', where again Freud is defending his expansion of libido, he states more cautiously and accurately the grain of truth that there certainly exists in this comparison:

> Moreover, what psychoanalysis called sexuality was by no means identical with the impulsion towards a union of the two sexes or towards producing a pleasurable sensation in the genitals; it had far more resemblance to the all-inclusive and all-preserving Eros of Plato's *Symposium.* (1925, SE vol. XIX, p. 218. In a similar vein, see 1930, SE vol. XXI, p. 210)

It is certainly true that Platonic Eros (even the *specific* eros of the *Symposium* and the *Phaedrus*) is wider than an impulse towards sexual union or genital pleasure, and in that respect it is indeed similar to Freud's love and libido. But whether it is as wide as

Freud's, and whether its non-sexual manifestations are sublimations, or aim-inhibited sexuality (Freud's 'affection'), that is extremely controversial. Nachmansohn and Pfister are of no help here.

Despite the failure of these two writers to support Freud's comparative claims, these claims may of course still be true. And we must now turn to this issue, remembering that our comparisons are rather complex. Part of the complexity is that in the case of Plato we must keep in mind the distinctions between eros and philia, between generic and specific eros, and the important differences (especially with respect to the role of pleasure) between the *Symposium* and the *Phaedrus*. In the case of Freud we must remember the differences between the anaclitic and the narcissistic concepts of love, and the still different concept of Eros (after 1919) which comprises both the sexual and the self-preservative instincts. To complicate matters still more, sometimes Freud makes comparisons to Aristophanes' speech rather than to what is usually taken as Plato's view (the speech of Socrates). All this makes our task harder, but unless we keep these distinctions in mind we run the risk of much confusion.

The Function of Love in Plato and Freud

Function is an important concept in the systems of Plato and Freud, and both use the concept to clarify the nature of love.[6] It may sound strange to speak of the function of love, but we can understand the concept here in terms of the distinction between object and aim, which both writers make: the function is given by the aim. Moreover, it will be recalled, Plato distinguished mental powers or faculties by aim and object, while Freud distinguished instincts by aim and somatic source. So for both writers the aim or function of love tells us something about the very nature of love. If the function or aim of love in the two theories is the same, this is a significant agreement.

Now there seems little hope of discovering any significant coincidence in function or aim between Plato's *generic* eros and Freud's anaclitic or narcissistic love. Generically, Platonic eros is for the good to be one's own forever: the aim is the everlasting possession of the good. We find nothing like this in Freud, and if we look we can find evidence of disagreement.[7]

It will be recalled that the immediate aim of the libido or sexual instinct in Freud is pleasure or satisfaction; while there are several intermediate aims such as looking and touching, and of course sexual union, which brings the most intense pleasures, and also serves the function of reproduction and the preservation of the species. This seems to be the view until *Beyond the Pleasure Principle*. Now if we compare this view with Plato's concept of *specific* eros in the *Symposium*, we see some crucial differences and one significant similarity. In specific eros, it will be recalled, the object is the beautiful (rather than the good), the ultimate aim is the immortality of the lover, and the intermediate aim, by which immortality is to be achieved, is biological or spiritual creation. Here the two theories diverge radically on the immediate or final aim of love: there is no role assigned to pleasure in Plato's theory in the *Symposium*. In the *Phaedrus* sexual gratification is indeed the aim of the lovers in Socrates' first speech, the lovers who have human madness. But this is the lowest kind of love for Plato. Sexual gratification is not the aim of the divine lovers. The pleasures they enjoy, in contemplating divine Beauty and its earthly shadows, seem to be aesthetic rather than sexual. And though Plato does not tell us explicitly what the aim of this lover is, it seems to be to keep the embodied soul free of sexuality so that when it leaves the body it can soar to the world of Forms and be like the divine soul. So the ultimate aim of Plato's specific eros seems totally different from the immediate aim of Freud's libido.

But don't we have a coincidence in *intermediate* aims? And isn't this the important comparison? Of course Freud does assign sexual union and reproduction as intermediate aims of the sexual instinct; and in Plato's specific eros the desire to create offspring does sometimes take the form of biological procreation through sexual union. Even here there are important differences: in Freud sexual love is 'the nucleus' of love, and sexual union is its normal aim; whereas for Plato sexual love with sexual union as its aim is the lowest kind of love, and achieves the lowest kind of immortality (the ultimate aim of love). But in any case, this agreement in aim or function between the two theories is too weak to support the comparative claim Freud makes. One would suppose that all theories of love, which include sexual love as a special case, would assign sexual union and/or reproduction as functions of such love. There may be disagreement whether sexual union or reproduction are *the* aims or the *normal* aims or the *highest* aims of sexual love; but that they are aims of some sort is hardly ever in dispute.

So the two theories touch hands on the functions of sexual union and reproduction. But when we remember their radical differences in ultimate aims, they so far appear to be quite distinct. Platonic eros, sparked by the perception of beauty, is an urge to create for the sake of personal immortality. Compelled by periodic accumulation of sexual products, Freudian libido is the urge to discharge them to obtain relief and pleasure. Both are allowed to serve the crucial function of biological reproduction, but after that the two theories part company.

But how, then, could Freud think that the libido of psychoanalysis and the eros of Plato coincide exactly in function? One possibility is that he was simply misled by Nachmansohn and Pfister, the only authorities he cites for his claim, both of whom present faulty accounts of Plato's view.

A second possibility is that the comparison Freud had in mind was not between his pre-1919 theories of love and libido and Plato's view, but rather between his new concept of Eros – under his new classification of instincts beginning with *Beyond the Pleasure Principle* – and Plato's view as presented by Nachmansohn. This at once presents the difficulty that for this comparison itself Freud could not possibly cite Nachmansohn for support, since the latter's paper was published in 1915 – four years before Freud published his new classification of the instincts. Perhaps he was relying on Nachmansohn just for Plato's view. In any case, this possibility has some plausibility. For one thing, the comparisons we are examining were made by Freud in 1920 and 1921, after he had already made his new classification of instincts. Moreover, two paragraphs after the comparison with Plato, where Freud returns to his main task in *Group Psychology* he says:

> Our hypothesis finds support in the first instance from two passing thoughts. First, that a group is clearly held together by a pwoer of some kind: and to what power could this feat be better described than to Eros, which holds together everything in the world? (SE vol XVIII, p. 92)

In a footnote appended to this question Strachey refers us to *Beyond the Pleasure Principle* (SE vol. XVIII, p. 50)

In this work Freud is taking a biological rather than a purely psychological perspective: he is reviewing phylogenetic evolution of the sexual instincts in species rather than ontogenetic developments of the instincts in the individual. In this context he sees a far closer connection between the sexual instincts and reproduction and the preservation of the species; whereas in the earlier ontogenetic discussions the sexual instincts were seen as being originally independent of reproduction. Moreover, the introduction of narcissim earlier threatened the older dualism between the sexual and the self-preservative (or ego) instincts: in object-libido the individual gives himself up in favour of the object, in ego-libido the individual exhausts himself; the instincts of self-preservation now appear to be also libidinal (SE vol. XVIII, p. 257). In this phylogenetic context and in response to this threat, Freud proposes a reclassification of instincts: the sexual and self-preservative instincts are brought together as 'the life instincts' and given the Greek name 'Eros', and a new basic instinct is postulated, the death or self-destructive instinct.[8] In a long footnote to ch. VI Freud himself brings biology and narcissism together:

> With the hypothesis of narcissistic libido and the extension of the concept of libido to the individual cells, the sexual instincts were transformed for us into Eros, which seeks to force together and hold together the portions of living substance. (SE vol. XVIII, p. 60–1)

To force together and hold together, to unite and preserve living things, these are the functions now assigned to Eros, in a phylogenetic framework.[9] Since Nachmansohn claims several times that for Plato eros is identical with the sexual drive for procreation, which is achieved through union, it would be understandable for Freud to suppose that in his own new classification of the instincts the function of his Eros is identical to that of the eros of Plato, to unite and preserve.

There is, however, a third possibility that may well be the correct explanation for Freud's comparative claims: the comparison Freud had in mind was between his new view of Eros and the view of eros put forward by Aristophanes in Plato's *Symposium*. On the face of it, this suggestion appears preposterous, since it would seem to involve some gross confusion about what 'Plato's view' is. Plato's view is usually assumed to be the view presented and endorsed by Socrates – that seems the usual working assumption concerning at least the middle and early dialogues. So in the *Symposium* Plato's view is usually taken to be that presented and endorsed by Socrates (and Diotima in this case). Further, Socrates' view of eros is certainly different from that expressed by Aristophanes in the same dialogue: the definitions of eros are different, and Diotima criticizes the view of Aristophanes. So they cannot both be 'Plato's view'. Nevertheless, in *Beyond the Pleasure Principle* Freud makes the comparison with Aristophanes explicitly; and we have a rather curious history in the references to Aristophanes' speech.

Besides the new classification of the instincts into Eros and the death instinct, the other novel element in *Beyond the Pleasure Principle* was Freud's notion that the instincts are essentially 'conservative': they exhibit a tendency to repetition (to which Freud gave the name 'repetition compulsion') and they aim at restoring an earlier state of affairs – two ideas that Freud apparently equated.[10] It is in the context of this new notion that Freud makes the comparison with the Aristophanes myth. He surveys the findings of biology for positive evidence of a death instinct or for the instincts being conservative but finds none. At this point, as Jones remarks in *Sigmund Freud*, 'he has recourse to the classical studies of his youth in support of his present conception of Eros' (vol. 3, p. 275).

> In quite a different region [than science], it is true, we do meet with such a hypothesis; but it is so fantastic in kind – a myth rather than a scientific explanation – that I should not venture to produce it here, were it not that it fulfils precisely the one condition whose fulfilment we desire. For it traces the origin of an instinct to *a need to restore an earlier state of things.*
>
> What I have in mind is, of course, the theory which Plato put in the mouth of Aristophanes in the *Symposium*, and which deals not only with the origin of the sexual instinct but also with the most important of its variations in relation to its object .... After the division [of the original pairs by Zeus] had been made, 'the two parts of man, each desiring his other half, came together, and threw their arms about one another eager to grow into one'. (SE vol. XVIII, pp. 57–58; Freud's italics)

In Aristophanes' speech Eros is 'conservative' in the sense Freud's view requires: as Jones puts it, 'the longing for union between them [the separated halves] was really a longing for reunion', that is, a longing for an earlier state. Given Freud's new view of the instincts, according to which 'the fundamental aim of all instincts is to revert to an earlier state, a regression',[11] the aim of Freud's Eros coincides with the aim of Aristophanes' eros. Moreover, it will be recalled, in the male–female case Aristophanic eros is said to serve reproduction and the preservation of the species, while in the other two cases it gives relief and pleasure; so union, preservation, and pleasure are aims of Aristophanic eros. And since to unite and preserve are the aims of Eros in *Beyond the Pleasure Principle,* while pleasure is still retained as an aim of Eros under the program of the pleasure principle, we can see that there is indeed a remarkable coincidence of functions in the two theories.

When we notice also that the framework of Aristophanes' myth is phylogenetic, the dominant framework of *Beyond the Pleasure Principle*, we can appreciate indeed how congenial Aristophanes' myth was to Freud's new views.

But did Freud think that the myth of Aristophanes represented Plato's view? The answer is unclear. In a footnote to the passage we quoted above Freud mentions some speculations about the myth being of oriental origin, and then adds:

> For Plato would not have *adopted* a story of this kind which had somehow reached him through some oriental tradition – to say nothing of giving it so important a place – unless it had struck him as containing *an element of truth*. (SE, vol. XVIII, p. 58, n. 1, my italics)

This suggests that Freud thought that Aristophanes' story did represent Plato's view; or perhaps more plausibly that Plato accepted from it 'an element of truth', namely that eros is desire to return to a previous state.[12] For the *Symposium* this can hardly be correct, if we suppose that the speech of Socrates represents Plato's view. In that speech there is nothing about eros being 'conservative': longing for an earlier state is not included as part of the aim of eros. On the contrary, it would seem that Platonic eros, both generic and specific, is forward-looking or future orientated: it is desire to have good things in the future or to continue to have them, or desire to create offspring and become immortal. It is in Plato's view (represented by the second speech of Socrates) in the *Phaedrus* that we might find a suggestion that eros is 'conservative': at least here we have reference to earlier states of disembodied souls and the theory of recollection. And it is the lover's previous acquaintance and love of the Form Beauty that explains his falling in love with one of its earthly shadows, a beautiful youth; so we have here what looks like a genetic explanation. But even if we were to suppose that what the 'god-maddened' lovers of the *Phaedrus* wanted was to get back to an earlier state of disembodied existence where they could contemplate the Form Beauty, this certainly is different from any earlier state Freud had in mind.

The Origin of Love in Plato and Freud

The question of the origin of love is crucial in Freud's theory. We noted earlier his preference for genetic explanations of choice of object and overestimation.[13] And we may note now that his main thesis about love is that all love is sexual in origin (SE vol. XVII, p. 91). All love – romantic love, self-love, love of parents and children, friendship and love of humanity, devotion to concrete objects and abstract ideas – is sexual in origin; though this origin may be disguised because of the psychic mechanisms of object displacement, aim-inhibition, and sublimation. Romantic love happens between man and woman when there is a confluence of sensuous feelings and feelings of affection on the same object. The sensuous feelings are obviously sexual, while the feelings of affection are aim-inhibited older sensuous feelings for the parent or parent substitute, now redirected to a new person. Thus both feelings that constitute normal romantic love are either sexual or sexual in origin. Self-love is a libidinal attachment to the ego, actual, past, or ideal, a case of ego-libido rather than object-libido. The love of parents and children is also aim-inhibited sexuality, where the aim of sexual union has been inhibited by the incest barrier and the feelings have turned into affection, or narcissistic love. Friendship is also aim-inhibited sexual love. And devotion to concrete objects and abstract ideas are cases of sublimation, where the aim of sexual union has been deflected, and the sexual energy is redirected toward more 'sublime' or more socially valued aims, such as the creation of works of art and science.

The question of the origin of love is crucial in Freud's theory for another reason: it bears directly on the expansion of the concept of sexuality, an expansion for which Freud claims support from Plato, as we saw. As Freud said, the 'stretching' of the concept of sexuality was 'necessitated by the analysis of children and what are called perverts' (SE, vol. VII, p. 134). As we saw in chapter 5, in his analysis of the perversions (deviations with respect to aim) Freud investigated the somatic sources of the perversions and found them in several erogenous zones besides the genitals; these were origins of sexuality physiologically or anatomically, and accordingly 'sexual' was expanded beyond the 'genital'. And in his analysis of children he found several manifestations of the sexual instinct in infants and children; so developmentally the origins of sexuality were found in infancy and childhood attachments to the parents; and accordingly 'sexuality' was expanded to cover periods earlier than puberty and adulthood. (Freud was also interested in the phylogenetic origins of sexuality but could not find enough scientific results in biology at the time to satisfy his curiosity – see SE 1919, vol. XVIII, p. 57.) In sum, the expansion of the concept of sexuality was the direct result of investigations of the somatic and ontogenetic origins of the sexual instinct.

Comparisons in origin are more difficult than the comparisons in function or aim that we made earlier. Here we seem to come up against general and fundamental differences between Plato and Freud. For one thing, Plato worked mostly with formal and teleological models and explanations, rather than with genetic ones. He did not know the theory of evolution, which directed investigators such as Freud away from final causes; and though Plato was interested in questions of origin, he would not be inclined to suppose, I believe, that the origin of something tells us what it really is. We can see this difference reflected in the different principles of individuation they had for what is sexual. For Freud an instinct or impulse is sexual if its *sources* and/or aims are sexual; a change in the object does not imply a change in the nature of the desire. This directs him to investigate the somatic sources of sexuality, and eventually he finds its essence in the excitations of the erogenous zones. But in Plato it is not even clear that the body is the source of sexuality; in the *Phaedrus*, as we saw, discarnate souls are tripartite and so presumably they have sexual appetites.[14] For Plato a desire or impulse is sexual if its object and aim are sexual. So, for the nature of sexuality, he looks to what it attaches itself to and what it wants, not to its antecedent somatic condition.

A second and more decisive difference lies in Freud's theory of infantile sexuality. Plato of course had no such theory, even according to Freud himself who wrote that no previous author had recognized the regular existence of sexual impulses in infants and children! When Freud speaks of the sexual origin of all love he is referring to its origin in infantile and childhood sexual impulses. But when Plato discusses eros and philia his subjects are always people at puberty and beyond; he seems to have no inkling of and no interest in earlier sexuality. When he uses genetic or historical accounts to explain Eros, in the *Phaedrus*, the reference is not to infancy and childhood, but to a previous existence of souls, and disembodied souls at that!

A third difference relating to origin, as least as fundamental as the others, is that Plato did not have Freud's theory of repression and the unconscious or anything remotely resembling it.[15] It follows, and I think it is certainly true, that Plato had no notion of 'repressed sexuality' or 'aim-inhibited love': that is, of something (such as familial love or friendship) which appears non-sexual in consciousness but is sexual in origin (i.e. was sexual in the infant or the child), and is still sexual in the unconscious. As Freud says when speaking of familial love : 'love with an inhibited aim was in fact originally fully sensual love, and it is still so in man's unconscious' (SE 1930, vol. XXI, pp. 102–3).

In view of the fact that Plato had no theories of infantile sexuality and of repression and the unconscious – two of the most original and fundamental doctrines of psychoanalysis – it would indeed be truly amazing if the eros of Plato and the love of psychoanalysis coincided in origin! And though Plato did expand the Greek concept of eros and Freud did expand our concept of sexuality, it would be equally amazing if these two expansions coincided!

Let us compare the two authors on the origin of friendship, familial love, self-love, and (in the next section) sublimation.

I know of no evidence whatsoever that Plato thought that friendship is always sexual in origin. We are not of course dealing here with the uncontroversial proposition that sometimes sexual relationships can turn into friendships with the sexual component dropping out, or the proposition that lovers can also be friends, but with Freud's controversial view that friendship is aim-inhibited sexuality or a derivative of the sexual instinct. In the *Lysis* friendship is analyzed without any reference to eros or to sexual desire: the preferred analysis is that a person who is neither good nor bad is friend to a good person or object out of desire for the benefits such a good can confer upon him. In the *Republic* friendship receives a different analysis: roughly speaking, two people can be friends only if they share the same evaluational attitudes and beliefs toward the same things; they think the same things good or bad, they love and hate the same things, they take pleasures and pains in the same things. Again, there is no reference whatsoever here to eros or sexual desire. In the *Symposium* itself Plato tells us that lovers who create spiritual offspring will have a 'surer friendship' (philia) than those who create children, since spiritual offspring are more beautiful and more immortal. This implies that eros can bring and perhaps normally does bring friendship; and presumably soul-eros brings a surer friendship than body-eros because its offspring, being more beautiful and more immortal, create a more abiding and permanent common interest in it. But there is no implication that all friendship has its origin in sexual impulses. Here we can see how different Plato's and Freud's views of friendship are by noting the different accounts they give of its constancy and abiding nature. For Plato this varies with the constancy of the object the friends share and the constancy of their beliefs (or knowledge) about it. Those who are friends, for example, because they share knowledge of the Good, would be the most constant and abiding of friends: for the

Good is eternal and knowledge of it the most comprehensive and constant of all knowledge. But for Freud the constancy of friendship, in contrast to the instability of sexual love, is accounted for by the fact that it is aim-inhibited sexuality: being aim-inhibited it is not capable of complete satisfaction, which brings with it loss of energy and reduction in the strength of the instinct. (See e.g., SE, vol. XVIII, pp. 111, 139 and 258.)

The story is similar with another case of *philia*, familial love. In the case of *parental* love, Plato implies in the *Symposium* that parents love and care for their children because of their own desire for personal immortality, the final aim of eros proper. Here parental love is given a teleological explanation in terms of the ultimate aim of personal immortality, not a genetic explanation that traces such love to infantile, narcissistic libido.

But what of *filial* love, the love of children for their parents? For Freud, it will be recalled, this consists of older incestuous impulses which have been inhibited in their aim and have turned into feelings of affection. Now there is indeed a remarkable passage in the *Republic* (pp. 571–2) in which Plato acknowledges incestuous desires for the mother and cites dreams as evidence! This has been hailed as an anticipation of Freud's theory of dreams and the Oedipus complex.[16] Plato says that all of us, even those who appear most moderate, have wild and lawless appetites, something revealed in our dreams, when the rational part of the soul is asleep, and the beastly and wild part will not refrain from anything, not even from 'attempting to lie with a mother in fancy, or with anyone else, man, god or brute'. Perhaps Plato thinks that these desires we are not aware of, or at least, would not acknowledge, though he does not say so. In the *Interpretation of Dreams* Freud refers to Plato twice, both times approvingly attributing to him the view that the virtuous man dreams what the wicked man does, and Strachey says that Freud is referring to this passage in the *Republic* (SE, vol. IV, p. 99, and vol. V, p. 658). But in the opening chapter of this work, where he reviews previous theories of dreams, including ancient ones, Freud does not even mention Plato (either in the first edition or in any of the later ones where he added many scholarly notes). As for incestuous dreams, such dreams had of course been mentioned earlier by Sophocles in *Oedipus Rex* (ll. 982 ff), a work and a passage that Freud knew quite well and discussed in some detail in the *Interpretation of Dreams* (SE, vol. IV, pp. 294–8). The *Republic* passage certainly shows that Plato was aware of incestuous desires and of the importance of dreams in revealing the irrational part of our souls – and these are propositions that Freud would certainly accept. The crucial question here, though, is whether we have any evidence that Plato thought that the incestuous desires of our dreams go back to infantile incestuous impulses, and that the love we as adults have for our fathers or mothers derives from these infantile incestuous impulses, now disguised because of repression or aim-inhibition. I know of no passage where Plato connects the incestuous desires of our dreams with infantile incestuous impulses, or either of these with the affection adults have for their fathers and mothers. Since he had no theories of infantile sexuality or of repression and the unconscious, it would be extraordinary if he had made such connections.

Turning to self-love, we might bring in another famous comparison between Plato and Freud, their tripartite division of the soul and the personality: Reason, the Appetitive element, and Spirit, which we have already mentioned in our discussion of the *Republic* and the *Phaedrus*; and the Ego, the Id, and the Super Ego in Freud's *The Ego and the Id*. Freud himself never refers to Plato when he proposes his so-called structural model of the mind: he only says that of the distinction between the ego, 'which represents what may be called reason and common sense', and the id, 'which contains the passions', that 'All this falls in line with popular distinctions we are all familiar with' (SE XIX, 1923, ch. II). But the striking similarities between the two divisions have not passed unnoticed.[17] Not only are both divisions tripartite, but the corresponding agencies have many similarities. For example, the Id is the source of impulses and wishes, it is wild and irrational, and it is governed by the pleasure principle. Similarly, the Appetitive element in Plato is irrational, it aims at the pleasures of food, drink and sex, and it is wild and lawless, containing even incestuous desires. The Ego deals with the external world and looks after the self-preservation and the interests of the individual; similarly Reason in Plato deliberates and makes decisions for what it judges to be the good of the whole person. And in sleep, as we have seen, both Reason and the Ego are asleep, and the lawless demands of the Id and Appetite break through and run wild in dreams.

It is also striking that both thinkers use the tripartite divisions to illuminate inner psychic conflict and its consequences, though Freud's interests here are more empirical and medical, Plato's more normative. Psychic harmony is a necessary condition of mental health in Freud, and psychic conflict results in several kinds of neurotic disturbances.[18] Psychic harmony is part of complete virtue in Plato (the virtue of temperance), and psychic conflicts characterize various types of vice; and since Plato thinks of justice and virtue as analogous to the health of the body, he even comes close to thinking of vices as types of mental illness.

At the same time, there are several fundamental differences between these two models of the mind, which make the striking similarities somewhat superficial. To begin with, Freud's distinction between the conscious and the unconscious cuts across the tripartite structural division: the Id is 'unknown and unconscious', and parts of the Ego and the Super-Ego are also unconscious. There is nothing like this in Plato, except possibly in the suggestion that the individual may not be aware of some of his wildest desires, such as incestuous wishes, except in dreams. Second, Freud's model is developmental or genetic, as well as structural and functional: only the Id could be called innate; the Ego is formed out of the Id by the aid of perception of the external world and by identifications, and the Super-Ego is a purely cultural product, 'the heir of the Oedipus complex' (ibid., ch. III). Plato, on the other hand, seems to think that Reason, the Appetitive element, and Spirit are innate, essential elements of the soul, though Reason needs development and the appetites taming. (Thus, for example, when tries to distinguish Reason from Spirit in *Republic* 441b, he tells us that 'one can see in children, that they are from the very birth chock full of rage and high spirit ...'.) Finally, Freud does not have Plato's extreme dualism of body and soul: For Plato, Reason, Spirit, and Appetite are elements of the soul; though they may have physical counterparts, as he tells us in *Timaeus*, pp. 66–72, the disembodied souls of the *Phaedrus* seem to have all three elements. But for Freud the mental or the psychical is inseparable from the physical and the somatic: it is a fundamental assumption of psychoanalysis that 'mental life is the function of an apparatus to which we ascribe the characteristics of being extended in space and of being made up of several portions' (SE vol. XXIII, 1938, p. 145; see also p. 158 for the second fundamental hypothesis of psychoanalysis: 'It explains the supposedly somatic concomitant phenomena as being what is truly psychical.') For Freud mental life seems to be a function of the body, a view that Plato comes close to articulating in the *Phaedo* – only to reject it.

Before he distinguished between the Ego and the Id, Freud postulated, as we saw, a primary narcissism in everyone, which he called ego-libido. The infant is completely narcissistic. Libido flows out of the ego onto objects, or under certain conditions becomes displaced onto the Ego-Ideal; it can also be withdrawn again into the ego, a case of secondary narcissism or adult self-love. With the distinction between the Ego and the Id came a modification: at the very beginning, in infancy, 'all the libido is accumulated in the Id', which sends part of this libido out into erotic object cathexes. The Ego, as it grows stronger, tries to get hold of some of this libido, usually by identifying with the love objects of the Id. Thus the 'narcissism of the ego is a secondary one that has been withdrawn from objects'.[19] It would be difficult to find anything corresponding to these notions and mechanisms of self-love in Plato. The object of Platonic eros is always something other than the self, the good or the beautiful, or good or beautiful things. Moreover, the deficiency model of desire seems to rule out entirely love of one's *present, actual* self, since it arises out of the perception of some deficiency or lack in oneself, and is a desire for that which one lacks.[20] In terms of the anatomy of the self, it would be difficult to imagine Platonic Reason trying to identify with the objects of Appetite, or trying to win the love of Spirit.[21] In Aristophanes' speech we have the notion of eros as a yearning for a past state in which we were united with our other half. Perhaps this might be thought of as narcissistic love, as love for what really is, or at least *was*, one's own self. Once more we seem to find more similarities with Aristophanes' story rather than the theories put forth by Socrates.

Sublimation and the Ladder of Love

There remains to consider the case of devotion to concrete objects and abstract entities, which presumably corresponds to cases in the ladder of eros in Plato. For Freud these are cases of sublimation, and on the basis of Nachmansohn's account of Plato, Freud would presumably view the ladder of eros as a series of successive sublimations. Hence in these cases also he would claim that Freudian libido and Platonic eros coincide in origin.

This comparison is difficult to make. Plato had no word for sublimation, and he obviously did not have anything like Freud's theory of libido and the vicissitudes of its development, of which sublimation is one. Freud himself did not have a complete and entirely clear theory of sublimation, and changed his mind several times about the mechanisms of sublimation.[22] Our question is not whether Plato had Freud's concept or theory of sublimation – which he clearly did not – but whether the succession of cases of eros in the ladder, as Plato describes them in the context of his theory, can be accurately characterized as cases of Freudian sublimation.

Now there are indeed certain similarities between Plato's treatment of cases in the ladder and Freud's account of sublimation, which have probably led writers of diverse backgrounds to view Platonic love as sublimation.[23] Platonic eros in the ladder and Freudian sublimation seem to cover the same kinds of cases: artistic, scientific, and philosophical creativity. Both men think that few people are capable of such creativity. Moreover, Plato views the objects and aims of eros in the ladder as higher and more valuable than the aims and objects of sexual eros below the ladder; and Freud supposes that in cases of sublimation aims and objects are more highly regarded, are thought to be more sublime, by society and the individual, than sexual aims and objects. Further, the chief mechanism of sublimation is some sort of displacement of intermediate aims, from sexual to artistic and scientific aims. And as we go up the ladder we seem to have a series of changes of intermediate aim and object that look like displacement, from sexual reproduction to artistic and scientific creations, and from bodies to souls to constitutions and so on. Further still, Plato seems to arrange the cases in the ladder of eros into some sort of causal, developmental series that starts with sexual love just below the ladder; it looks therefore as if it is the original sexual energy that motivates and fuels the whole ascent, much like what happens in Freudian sublimation.[24] And both men seem to think that when eros is joined with artistic, scientific, or philosophic talent, it is responsible for the highest achievements of civilization.

These similarities are certainly striking. Yet it is very doubtful that Plato would have accepted the Freudian characterization of the ladder of eros as a series of successive sublimations. Though Freud's theory of sublimation is not entirely clear, certain features of it are clear, and they all point to crucial differences between his concept and Plato's. Sublimation in Freud is an unconscious process; there is nothing that corresponds to this in Plato. On the contrary, the ascent up the ladder seems to be a conscious process: as reason apprehends new beautiful objects or kinds of beauty and by comparison sees that they are greater or more beautiful, the lover becomes inspired to new and higher creativity. Moreover, it is an essential feature of Freudian sublimation that the original aim of the sexual instinct, sexual union, or the aims of components of the instinct, such as looking and touching, are blocked perhaps through 'reaction formations' ('the dams of disgust, shame, and loathing') or because of the incest barrier; the instinct then is 'deflected' to new, more socially acceptable or sublime aims. But there is nothing like this mechanism recognized by Plato. As

Moravcsik points out,[25] in the ascent reason does not block the aims of eros but rather guides the lover to new creations through the apprehension of greater beauty and greater immortality. To be sure, Plato says that the lover who has attained the higher steps will 'disdain and think little' of lower beauties, especially the beauty of the body; but this is a feeling the lover has after he has climbed higher and compared the new beauties to the old ones; it is not something earlier that blocks lower aims. The Greeks may have had some negative feelings toward sexuality, Plato perhaps more than the average Greek, but less so than in the post-Christian, Victorian culture of Freud's time; and in any case Plato makes no use of this in the ladder of eros.

We can go further. It is essential to Freudian sublimation that there is a change of aims: the original sexual aims are displaced and replaced by new non-sexual ones. But in the ascent in the ladder of eros there is no change of aims: the aims throughout are creation of offspring and personal immortality. What changes is the attracting beautiful object and the kind of offspring that is created. And partly as a result of this difference, we get another one. Freud thinks that the new, sublimated non-sexual aims will never give complete satisfaction, certainly not as complete as the original sexual aims, just as the new love object chosen at puberty will never satisfy as much as the original incestuous one it replaces. But Plato has no such notion: on the contrary, he thinks that as the lover goes up the ladder he will gain greater immortality, blessedness and happiness; for he will have a greater share of beauty and the good.

Finally, though Plato arranges various cases of eros in the ladder in some sort of developmental series, so that it looks as if it is the original sexual energy that fuels the ascent, this is somewhat illusory as a parallel to Freud. Freud produces essentially two reasons for thinking that a case of devotion to concrete objects and/or abstract ideas – a case of artistic or scientific creativity – is sublimation, that is, sexual in origin. One reason is that though in sublimation the sexual impulses are disguised, they always preserve 'enough of their original nature to keep their identity recognizable (as in such features as the longing for proximity, and self-sacrifice)' (SE, vol. XVIII, pp. 90–1). Other features such as possessiveness, jealousy and passionate attachment may also be present. And as Vlastos points out, there is a parallel to this in Plato:

> Plato was the first Western man to realize how intense and passionate may be our attachments to objects as abstract as social reform, poetry, art, the sciences and philosophy – an attachment that has more in

common with erotic fixation than one would have suspected in a pre-Freudian view of man. (Ibid., p. 27)

But this would not be sufficient reason, for Plato or Freud, to justify the belief that the energy in these cases is sexual and thus that the devotion to abstract entities is sexual in origin. Symptoms alone do not prove that sexuality has a monopoly on passion.

Now Freud has a second and far more important reason for believing this: he is able to give genetic accounts, more or less successful perhaps, of the origins of such devotion. He is able, through dreams, memories, and associations to trace such devotion to sexual instincts in childhood and infancy. But Plato has no such genetic accounts, no knowledge of infantile sexuality, and shows no inclination to work in that direction. The ladder of love is not developmental or genetic in a Freudian sense: it does not begin with infantile sexuality and go on to describe actual stages and patterns of psychosexual development; it begins with adult love and prescribes the most desirable progression, that is, a movement towards the best kind of love according to Plato's ethics. The primitive model for the structure of Platonic eros proper may indeed have been the case of heterosexual love, where an attractive object arouses the sexual drive for union, where we have procreation and immortality by replacement. But even in this case we have no reason to think that Plato supposed that all the energy is sexual. We must remember that eros proper is a species of generic eros, and that the drive for immortality is derived from the latter, and is probably conceived as a perfectionist or self-preservative drive. When we go to higher cases of eros we retain the structural similarity. But Plato, lacking genetic accounts, would have no reason to believe that in the higher cases the desire for immortality or the desire to create is sexual. For him a desire is sexual only if it has a sexual object and/or a sexual aim. The aims are not sexual, and at the highest step the Form Beauty is as non-sexual an object as one could possibly construct. Far from sexualizing all love, it looks as though, in making eros proper a species of generic eros, he was trying to desexualize even sexual love. The Platonic lover is not driven by sexual desire, but pulled, attracted by immortality, beauty and the good.

Choice and Overestimation

We have seen that an important question for any theory of love is how the lover selects his beloved. Plato did not raise this question explicitly, but there is some evidence that he paid some attention to it. Freud on the other hand investigated love choices systematically, and his new theories of psychosexual development together with clinical data seem to have enabled him to break new ground.

In the *Symposium* Plato has Aristophanes explain homosexual and heterosexual selection by reference to Aristophanes' hypothesis of the development of the human species – a phylogenetic explanation. But this is not of course Plato's own view. In his own theory the hypothesis that guides selection seems to be that the lover is attracted by what he thinks or perceives is beautiful or good. In the ladder of love the initial selection is based on the perception of one particular beautiful body; beauty of body becomes an object of love when the lover reflects that one beautiful body is akin to another; beauty of soul when the lover sees that this is a greater or more valuable beauty. Subsequent selections are made on a similar basis, until the lover contemplates the Form Beauty and realizes that this is the most beautiful and immortal object possible. Below the ladder, in the case of animals and humans, heterosexual selection is perhaps partly explained by the desire to create biological offspring. So far as I can see this is all we can extract about selection from Plato's theory in the *Symposium*.

In the *Phaedrus* (252–3), in Socrates' second speech, Plato tells us that some people are followers of gods, each imitating and honoring a particular god. Such people choose as beloveds, among the ranks of the beautiful, those who are like the gods they follow. Here the gods seem to be symbols of personal ideals: the followers of Zeus seek someone of a philosophical and lordly nature, those of Hera seek those of a kingly nature, and so on. Thus lovers select among the ranks of the beautiful those who exemplify the personal ideals the lovers were already attached to in a previous disembodied existence. Here we have a genetic or historical explanation or selection. But the past being appealed to is not the lover's infancy or childhood, but a non-sexual disembodied previous existence.

Plato's theory of eros in the *Symposium* seems too general to explain the considerable individual and cultural variations we encounter in the selection of beloveds. Beauty or goodness characterize many objects and the lover selects among these: a lover's perceiving his beloved as beautiful is not, therefore, an adequate explanation of his selection of that particular person. The passage in the *Phaedrus* seems to be an attempt to fill this gap; but here Plato seems to rely on his speculative metaphysics about the pre-existence of human souls, something that makes such explanations difficult to assess. In the *Symposium*, where we have a coherent and grand theory, there is nothing that would begin to explain exclusive attachment to a particular individual. Plato seems more interested in getting us away from such attachments, rather than attempting, like Freud, to explain their mysteries or irrationalities.

Even at the level of some generality, it is difficult to see if any explanatory work is done by the proposition that we love only what [we think, perceive, or judge] is beautiful or good. Is this proposition necessary at all, for example, to understand homosexual selection? It is perhaps true of every case of love that the lover finds something attractive in the beloved, but this attraction need not be characterized in terms of beauty or goodness. Initial attachments of children, for example, may be understood without recourse to such characterizations, and subsequent selection may be explained in terms of such original attachments. It is striking that in Freud's detailed explanations of selection, whether anaclitic or narcissistic, terms such as 'beauty' and 'goodness' rarely if ever occur.

Plato's theory of love, especially in the *Symposium*, may be too object-oriented, and modeled too much after conscious rational choice, to explain love selections adequately. Plato seems to concentrate entirely on the object of love, as if variation of selection can be explained entirely or even mainly by characterizations of the object. What Freud sees clearly is that this cannot succeed. To explain selection we need to consider the personality of the lover and the development of that personality. It is attention to this development that provided Freud with the models of selection he constructed. When we consider the vast variety of love choices – they range all the way from the rational to the irrational, from the obvious to the incomprehensible, from the normal to the neurotic and even the pathological – it is highly doubtful that we can understand the phenomena without recourse to genetic explanations. Even sexual selection among animals may have to be brought in to complete our understanding. Plato's theory of love seems innocent of such considerations, and especially of ontogenetic explanations.

The story on the question of overestimation is somewhat similar. Freud noticed the phenomenon early, thought that over- estimation is characteristic mainly of male lovers, and proposed several explanations of it, some anaclitic, some narcissistic. Plato's theory in the *Symposium* seems to contain little if anything that can be used to explain overestimation. Perhaps Plato in this dialogue did not even recognize overestimation?

In this connection Professor Vlastos makes an interesting claim. He contrasts Platonic eros with Rousseau's extreme idealization of Madame d'Houdetot, and says:

> But no Platonist could have confused the idol of *his* heart with a Madame d'Houdetot. Even in the heat of passion the Platonic idea does not lend itself to this kind of mistake ... the ontology of the paradigm-form ... that harshly dualistic transcendentalism ... proves a sterling asset in this area. It sustains a kind of idealism less addicted to the pathetic fallacy than are most other kinds. It makes for a more truthful vision of that part of the world which we are all most tempted to idealize and so to falsify – the part we love. (*Platonic Studies*, pp. 29–30)

This explains why Plato does not explicitly recognize overestimation or idealization in the *Symposium*: his theory of eros leaves no room for it. I think, though, that this is true only of eros at the very top of the ladder, where the object of love is the Form Beauty itself. The Form Beauty cannot be overestimated because it is the most beautiful object there is or can be; it is perfectly beautiful, beautiful without qualification, and so overestimation is conceptually impossible. But it does not follow from this, nor is it true, that below the top of the ladder there is no room for overestimation. The objects of love below the top are imperfectly beautiful and overestimation is possible. Moreover, Plato tells us that as the lover becomes attached to higher objects he views the lower ones 'with disdain', and at the top he may come to regard the beauty of the flesh as 'mortal trash'. This suggests that at earlier stages the lover overestimated the beauty of the body. Thus the theory leaves room for overestimation, and Plato even in the *Symposium* may have been aware of the phenomenon. Unfortunately the theory contains little that would explain overestimation, unless it be the implied proposition that the lover overestimates a beautiful body or the beauty of the body because at the lower stage he does not know yet what beauty really is – he has not yet become aware of perfect beauty. This would be an attempt to explain overestimation as an intellectual error due to lack of awareness of a higher standard: we overestimate bodily beauty because we are not aware of a beauty incomparably greater or more valuable.

In the *Phaedrus* there are passages in which Plato seems to recognize overestimation explicitly (233ab, 251ab), but he says very little about it. In the first passage he attributes to Lysias the view that lovers praise their beloveds 'beyond due measure' because they fear incurring their displeasure or because their own judgment is 'obscured by passion'. The first reason suggests flattery rather than overestimation, while the second does not seem sufficient to explain it: granting that the lover's judgment is obscured by passion, why should the error be in the direction of overestimation? In the second passage Socrates himself tells us about someone who has already contemplated Beauty itself, 'when he sees a god-like face or form which is a good image of Beauty ... reveres the beautiful one as a god, and if he did not fear to be thought stark mad, would offer sacrifices to his beloved as to an idol or a god'. This suggests overestimation, though as Vlastos points out 'the lover is in no danger of confusing the boy with the Idea' (ibid., p. 30, n. 88). The context suggests that this is the best kind of Platonic lover: one who has recently 'initiated', 'beheld' Beauty itself, had eros it, and now falls in love with an earthly image of it – a particularly good image, a boy of god-like face or form. By why should this result in overestimation? The ladder of love in the *Symposium* would suggest just the contrary: it is hard to see how the Platonic lover who has reached the top of the ladder could fall in love with earthly images at all; but if he did, how could he possibly overestimate what he regarded from the top of the ladder as 'mortal trash'?

Here too, as in the case of selection, Plato seems to focus too much on the objects of love. His tendency is to understand mental states, whether emotional or intellectual, in terms of their objects and aims. The causal conditions that give rise to such states largely escape his attention or are perhaps beyond the data that were available to him. In addition, he imposes on the objects of love the harsh dualism of the theory of Forms, the rigid distinction between the sensible world and the Forms. In this context his tendency is to think that those who overvalue things in the sensible world do so because they are not aware of the perfect paradigms, the Forms of which these things are only imperfect shadows. But in the *Phaedrus*, where the passionate – even manic – intensity of love is recognized, he realizes that even the best Platonic lover, the one who has contemplated perfect Beauty, may develop passionate love for its earthly images, and may display the overestimation that his metaphysics and epistemology allows only to lesser lovers. And though perhaps he suggests some causal connection between the lover's passion and his overestimation, Plato seems to make no sustained effort to explain the phenomenon. In any case, idealization had not probably attracted the attention it did later in the cultures of courtly and romantic love.

Plato and Freud

Our results in this chapter should not be surprising when viewed in proper perspective. The divergences we have emphasized may well be expected when we reflect on the differences in culture and language, the great advances in medicine, biology, and psychology, and the fact that Plato was primarily a speculative philosopher, Freud an empirical psychologist. Both were men of genius but they came to our subject with different theoretical backgrounds, different resources, and different methods of investigation.

Freud's medical background led him to think of love in terms of symptoms and causes, almost as if love were an illness. His theory of love could be called the symptomatology and aetiology of love. The symptoms of love are to be catalogued, their causes discerned, the lover, if necessary, to be cured. His knowledge of the theory of evolution led him away from teleology and final causes towards an investigation of the origins and development of the experience of love; and his investigation and treatment of neuroses revealed the significance of early sexuality for later life. The aetiology of love turned into a sexual archaeology of love. Biology and the theory of evolution also led him to think in terms of longer and longer time frames and to regard the human species as continuous with the rest of the animal kingdom. He came to believe that 'the development of human beings requires ... no different explanation from that of animals' (SE vol. XVIII, p. 42). Ontogeny recapitulates phylogeny, and there is no hope of understanding the former without the latter. His new theories of the unconscious, of infantile sexuality and psychosexual development gave him new and powerful theoretical tools for investigating sexual and emotional phenomena. His clinical practices, hypnosis, free association, and the interpretation of dreams, made available to him empirical data that had never come under the purview of a single great mind earlier. It is this formidable array of concepts, tools and data that he brought to the investigation of love. He was without doubt in a far better position than any man earlier to try to understand especially the mysteries and irrationalities of love.

A much earlier pioneer, Plato had fewer and different resources. He had no theories of the unconscious and of infantile sexuality, no privileged data, and he did not have the benefit of the theory of evolution. He brought very different theories to this study of love: his perfectionist ethics, his rationalistic psychology, the metaphysical theory of Forms, his speculation about the previous existence and immortality of the soul, and his belief that human beings are different in kind from animals in their possession of reason. His principal tools of investigation were definition, hypothesis, and argument, with nothing but very general facts to check the truth of his conclusions. And he showed a marked tendency toward teleological explanations of behaviour within certain assumptions about goodness, beauty, and human rationality. Instead of a sexual archaeology, he gives us a perfectionist teleology of love. He was not in the best position to explain the mysteries and irrationalities of love, though the *Phaedrus* shows clearly that he appreciated well enough the madness of the erotic.

At the same time, perhaps precisely because of his great metaphysical vision of the ideal Forms and his perfectionist ethics, Plato was in a great position to extend the scope of beauty beyond the physical, to appreciate the creativity of love in the arts and sciences, and elevate the best kind of love to an aspiration for immortality and the Good. Instead of making erotic love the root of all love, Plato superimposed on eros his theories of happiness and the good, his theory of the Forms as ideal exemplars and his moral psychology. He started with the primitive model of bodily beauty and attraction, and the desire for physical union and reproduction. But he assimilated or subsumed this model under another one derived from his ethics and metaphysics: the desire is sparked and directed by the perception of beauty, and is made to serve another independent desire, the desire for the good and immortality. Every love is a species of the desire for the good. The desire for the good is deeply rooted in the finitude and imperfection of human nature, but it does not necessarily or always have a somatic source. There are other goods besides pleasure and the preservation of life, such as knowledge and the perfecting of our potentialities; and even pleasure need not always be somatic. For Plato the desire for the good and immortality is an independent drive for perfection, a drive to the Form, a view that Freud explicitly denied and called a 'benevolent illusion' (SE, vol, XVIII, p. 42). Love of beauty is subsumed under this drive. Love of physical beauty arouses the sexual drive which is somatic and leads to sexual union and reproduction. But this is the lowest grade of love, a love we have in common with animals. Plato would never have accepted the view that the development of human beings requires no different explanation from that of animals. Even this low grade love is made to serve the low grade immortality that children can bring. At higher stages of love, which only human beings can attain, the beauty is not physical but abstract, the desire it sparks is not sexual or somatic but purely psychic, and the final motivation is to come as close to the divine immortality of perfect beauty as is humanly possible. The drive to beauty, immortality, and the good is the divine part of human nature, the part we do not share with animals, the part that human reason makes possible. It is this drive that is responsible for the highest achievements in art, culture and science.

Notes

1 In *Beyond the Pleasure Principle,* where Freud adopts his second system of instincts, he is quite explicit on this: 'Our views have from the very first been *dualistic,* and today they are even more definitely dualistic than before – now that we describe the opposition as being, not between ego-instincts and sexual instincts but between life instincts [these are the sexual instincts and the self-preservative instincts which Freud now groups under Eros – see e.g. p. 52] and death instincts (SE, vol., XVII, 1920, p. 53). See also Jones, E. *The Life and Work of Sigmund Freud,* vol. 3, pp. 266–80.

2 The longest reference to the myth of Aristophanes is in *Beyond the Pleasure Principle,* SE, vol. XVIII, pp. 57–8, and p. 58, n. 1. We shall return to the curious story of these references.

3 Freud himself may have had some misgivings about the accuracy of Nachmansohn's and Pfister's claims: 'Freud's Libidotheorie verglichan mit Evoslehre Platos', 'Internationale Zeitschrift Feur Aerztliche Psychoanalyse', vol. 3 (1915) and 'Plato als Vorkufer dur Psychoanalyse', 'Internationale Zeitschrift Fur Psychoanalyse', vol. 7 (1921) respectively. At any rate in the paragraph immediately following his comparative claim, he says that he could have avoided the controversy over his expansion of sexuality if he had adopted 'the more genteel expressions "Eros" and "erotic"' (SE, vol. XVIII, pp. 90–1). This is a suggestion that Nachmansohn in fact made. But, Freud goes on to say, this would have been a concession in words, which could lead to a concession in substance. Now this is strange indeed, for at least two reasons. If the eros of Plato 'coincides exactly' with the libido of psychoanalysis in function, origin and relation to sexual love, why would it be a concession at all to adopt the term 'eros'? And secondly, Freud *already* adopted the term 'Eros' – to cover both sexual and self-preservative instincts – one year earlier in *Beyond the Pleasure Principle* (1920). It is really a pity that Freud did not have the time to study or re-study Plato's views, especially in the *Symposium* and the *Phaedrus,* and make up his own mind about Plato's view of love and its similarities to his own theory.

4 Nachmansohn (ibid.) quotes passages almost entirely from *Symposium* and the *Phaedrus*. He takes no note at all of the definition of generic eros, but since he relied mostly on passages which speak of procreation, immortality, and the ladder, we can say he is talking about Plato's concept of specific eros. There is also some evidence that Nachmansohn misunderstood Freud's concept of sublimation since he tells us that sublimation concerns the object not the instinct, whereas Freud is explicit that 'sublimation describes something that has to do with the instinct' (that is, it is a deflection of the sexual aim). See e.g., SE vol. XIV, p. 94. Besides problems of accuracy, Freud's reliance on this essay poses other difficulties. Nachmansohn's essay was written at or before 1915, before Freud changed his system of instincts four years later – a change that brought about changes in the origin and function of what Freud after 1919 called 'eros'. So Nachmanson was comparing Plato's eros with Freud's libido in Freud's first classification of instincts, and Freud was endorsing the comparison after he had changed this classification.

5 Pfister's shorter article is no help at all. He refers us to Nachmansohn's article for support. And in his own short exposition of Plato's view he seems hopelessly confused: He quotes indiscriminately from the speeches of Eryximachus, Agathon, and Socrates as if they all represented Plato's view, including even the part of Agathon's view that Socrates criticizes!

6 Thus, e.g. sometimes the reality and pleasure principles are stated in terms of their relations to the function of the mental apparatus. See e.g. 'Formulations of the two Principles of Mental Functioning', SE vol. XII. And in the *Ego and the Id*, the ego, the id, and the super-ego are constantly described in terms of their functions. Plato's reliance of some notion of function is well known, for example, in the *Republic*; for the evidence see, e.g. Santas [1973] and [1985].

7 Plato has used his most general value concept – goodness – to define generic eros. Freud shows no inclination ever to define love in value terms, and shows marked distrust of all value-judgements (SE, vol. XXI, 1930, p. 145). See also his remarks in SE vol. XVIII, p. 42, where he says that the belief that 'there is an instinct towards perfection is a benevolent illusion'.

8 For Freud's own account of the developments that led to the new classification see, e.g. *Beyond the Pleasure Principle*, SE vol. XVIII, pp. 50–3, and 'The Libido Theory', ibid., pp. 256–9. Jones also describes these developments in ibid., vol. 3, 272–3.

9 It is important to note that in *Beyond the Pleasure Principle* Freud does not of course give up the pleasure principle: The immediate aim of the sexual instinct is still pleasure, and sexual union is of course one of the immediate aims. But the Pleasure Principle is now modified not only by the Reality Principle but also by the new principle, the compulsion to repeat. The new functions assigned to Eros are

presumably within a phylogenetic framework: what this Eros preserves, for example, is the species, not the individual.

10 At least so Jones claims, arguing further that the two ideas are distinct, ibid., vol. 3, p. 271.

11 Jones, ibid., vol. 3, p. 271. The aims of Freud's Eros and Aristophanes' eros would coincide *in general,* in both aiming at an earlier state of affairs. Freud makes no comment on whether they would coincide more specifically. Jones offers what seems to be a curious suggestion: 'If we are to follow Plato's, and Freud's, thought in its entirety we must conclude that the ultimate reunion it betokened could only be with the mother, from whom one had unfortunately been separated at the beginning of life', ibid., p. 275. There is no suggestion or implication of this in Aristophanes' story; in fact it seems to make no sense since some reunions would be male–male! Finally it should be noted here that in *An Outline to Psychoanalysis* (1940) Freud gave up the hypothesis that Eros is 'conservative' (SE vol. XXIII, p. 149 and n. 1). This hypothesis, he now says, would imply that 'living substance was once a unity which had later been torn apart and was now striving towards reunion.' And in a note, in a clear reference to Aristophanes' speech in the *Symposium,* he says that 'creative writers have imagined something of the sort, but nothing like it is known to us from the actual history of living substance'.

12 Jones notes that nearly forty years before 'Freud had quoted this idea of Plato's to his betrothed to illustrate the intensity of his longing for union with her', ibid., p. 275. Strachey thinks that on p. 136 of the *Three Essays,* SE vol. VII, Freud was alluding to 'Plato's myth', even though Freud there speaks of 'the poetic fable which tells us how the original human beings were cut into two halves – man and woman – and how these are always striving to unite again in love'. That is, Freud writes as if the original human beings were all man–woman combinations, which of course is not Aristophanes' myth, but possibly the oriental version to which Freud refers in *Beyond the Pleasure Principle,* p. 58, n. 1. In this latter work Freud describes Aristophanes' myth correctly. This confusion was possibly what led Ellenberger to claim that 'Both Plato and Freud taught the original bisexuality of the human being ...' *The Discovery of the Unconscious,* p. 503. According to Aristophanes' myth in the *Symposium* only one of the three original pairs was bisexual, the other two were all male and all female. Nearly all of the references by Freud and his commentators to the speech of Aristophanes are ambiguous: 'Plato's thought', 'Plato's idea', 'Plato's myth' – they nearly always seem to suggest that this is Plato's own view. Of course in a sense all these phrases are correct: the writer is Plato. But we cannot attribute all the views he puts in the mouths of his characters to Plato, especially since often they contradict each other. In this respect we noted earlier an outright mistake: the Walsters emphatically express that

Aristophanes' speech is 'Plato's theory of love', and make no mention of any other views in Plato!

13 For Freud's notion of 'genetic' explanations, see e.g., Rapaport, D., *The Structure of Psychoanalytic Theory, Psychological Issues*, vol. III; Hall and Lindsay, ch. 1; and Neu, Jerome, 'Genetic Explanation in *Totem and Taboo*', in *Freud: A Collection of Critical Essays*, ed., R. Wollheim, pp. 366–7.

14 Whether Plato held this view consistently throughout the dialogues – that disembodied souls have not only reason but also spirit and appetites – is problematic. For a brief discussion see Hackforth, *Plato's Phaedrus*, Cambridge U.P., London, 1952, pp. 75–7, and Guthrie, HGP, vol. IV, pp. 421–6.

15 In his massive and scholarly investigations of the origins of the concept of the unconscious and theories about it, Ellenberger does not include Plato as one of those who anticipated Freud. See *The Discovery of the Unconscious*, e.g., pp. 311ff.

16 See e.g., Paul Shorey, tr., Plato's *Republic*, vol. 2, pp. 334ff n. d.

17 For a recent judicious comparison see A. Kenny, *The Anatomy of the Soul*, Blackwell, Oxford, 1973, pp. 10–14. For a comparison that finds more similarities than I think there are, see Simon, B. *Mind and Madness in Ancient Greece*, chs 8 and 10.

18 See e.g. vol. XIX, p. 149, where the neuroses are said to result from conflicts between the ego and the id, and narcissistic neuroses such as melancholia from conflicts between the id and the super-ego.

19 SE, vol. XIX, 1923, *The Ego and the Id*, ch. IV. But see Strachey's Appendix B for some complications.

20 Kosman, L.A., 'Platonic Love' (in *Facets of Plato's Philosophy*, ed. by W.H. Werkmeister) seems to disagree. I find Kosman's discussion valuable, especially his sorting out of the different criticisms that have been made against Plato's theory. But I cannot agree with his view that 'Erotic love is thus primarily for Plato self-love …' (p. 60). He seems to reach this conclusion by a series of inferences from a passage in the *Lysis*, which is primarily about philia rather than eros, and from a conclusion there that is rejected. I don't think that Kosman appreciates sufficiently the contrast between the Aristophanic myth and Plato's own view. He allows that Aristophanes' view is 'corrected by Diotima' (p. 62), but in the relevant passage in the *Symposium* it is more accurate to say, I think, that the view is rejected: *to oikeion* is replaced by *to agathon* as the object of eros. Kosman's view is not entirely clear to me, however. He may mean that the object of eros in Plato is some future *ideal* state of oneself (the lover); such a case would be comparable to Freud's love of one's ego-ideal in the paper on Narcissism, and it is not excluded by Plato's deficiency model.

21 See e.g., at the end of *The Ego and the Id*, Freud's striking statement: 'To the Ego, therefore, living means the same as being loved – being

loved by the super-ego ...' To Plato's Reason, on the other hand, living means learning and knowing.

22 See Harry B. Levey's extensive review of Freud's view of sublimation, 'A Critique of the Theory of Sublimation', in *Psychiatry*, vol. 2, 1939, especially pp. 248–9.

23 See e.g. Dodds, E.R., *The Greeks and the Irrational*, p. 218, and Ellenberger, ibid., p. 503.

24 There is a striking passage in the *Republic*, which might be appealed to here:

> But, again, we are surely aware that when in a man the desires incline strongly to any one thing, they are weakened for other things. It is as if the stream had been diverted into another channel ... So, when a man's desires have been taught to flow in the channel of learning and all that sort of thing, they will be concerned, I presume, with the pleasures of the soul in itself, and will be indifferent to those to which the body is the instrument, if the man is a true and not a sham philosopher (485d).

There are several similar similies in Freud: 'the libido behaves like a stream whose main bed has become blocked. It proceeds to fill up collateral channels which hitherto have been empty, (SE, vol. VII, p. 170)'; 'The various channels along which the libido passes are related to each other from the very first like intercommunicating pipes, and we must take the phenomenon of collateral flow into account' (ibid., p. 151, n. 1).

> Next, we must bear in mind that the sexual instinctual impulses in particular are extraordinarily *plastic*, if I may so express it. One of them can take the place of another, one of them can take over another's intensity; if the satisfaction of one of them is frustrated by reality, the satisfaction of another can afford complete compensation. They are related to one another like a network of intercommunicating channels filled with a fluid ... Further, the component instincts of sexuality as well as the sexual current which is compounded of them, exhibit a large capacity for changing their object, for taking another in its place – and one therefore that is more easily attainable. This displaceability and readiness to accept a substitute must operate powerfully against the pathogenic effect of a frustration. Among these protective processes against falling ill owing to deprivation there is one which has gained special cultural significance. It consists in the sexual trend abandoning its aim of obtaining a component or a reproductive pleasure and taking on another which is related genetically to the abandoned one but is itself no longer sexual and must be described as social. We call this process 'sublimation', in accordance with the social estimate that places social aims higher than the sexual ones, which are at bottom self-interested. (SE vol. XVI, p. 345)

It is unclear how far the Platonic passage 'anticipates' this so-called 'hydraulic model' of the libido in Freud. At a minimum it would seem that Plato assumes that the total 'emotional' or 'psychic' energy available to an individual is limited and so the more that is expended in one direction the less that will be available for others; and this is similar to Freud's 'economics' of the distribution of the libido. But whether Plato had in mind any of the mechanisms of plasticity which

Freud mentions here and elsewhere is, to say the least, dubious. We saw, for example, that in *The Ego and the Id*, ch. III, Freud speculates that all sublimation may take place through the mediation of the ego: the ego tries to get hold of some of the sexual energy of the id by taking on (identifying with) the characteristics of a lost love object of the id. This is anything but Platonic: in the ladder of love reason guides the ascent by finding out new and more beautiful objects for desire, certainly not by identifying with the objects desire already has. Moreover, since Plato and Freud had different principles of individuating desires, impulses, or instincts it is doubtful that they could both allow the same mechanisms: for example, for Freud there is no conceptual problem in displacement of objects, since he relies on aim and source for individuation, whereas for Plato there would be since he relies on objects and/or aims for classifying and individuating desires. Similarly, change of aims, what is involved in sublimation, is difficult for Plato, whereas for Freud it is perhaps not as problematic because he can rely on the source of the instincts, the erogenous zones. Also Freud can give genetic accounts, on the basis of dreams and free associations, of the connection between the sublimated impulse and the older sexual one, whereas Plato has no such conception or the data for it.

25 Ibid., p. 291.

Epilogue: More Questions About Love

> 'Your words and my own eager mind reveal exactly what love is', I said, 'but now there is an even greater doubt, I feel' ...
>
> Dante

We started our study with questions about love and we discussed two theories that give more or less systematic answers to them. It is perhaps appropriate to close with a brief reconsideration of questions about love.

This is prompted by several reasons. First, if we knew that our original set of questions was correct and complete we could think of different theories of love as providing alternative answers to our questions. The questions would always be the same and we would seek the true answers among the alternative theories. But we don't know this. We must therefore be open to the possibility of new and perhaps more fruitful questions. Apart from this, our original questions were really pretty general. It is reasonable to expect that theories of love worthy of serious consideration will suggest new or at least more specific questions about love that can guide and shape further study and research.

Is this true of our theories? I believe so.

In his use of the deficiency model Plato supposed that all love, whether of family, friends, or lovers, arises out of the finitude, mortality, and imperfections of human beings. Whether this is true or not, it gives a definite shape to Plato's concept of love and it clearly implies that a being which is infinite, perfect, and immortal, cannot love. Is this true? Is the Christian notion, for example, that such a being loves, a senseless illusion? Or can there be such a love, to which even human beings can occasionally if rarely aspire, transcending or at least forgetting for the moment their own finitude and thinking only of the need of another? What is this love? Plato's theory certainly raises this question, and the case of beings free of our imperfections becomes a test case for what love is.

In making the object of all love the good or the beautiful Plato gave an evaluational and rationalistic cast to the concept. Our emotional attachment in love arises out of our needs, our mortality and imperfections, but our choice always rests on the perceived value of the object, its beauty or goodness. The strength of our emotional attachments may vary somewhat with our needs, and it may even influence our judgment about the goodness or beauty of the object. But though our choices in love might for this and other reasons be more or less mistaken, they are never really irrational. There can be no love without valuation, and our choices always rest on it. Thus Plato's theory raises the question whether love is always rational, and whether evaluative teleological models are the only models by which we can understand the concept and the experience of love.

Finally, in making the Forms Beauty or Goodness the objects of the best and highest kind of love, Plato implies that the value of love depends entirely on the value of the object. The best love is the love of the best or most beautiful object, and it happens when we know or truly believe that what we love is Beauty or the Good itself. The best love is the love of the best object because only the best object can best remedy our imperfections and spark and guide our creativity. This is an inspiring ideal that may help us transcend our humanity, but it inevitably raises the question whether the value of the object is the only basis for judging the value of love. What, for example, of the value of our love to the object? This may be a senseless question about love of abstract entities, but the case may be very different for love of human beings. Plato's theory, especially in the *Phaedrus* allows and even directs the lover to benefit the beloved. But the beloved is still seen as an image of an abstract entity which remains the source of value for that love, the model that guides the lover. Love of the weak, the deformed, the sick, the untalented, even of the cruel and the arrogant, not only has no value, it seems, but it is not even a theoretical possibility. Can the object so totally dominate the concept, define its nature and give it its only value?

The questions about Freud's theory come from the other end of the spectrum, for Freud's theory of love is almost diametrically opposed to Plato's. The essence of Freud's theory lies in the relation he sees between all love and sexuality, and in his explanations of choice and overestimation which always rely on the past sexuality of the lover. Behind this lies Freud's theory of the unconscious which knows nothing of time, contradiction, or rationality; and his new theory of sexuality in which the connection between instinct and object has been severed, the nature of the love instinct is thought to depend entirely on its somatic sources, and the value of love entirely on satisfaction. Behind every love, inside every lover there rages a titanic struggle of which the individual is not even aware; a struggle between the childish, irrational and peremptory demands of the unconscious and the inexorable demands of reality, of nature and civilization. In a state of semi-hypnotic compulsion, almost in desperation, the individual falls in love with himself, his mother, a laughing face, an enigmatic smile, a boyish figure, the elusive beauty of an abstraction, or the benevolent illusion of a cause greater than himself.

Does all love really have its source in the unconscious and the irrational? Don't we ever love anything simply because of what we see, hear, touch or imagine? Does my love of Mozart require any further explanation than the fact that I cannot imagine a more harmonious blend of form and feeling?

Is love always marked by overestimation, of myself or an external object, and therefore always based on an illusion? Perhaps Juliet overestimated Romeo when she called him 'the god of my idolatry', and Dante Beatrice when he made her 'the glorious mistress of my mind'. Perhaps even Paris overestimated Helen, even though he had plenty of company and in his case we shall have to speak of a mass illusion. But aren't some things so truly good and beautiful that no illusion is required to spark or explain our love of them? Can't our beloveds ever turn out to be as we first imagined them or even greater? Do we need to be under some illusion to love the beauty of Praxitelis or Michelangelo? Above all, must we be under an illusion to love the truth?

Can the object of love be almost totally divorced from love, and be thought of only as a more or less suitable instrument for satisfaction? Isn't Freud's love of truth and knowledge defined by its objects and thus distinguished from his other loves? And don't we admire and value it no matter what its sources because we value truth and knowledge?

Above all, is sexuality really as wide a concept as love? Do their objects always coincide? Is truth or justice a sexual object? If not, and we can love truth or justice, the two concepts are not co-extensive. Freud might reply that we have now reverted to Plato's, the Philosopher's obsessive preoccupation with objects. This deceives us, he will say. To see that all love really originates in sexuality we must take into account the unconscious and the psychic mechanisms of displacement of objects, of repression or inhibition of aim, and sublimation. Then psycho-analytic data will confirm that the tender feelings of affection and care for the beloved, the apparently non-sexual component of normal romantic love, are older, aim-inhibited sexual impulses. And devotion to an abstraction is aim-deflected sexuality; in sublimation neither the object nor the aim need be sexual, but the source is. Is this really sufficient for supposing that Mill's love of liberty is sexual? And even if it is, does this really have one iota of significance for the value of that love or for his eloquent defense of liberty? Apart from this, do we really have a clear view of the psychic mechanisms of aim-inhibition, of the supposed transformation of sexual impulses into affection, and of sublimation? The non-dogmatic Freud did not hesitate to admit that we have not:

> A psychology which will not or cannot penetrate the depths of what is repressed regards tender emotional ties as being invariably the expression of tendencies which have no sexual aim, even though they are derived from tendencies which have such an aim. We are justified in saying that they have been diverted from these sexual aims, even though there is some

> difficulty in giving a representation of such a diversion of aim which will conform to the requirements of metapsychology. (SE vol. XVIII, 1921, p. 119)

Plato's and Freud's theories of love have dominated our thought and life so much, and reactions to them are sometimes so emotional, that we would do well to remember that Plato and Freud were not dogmatic. Near the end of his life Freud remarked that we know very little about love, and Plato left us the legacy of continuous and open philosophical dialogue. They were both capable of passionate defense of their views, but both loved truth and clarity more than they loved their own theories of love.

Bibliography

Adams, R.M., 'Pure Love', *Journal of Religion and Ethics*, vol. 8, 1980.

Allen, R.E., 'A Note on the Elenchus of Agathon: *Symposium* 199c–201c', *The Monist*, no. 50 (1966) pp. 460–63.

Anton, J. & Preus, A., *Essays in Ancient Greek Philosophy*, vol. 2, State University of New York Press, Albany, 1983.

Arieti, S. and J.A., *Love Can Be Found*, Harcourt Brace Jovanovich, Inc., New York, 1977.

Benoit, H., *The Many Faces of Love*, Pantheon Books, New York, 1955.

Bolotin, David, *Plato's Dialogue on Friendship*, Cornell University Press, 1979.

Bretlinger, J., ed., *The Symposium of Plato*, University of Massachusetts Press, 1970.

Brown, Norman, *Life Against Death*, Wesleyan University Press, 1959.

Burnet, J., ed., *Plato's Phaedo*, Oxford University Press, 1911.

Bury, R.G., *The Symposium of Plato*, 2nd edn, Cambridge University Press, 1969.

Carson, Anne, *Eros: The Bittersweet*, Princeton University Press, 1986.

Cioffi, F., ed., *Freud: Modern Judgments*, Macmillan, London, 1973.

Cooper, John M., 'Aristotle on Friendship', in *Essays in Aristotle's Ethics*, ed. A. Rorty, University of California Press, Berkeley, 1980.

Cornford, F.M., 'The Doctrine of Eros in Plato's Symposium', in *The Unwritten Philosophy*, ed. W.K.C. Guthrie Cambridge University Press, 1950.

Cornford, F.M., *Principium Sapientiae*, Cambridge University Press, 1952.

D'Arcy, M.C., *The Mind and Heart of Love*, Henry Holt, New York, 1947.

Daly, M. and Wilson, M., *Sex, Evolution and Behavior*, Willard Grant Press, Boston, 1983.

Derrida, J., *La Carte Postale: de Socrate à Freud et au dela*, Paris, Flammarion, 1980.

de Rougemont, D., *Love in the Western World*, tr. M. Belgion Harcourt Brace Jovanovich, New York, 1940.

De Sousa, R., 'Norms and the Normal', in *Freud*, ed. R. Wollheim.

Dodds, E.R., *The Greeks and the Irrational*, California University Press, 1951.

Donagan, A., *The Theory of Morality*, Chicago, 1977.

Dover, K., *Greek Homosexuality*, Vintage, New York, 1978.

Dover, K., *Plato, Symposium*, Cambridge University Press, 1980.

Ellenberger, H., *The Discovery of the Unconscious*, Basic Books, New York, 1970.

Ellis, A., ed., *The Encyclopedia of Sexual Behaviour*, Hawthorn Books, New York, 1961, 2 vols.

Ellis, Havelock, *Psychology of Sex*, R. Long and R.R. Smith Inc., 2nd edn, New York, 1966.

Eysenck, H.J. and Wilson, G.D., *The Experimental Study of Freudian Theories*, Methuen, London, 1973.

Fine, R., *Freud: A Critical Re-evaluation of his Theories*, David MacKay Co., Inc., New York, 1962.

Fine, R., *A History of Psychoanalysis*, Columbia University Press, New York, 1979.

Fodor, N., ed., *Freud: Dictionary of Psychoanalysis*, Philosophical Library, New York, 1958.

Foucault, M., *The History of Sexuality*, R. Hurley, tr., New York, Pantheon Books, 1978.

Freud, S., *Collected Papers*, vols IV and V, The Hogarth Press, London, 1957.

Freud, S., *The Standard Edition of the Complete Pscyhological Works of Sigmund Freud*, ed., J. Strachey, The Hogarth Press, London, 1953, vols. I–XXVI.

Fromm, E., *The Art of Loving*, Harper and Row, New York, 1956.

Gedo, J.E., and Pollock, G.H., *Freud: The Fusion of Science and Humanism, Psychological Issues*, vol. IX, nos 2 and 3, Monographs 34 and 35.

Gilby, T., tr., *Aquinus*, Oxford University Press, 1960.

Glidden, D.K., 'The *Lysis* on Loving One's Own', The *Classical Quarterly*, vol. 31, no. 1, 1981.

Gould, T., *Platonic Love*, London, 1963.

Grant, V.W., 'Sexual Love' in *The Encycolpedia of Sexual Behavior*, ed. Albert Ellis, Hawthorn Books, 1961, vol. 2.

Grant, V.W., *Falling in Love*, Spring Publishing, New York, 1976.

Greenberg, R.P., and Fisher, S., *The Scientific Credibility of Freud's Theories and Therapy*, Basic Books, New York, 1977.

Grundbaum, Adolf, *The Foundations of Psychoanalysis, A Philosophical Critique*, University of California Press, 1984.

Grundbaum, A., 'Freud's Theory,' the presidential address in *APA Proceedings*, Sept. 1983.

Guthrie, W.K.C., *A History of Greek Philosophy*, vols I–V, Cambridge, 1967–78.

Hackforth, R., *Plato's Phaedrus*, Cambridge University Press, London, 1954.

Hall, C.S., and Lindsay, G., *Theories of Personality*, Wiley, New York, 1970.

Hall, C.S., *A Primer of Freudian Psychology*, World Publishing, Cleveland, 1954.

Halperin, D., 'Platonic *Eros* and What Men Call Love,' in *Ancient Philosophy*, 5, Fall 1985 (This interesting paper reached me too late to be discussed).

Harper, R., *Human Love*, Johns Hopkins, Baltimore, 1966.

Harrison, Jane, *Prolegomena to the Study of Greek Religion*, World, New York, 1966.

Hazo, R.G., *The Idea of Love*, Praeger, New York, 1967.

Henriques, F., *Love in Action*, E.P. Dutton, New York, 1960.

Hitschmann, E., 'Freud's Conception of Love', *International Journal of Psychoanalysis*, vol. 33, 1952.

Hollitscher, W., *Sigmund Freud*, Routledge and Kegan Paul, London, 1950.

Hunt, M.M., *The Natural History of Love*, A. Knopf, New York, 1959.

Jones, E., *The Life and Work of Sigmund Freud*, 3 vols., Basic Books, New York, 1955.

Irwin, T., *Plato's Moral Theory*, Oxford University Press, 1977.

Kahn, Charles, 'Plato on the Unity of the Virtues', in *Facets of Plato's Philosophy*, ed. W.H. Werkmeister (Van Gorcum, Assen, 1976.)

Kahn, Charles, 'Drama and Dialectic in Plato's *Gorgias*', in *Oxford Studies in Ancient Philosophy*, ed. Julia Annas, Oxford University Press, 1983.

Kaufman, W., *Discovering the Mind*, vol. 3, McGraw-Hill, New York, 1980.

Kenny, A., *The Anatomy of the Soul*, Blackwell, Oxford, 1973.

Kosman, L.A., 'Platonic Love', in *Facets of Plato's Philosophy*, ed. W.H. Werkmeister (Van Gorcum, Assen, 1976).

Levey, H.B., 'A Critique of the Theory of Sublimation', *Psychiatry*, vol. 2, 1939.

Lillyman, W., 'Analogies for Love: Goethe's *Die Wahlverwandtschaften* and Plato's *Symposium* in *Goethe's Narrative Fiction*, ed. W. Lillyman, Walter de Gruyter, Berlin, 1983.

Lindsay, Gardner, 'Some Remarks Concerning Incest, the Incest Taboo and Psychoanalytic Theory', *American Psychologist*, 1967, vol 22, pp. 1051–9.

McDougall, W., *Social Psychology*, 14th edn, Methuen, London, 1963.

Marcus, R.A., 'The Dialectic of Eros in Plato's Symposium', in *Plato*, vol. II, ed. G. Vlastos, Doubleday, 1970.

Marshall, D.E., and Suggs, R.C. eds, *Human Sexual Behavior*, Basic Books, New York, 1971.

Maslow, A.H., 'Love in Healthy People', in *The Practice of Love*, ed. A. Montague, Prentice Hall, New Jersey, 1975.

May, R., *Love and Will*, N.N. Norton, New York, 1969.

Montague, A., ed., *The Meaning of Love*, Greenwood Press, Westport, Co., 1953.

Montague, A., ed., *The Practice of Love*, Prentice Hall, New Jersey, 1975.

Moravcsik, J.M.A., 'Reason and Eros in the "Ascent" – Passage in the *Symposium*', in *Essays in Ancient Greek Philosophy*, ed. J. Anton, Albany, 1971.

Morgan, D.N., *Love: Plato, the Bible and Freud*, Prentice Hall, Englewood Cliffs, N.J., 1964.

Md. Mujeed-ur-Rahmann, ed., *The Freudian Paradigm*, Nelson Hall, Chicago, 1977.

Nachmansohn, M., 'Freuds Libidotheorie verglichen mit Eroslehre Platos', *Internationale Zeitschrift Feur Aerztliche Psychoanalyse*, vol. 3, no. 65, (91), 1915. Tr. for *Plato and Freud*, by Craig Decker.

Nagel, Thomas, 'Sexual Perversion', *Journal of Philosophy*, vol. 66 (1969).

Nakhnikian, G., 'Love in Human Reason', *Midwest Studies in Philosophy*, vol. III, 1978.

Neu, Jerome, 'Genetic Explanation in *Totem and Taboo*', in *Freud*, ed., Wollheim, Anchor Books, New York, 1954.

Norton, D.L., and Kille, M.F., *Philosophies of Love*, Chandler, San Francisco, 1971.

Nussbaum, M., 'The Speech of Alcebiades: A Reading of Plato's *Symposium, Philosophy and Literature*, nos 2 and 3, 1979.

Nussbaum, M., *The Fragility of Goodness*, Oxford University Press, 1985.

Nygren, A., *Agape and Eros*, tr. P.S. Watson, University of Chicago Press, 1982.

Pfister, O., 'Plato als Vorlaufer der Psychoanalyse', *Internationale Zeitschrift Fur Psychoanalyse*, vol. 7, no. 269 (91), 1921.

Pope, K.S., et al., *On Love and Loving*, Jossey-Bass Publishers, San Francisco, 1980.

Rapaport, D., *The Structure of Psychoanalytic Theory, Psychological Issues*, vol. II, no. 2, 1960.

Plato, with an English Translation, Loeb Classical Library, Harvard University Press, Mass., 1953.

Rawls, J., *A Theory of Justice*, Harvard University Press, Cambridge, Mass., 1972.

Reik, T., *Of Love and Lust*, Farrar, Straus, New York, 1957.

Rhodes, C., *The Necessity of Love*, Constable, London, 1972.

Ricoeur, P., *Freud and Philosophy*, Yale University Press, New Haven, 1970.

Robert, M., *The Psychoanalytic Revolution*, Harcourt Brace Jovanovic, Inc., New York, 1966.

Rosen, S., *Plato's Symposium*, New Haven, 1968.

Ross, D., *Plato's Theory of Ideas*, Oxford University Press, 1951.

Ryan, J., tr. *The Confessions of St. Augustine*, Doubleday, New York, 1960.

Sachs, D., 'On Freud's Doctrine of Emotions', in *Freud*, ed. R. Wollheim, 2nd edn, Anchor Books, New York, 1954.

Santas, G., 'The Form of the Good in Plato's Republic', *Philosophical Inquiry*, 1980. Reprinted in *Essays in Ancient Philosophy*, vol 2, (eds) J. Anton and A. Preus, 1983.

Santas, G., 'Plato's Theory of Love in the *Symposium*', *Nous*, March, 1979.

Santas, G., 'Plato on Love, Beauty, and the Good', in *The Greeks and the Good Life*, ed. D. Depew, Hackett, 1980.

Santas, G., 'Hintikka on Knowledge and its Objects in Plato', in *Patterns in Plato's Thought*, ed. J.M.A. Moravcsik, 1972.

Santas, G., *Socrates*, Routledge and Kegan Paul, London, 1979.

Santas, G., 'Two Theories of Good in Plato's *Republic*', *Archiv fur Geschichte der Philosophie*, 1985, pp. 223–45.

Shakow, D. and Rapaport, D., *The Influence of Freud on American Psychology*, *Psychological Issues*, vol. IV, no. 1, Monograph 13.

Simon, B., *Mind and Madness in Ancient Greece*, Cornell University Press, Ithaca, New York, 1978.

Shorey, P., tr., *Plato's Republic*, Harvard U.P., Cambridge, Mass., 1952.

Singer, I., *The Nature of Love*, 2 volumes, 2nd edn, University of Chicago Press, 1984.

Stendhal, *Love*, tr. G. and S. Sale, The Merlin Press, London, 1957.

Strachey, J., ed., *The Standard Edition of the Complete Psychological Works of Sigmund Freud*, The Hogarth Press, London, 1953, vols. I–XXVI

Stokes, M.C., *Plato's Socratic Conversations*, The Athlone Press, London, 1986.

Sulloway, F., *Freud: Biologist of the Mind*, Basic Books, New York, 1979.

Suttie, I.D., *The Origins of Love and Hate*, The Julian Press, New York, 1952.

Vlastos, G., 'The Individual as Object of Love in Plato', in *Platonic Studies*, 2nd edn, Princeton, 1973.

Walsh, Gerald, *Dante Alighieri*, The Bruce Publishing Co., Milwaukee, 1946.

Walster, E. and G.W., *A New Look at Love*, Addison-Wesley Pub. Co. Inc., Massachusetts, 1978.

Williams, Charles, *The Figure of Beatrice*, Noonday Press, New York, 1961.

Wollheim, R., ed., *Freud: A Collection of Critical Essays*, Anchor Books, New York, 1954.

Wollheim, R., *Sigmund Freud*, Viking Press, New York, 1971.

Woodruff, P., *Plato: Hippias Major*, Hackett, Indianapolis, 1982.

Zanuso, Billa, *The Young Freud*, Blackwell, Oxford, 1986.

Index